To Aunt
with best.
Elizabeth Taylor.

NEXT STOP
SIBERIA

by

Elizabeth Taylor

Grosvenor House
Publishing Limited

This book is published by
Grosvenor House Publishing Ltd
28-30 High Street, Guildford, Surrey, GU1 3EL.
www.grosvenorhousepublishing.co.uk

A CIP record for this book
is available from the British Library

ISBN 978-1-78148-533-0

I dedicate this book to my sons Stephen and Andrew, who have encouraged me throughout the project. I hope it gives them an insight into their own identity and highlights the culture which they have inherited from their Polish grandparents.

I also thank my English husband Graham, who has patiently helped me to research some of the factual elements in the writing of this book and accompanied me in 2009 to retrace and visit my parents' home in Lwów and the territories which were lost to my family in the post-war movement of Poland's borders.

About the Author

Elizabeth Taylor (née Zatorska) was born in 1952 in Cambridge and from 1957 lived in Hitchin Hertfordshire for forty-five years. Her parents originated from Poland and came to England as immigrants directly after the Second World War, when her father completed his military wartime service with the Allied Forces.

Having the good fortune of being bi-lingual, she interpreted for her family and the Hitchin Polish community from a very early age and later became a qualified professional freelance interpreter in the 1990's working within the legal system, immigration and the healthcare service. Since 1973, she has also worked in a number of Hertfordshire schools as a consultant and an administrator.

Having listened to the wartime accounts of family and friends, who endured unimaginable horrors of Stalin's gulag camps, she decided to write a book as a tribute to the minority who survived and a testament to the majority who perished whilst prisoners in Siberia.

Introduction

It is probably easier to write a book based on fiction, as one can design and unfold the drama and storyline from the resources of one's skill in creativity and wild imagination, then building on these, unfold and create a thriller, romance or science fiction novel. Of course, in order to attract enough interest to achieve a best seller, the writer has to bear in mind any particular popular theme which people are drawn to reading at that period of time. However, when writing about events which actually occurred, the storyline has to run parallel with historical accounts, which is more difficult, in order to put the picture into perspective.

Sometimes we look to Hollywood or further afield, in order to find stars on which to base a novel because it is hard to imagine and recognise that such heroic people could possibly exist within our own families. However, if we look more closely, such heroes can be uncovered in ordinary mortals who have led their lives in some remarkable way, either through performing spectacular deeds of courage or surviving some tragic circumstances which 'the rich tapestry of life' has weaved and presented to them. When looking at the lives of such people, it is easy to see that in order to preserve their own sanity, they have put to use the wise anecdote that says "*One must have serenity to accept what cannot be changed, courage to change what is possible, but wisdom to recognise the difference.*"

The story in this book is based on the lives of a group of ordinary people who, having been caught up in the outbreak of the Second World War in Poland and deported by the Soviets to the frozen wastelands of Siberia and Asiatic Russia, endured unimaginable danger, abuse, deprivation and upheaval thrust upon them. They faced these with courage and sometimes despair, using their initiative and resourcefulness to cope with all the obstacles and challenges which they faced to merely survive on a daily basis. The outbreak of World War II for them started immediately in 1939 but its effects made them homeless refugees for seventeen years, long after the war had ended for most people in Europe, and moreover, it left them in exile from their beloved homeland for the rest of their lives.

My story aims to provide a written account of the terrible events which the conflicts of the Second World War imposed on so many nations and tragically affected millions of innocent civilian lives, especially in Europe and particularly Poland.

Whilst there are countless books written and many films produced on the holocaust and atrocities suffered as a result of the Nazi invasion of Europe, it is only with the fall of Communism in 1989, when Poland regained its independence, which lifted the ban on press articles depicting crimes against humanity at the hands of Stalin's government during World War II. During the invasion of the Russian armies onto the Eastern parts of Poland and throughout the twenty months of Soviet occupation, Poland lost 1,700,000 of its innocent citizens, mainly through deportations to Siberia.

A secret military agreement forming part of the Soviet-German Molotov-Ribbentrop pact of 23rd August 1939, planned to divide Poland between them and thus annihilate it from the world map. The deportations were organised with fine precision on the part of the Soviet government, resulting in most of the citizens of Eastern Poland being systematically taken in cattle trucks to the depths of Russia, a journey lasting some four weeks. The majority of people who were deported to Siberia, either lingered for years in that God-forsaken frozen hell or perished without trace as a result of starvation and extreme temperatures below -50°C. Others died of diseases such as typhoid and dysentery and the unachievable demands of the heavy work targets set in the labour camps. Looking at statistical records, the number who finally survived, as compared to those who were deported, is staggeringly few. To put into perspective the magnitude of this ethnic cleansing of the Eastern borders of Poland, out of 1,500,000 people who were deported as prisoners to Russia, only 7% miraculously emerged from years of inhumane suffering and struggled to reshape what was left of their lives, having no choice but to live as refugees in exile. Many who did not manage to escape, were left in those Soviet wastelands for ever.

As Germany unleashed its military might and attacked Russia on 22nd June 1941, the Soviet Union agreed to fight as an allied force with Britain and Europe against Germany. Prime Minister Winston Churchill and The Polish Government in Exile based in London, persuaded Stalin that it would make sense to release all Polish prisoners of war detained in the hundreds of scattered Siberian labour camps, as they could be trained and incorporated into strengthening the allied forces in the war efforts. This agreement also specified that the wives, children and dependents of these potential soldiers should also be released as they now represented families of service men. There followed the Sikorski-Mayski agreement, which was signed in London on 30th July 1941, between Polish Prime Minister General Sikorski, British Foreign Secretary Antony Eden, Churchill and the Soviet ambassador to the United Kingdom Ivan Mayski. As a result, 115,000 Polish prisoners from the labour camps were eventually evacuated out of Russia in 1942, led by General Anders and from these, emerged the Polish allied forces of over 41,000 under the title Polish II Corps. They went on to fight in the major campaigns travelling through Iran, Iraq and Palestine, onto Tobruk in North Africa and later Monte Cassino and Ancona in Italy.

However, although Stalin initially agreed to this release of prisoners from Siberia, as with many other agreements which the world believed him to honour, he later revoked the arrangement, resulting in only a proportion of Siberian exiles being released before Russia clamped down the evacuation efforts. Those remaining were 'persuaded' to take on Soviet citizenship and in so doing, lost their Polish nationality and the right to leave Russia and found themselves incarcerated in the depths of the vast Soviet territories forever as cheap labour.

This book serves to describe how a particular group of people, faced with ongoing life-threatening situations, never lost hope that the conflicts would eventually cease and the world would once again return to peace and stability which would enable them to return home to Poland. It was their steadfast faith and hope which ultimately defeated despair and evil. Above all else, they never lost their deep imbedded faith in God and wholeheartedly trusted that in some way, which in the upturned world they found themselves in was not always obvious, He was looking after them and would either redeem them from the evil encounters which they faced on a daily basis, or ultimately relieve them from their suffering into His care through death.

I do not profess to be a fanatically religious person, although I was brought up within a Catholic family which I try to live my life by. However, as I have traced the scenario of challenges and incidents which my characters in the story lived through, I cannot dismiss that it was not just a mere coincidence they survived through so many tragedies and am convinced that someone was looking after them and had a plan and purpose for their life ahead. They lived with God at their right hand and never lost faith.

If one could look inside a crystal ball at a time of a major life threatening crisis, it would be easy to say "I will survive this, if I just persevere through the storm, because I can see myself thirty years in time portrayed in this glass, so I know that I pulled through!" However, without such a clairvoyant device, it is only faith and hope that gives a person that inner stamina amidst utter desolation, in order to conquer, triumph and come out the other side.

Unfortunately, looking back through history, human beings do not seem to learn the disproportionate price eventually paid by any nation as a consequence of embarking on invasions of other countries and the despair, destruction and deprivation that inevitably follow for many years. Looking at the conflicts which have happened over the 20th century alone, including wars which were supposed to 'end all wars', and those which are ongoing in the world today, I cannot say with complete confidence that a World War will never occur again at some point in the future. However, the survival of civilian people caught up in any such tragedies, undoubtedly depends primarily on their strength of mind and health, confidence in making decisions to promote that survival and the ability to integrate and socialise with other people. Human beings generally pull together in times of crisis, thus creating mutual moral support and strength in teamwork to overcome each difficult scenario as it occurs and not facing it alone.

In comparing my own life which began, shortly after the end of the war in 1952, I regard myself truly fortunate that no such major world conflicts have reoccurred in my lifetime which might have had a direct impact on me and my immediate family. However, I sometimes wonder whether I would have been equipped with the exceptional strength of mind and character needed to survive the upheaval which I would have undoubtedly had to face had I been born in Poland only fifteen years earlier. In considering this, one cannot help thinking if it is simply the sheer luck of the draw that presents a person to face and endure such a tragedy or maybe destiny maps out our life ahead. Perhaps there is a hero waiting in all of us and sometimes it is the element of surprise that saves us as, when faced with immediate threat or danger, people often tackle the unexpected situation with amazing courage. Deep down we need to possess a never-ending belief in our own capacity to recognise that life is worth the fight for survival.

Preview of the City of Lwów

The City of Lwów (*pronounced Le-voof*), which was sited on the Eastern side of Poland, was founded in 1272 and had developed and expanded into the trade centre of Poland with the East. It was the trail for merchants travelling from Western Europe to Moldavia and Italian colonies along the Black Sea where traders exchanged silks, furs, cloth and spices and this resulted in the city growing in wealth with dynamic speed. Over the years of history, it had been inhabited by many nationalities and eventually Jews, Polish, Germans, Italians, Scottish, Greeks and Ukrainians all lived together in harmony, proud to be citizens of Lwów which became a multi-cultural city full of industries, commerce and successful businesses which all prospered and grew.

This however made the city an attractive target to prospective enemies. In the course of its history Lwów had been seriously attacked seven times and invaded twenty one times by Swedes, Tartars and Turks but had defended itself successfully each time thanks to its fortifications which formed part of the key elements of the defence system of the country. Lwów also witnessed two great battles which took place alongside its city walls. In 1772 Lwów was under Austrian rule and during the 20th century, the First World War brought bloody battles between Ukrainians and Polish. Following this, Lwów recovered and blossomed again with the building of new specialist schools and libraries to improve and raise the profile of learning and education. A nationally famous Lwów radio station was set up and a good health care system was developed for employees with the co-operation of their employers and medical establishments. Between 1867 and 1918, Lwów held the status as the capital city of Galicia under the Austro-Hungarian Empire. It was also fortunate to be one of the first European cities to have an electric tram system in service.

The World War II Soviet occupation between 1939 and 1941 brought with it significant losses to Poland and Lwów. The University was a centre of learning excellence in Poland and ranked third largest after Kraków and Warsaw. It employed many professors who were world leading specialists in their field of medical research, science and teaching. Subsequently, the German invasion of the city, which lasted from June 1941 to July 1944, began by immediate execution of the many Polish professors belonging to the Lwów University. Because of their intellectual skills; the majority of them were arrested and shot as this was a means of eliminating the core of Polish intellectuals and valuable knowledge which generates power. In addition, a large proportion of Lwów's residents were Jews who owned the big department stores and shops as well as successful businesses and banks. They automatically fell victims of the Nazis cleansing programme and were either murdered or taken to concentration camps where they were exterminated.

At the end of the Second World War, Polish nationals remaining in Lwów were forcibly banished and sent to territories on the western part of Poland, which had been agreed by the superpowers in the shifting of her post-war borders. As a result, Lwów found itself in Ukraine and its Polish citizens were not permitted to return to their beloved city. This caused great heartache to Polish residents who originated from Lwów and the Lwówian poet J. Zahradnik, whilst in exile, accurately represented their feelings as he wrote this verse which I translate below:

"I will not abandon nor leave my beloved city
Why should half my life die off?
Maybe beyond Lwów, some other world emerges
But what is that world to me, in which there is no Lwów?"

The dialect of Lwów was very unusual with a melodic tone and certain phrases and expressions such as "Ta Yoy!" (which means *"so there!"*) originated from and depicted Lwów's individuality. Residents of Lwów were extremely proud of their citizenship and once established, were reluctant to move anywhere else except in unavoidable circumstances. The words of the famous song which the citizens of Lwów sang went as follows:

Let others travel wherever they like
To Vienna, Paris or London,
But I will not venture from the doorstep of Lwów
O mother, so help me God.

Where else is as grand for people as here?
There's no place like Lwów.
Where they wake you and lull you to sleep with a song
Only in Lwów.

The rich man and beggar are brothers there
And all wear a smile on their face.
The girls who belong to that wonderful town
Have the sweetness of juice, chocolate and honey!

If I had to choose where to be born once again
Only in Lwów. Ta joj! (So there!)

Hence, the tragedy of post war border movements imposed by the super powers was a bitter blow from which most Lwówians never recovered and certainly never forgave the political powers that offered Lwów as a pawn for a peace offering to appease Stalin.

The historic centre of Lwów with its buildings and cobblestone roads survived the Second World War largely unscathed along with the Polytechnic, University and Theatre of Opera and Ballet. Lwów features on the UNESCO World Heritage List and proudly celebrated its 750th anniversary in 2006.

CHAPTER ONE

The Realisation of a Dream

Jania Hunka had not imagined that taking the courageous step of leaving her home village of Waniów, near Bełz in Eastern Poland, along with it her entire family, would bring such rewards and fulfilment of her long held dreams. She wanted to be a cook ever since she was a small girl and was steadfast in her ambition of taking this to the very top to train as a chef. Opportunities such as she dreamed of only existed in big cities and she knew that the training she would need would best be found in the prestigious and elegant city of Lwów, where her family originated from.

She was born in Janów, a large town near Lwów, where Johann Kraus, her wealthy grandfather on her mother's side, had been the town mayor for many years until his sudden death on 26th December 1898 which coincided with Jania's arrival into the world. Unfortunately, with the mayor's death and her birth occurring almost simultaneously, there was much panic and commotion in the household on that bitterly cold day as doctors, midwife and visitors with condolences were all arriving and leaving, causing the large town house, where the family resided, to fall in temperature and chilled the newborn baby resulting in Jania almost dying of pneumonia shortly after her birth but somehow she survived.

It was now 1919, and the majority of young women were encouraged by their parents to find suitable husbands and enter a marriage to secure their future. Daughters in families were seen as an asset to marry off well and thus ensure they would be provided for, but Jania had decided that marriage to any man was no longer the dream which she wanted to pursue and this had met with disapproval from her parents. Although at the age of eighteen she had been in love, her father Jan Hunka, would not consent to giving his blessing to the relationship. He considered that Paweł Mechalski, the young man in question, was not from a family of sufficient social standing and the Mechalski family did not possess the financial security which he would have expected to see in place in order to give his eldest daughter away. He had after all worked hard all his life as a senior forestry commission gamekeeper which paid a handsome salary and had invested much of this money in a good education, through a fee paying boarding school, for both Jania and her younger brother Jozef. Jania had been an only child for six years and at the time she was completing her primary education, Jan recognised that she was very gifted in literature, history and geographical knowledge and decided to invest in educating her further.

Jozef her brother, was born in 1904 and after completing the village primary school, went to boarding school in 1916, as he was keen on mathematics and music being a gifted violin player. He was a kind and cheerful young man who was also a talented craftsman, having made his own violin and other instruments which he played. Unfortunately Jozef met with a tragic accident which eventually caused his death at the age of only twenty.

One summer, whilst on vacation from boarding school, he was working in a timber yard which was owned by a friend of his father. During the process of cutting large pieces of wood into planks, the industrial belt driven saw which he was operating, flew out of its setting, hitting him with full force on the side of the head knocking out some of his teeth and badly injuring his face. However, more seriously, this blow caused him to suffer from severe epileptic fits and convulsions throughout the rest of his young life. He sadly died of a brain haemorrhage after a serious fall caused by a fit resulting in terrible grief and sorrow to his parents having lost their only son. It devastated his three sisters who witnessed the death of their beloved brother.

Jania's two younger sisters, Tonia and Julia were only allowed to complete primary school and then were educated in housecraft skills at home by their mother Maria, as it was generally considered that formal education for girls was a waste. Daughters were after all, expected to marry someone from the village so as to remain in the local area. They were supposed to take up their duties as a wife, looking after a home with as many children as God chose to present them with, help their husbands with the work on the land and eventually provide care for their aging parents.

Jania knew that it was no use to argue with her Victorian father. He had always ruled the family with an iron fist and when he had set his mind on something, nobody could persuade him to reconsider. She decided that if she could not marry Paweł, she would not marry at all and so the idea of following her dream was the next obvious step to take. She would not be dependent on any man and end up being a submissive wife as her mother had been for so many years. If she moved to the city, she could complete proper training and make her own way to be a self sufficient and respected city lady with sought after catering skills. In this way, with hard work and perseverance, she could earn a considerable salary doing what she loved best.

Now that she was twenty-one, she had already completed three years of gastronomy training linked to an apprenticeship. Following that, she had seen an advertisement and applied for a position as cook at the Lubomirski Palace in Lwów. To her delight, they were so impressed with her skills, that they had accepted her in exchange for a generous salary. Recognising the golden opportunity, she decided to take that chance and excel at the career which she knew she was destined to follow. As part of her probationary period, her employer, Count

Lubomirski, had recommended her for a specialist Cordon Bleu course in an excellent Lwów catering college. She could put these skills to use when the Lubomirski family regularly entertained and dined their guests as, with the help of excellent cuisine set against the magnificent ambiance of their palace, they could impress their visitors who were often of nobility or influential members of high society. A good team of well selected and highly skilled staff was a prestigious asset to any society family, whose status in the elite ranks was achieved partly by the household which represented them, portraying them in the light of excellence, and wealth.

The Lubomirski Palace was situated in the heart of the city of Lwów, directly on the corner of the Market Square and next door to the former palace of the Roman-Catholic archbishops, where in 1673, King Michael of Poland had died. It had been built for Prince Stanislaw Lubomirski in the 1760's and styled in Baroque architecture. Between 1771 and 1821 it had served as the residence for Austrian governors of Galicia in the days of the Austro-Hungarian Empire, which Poland had been incorporated into and during which period, Lwów, known then as Lemberg, had held the status of capital city of Galicia.

From its many tall windows which spanned over three storeys, Jania could see the panorama of the city unfold, displaying its many varieties of buildings and their architectural splendour. These were broken up by green areas of parks and colourful public gardens set out with flowers, shrubs and cleverly designed borders. There, on warm summer evenings and Sundays, couples and pretty young women arm in arm would gracefully promenade in their fine clothes and beautiful hats, enjoying the sweet smelling air and exchanging polite conversation with acquaintances. Horse drawn carriages, some quite plain and others very grand and ornate, transported people in elegant comfort. The well maintained and groomed horses made a ringing clopping on the cobbled streets below with their hooves echoing as they briskly trotted to the command of their drivers.

The more affluent and fashionable society were now driving

automobiles which glided at a faster pace through the many tree lined avenues and boulevards. These were mainly shiny black vehicles with large polished lamps on the front and grooved running boards on either side to assist entry. Their drivers were well dressed city gents with either cream boater hats in the summer or felt black hats in the winter. As the limousines made their way through the streets, they occasionally hooted at pedestrians who got in their way. The red and cream trams glided along the criss-crossed rails on the wide streets and provided efficient transport around the city for shoppers and businessmen.

Immediately opposite the palace, there stood the magnificent cream coloured Latin Cathedral, originally dating back to the 14th century, with its delicately tiered green tower on top and curved green dome on its attached chapel below. Predominantly of gothic style, with additions and improvements over many years, it also contained architecture of the Renaissance period. The body of the cathedral was constructed of three sections, with the area dividing the nave and sanctuary dominated by late Baroque and Rococo style and very tall stained glass gothic windows. There was a main altar, soaring into the vastly tall arches of the cathedral's ceiling, designed mainly of dark marble and decorated with large carvings. In the side nave was an altar finished in light grey marble and gold, richly decorated with treasures from many historical periods. On the left was an additional chapel made of brown marble at which masses were also conducted. A number of illustrious or famous people had been buried there over the years and their ornate tombs were spaced amongst the huge supporting marble pillars. This was one of the many places of worship sited in the vicinity of the Market Square and it was always busy with citizens attending masses, particularly those which were held on special religious feast days and accompanied by one of its two powerful organs.

Silhouetted against the Lwów panorama, featured the Church of Corpus Christi with a large dome and façade richly decorated with carved figures and its internal architecture of

ELIZABETH TAYLOR

Italian design. This was run by the convent of Dominican nuns.
Within walking distance of this, was the monastery of the
Carmelite nuns. There were several monasteries in the city and
as well as spiritual support, they provided invaluable charitable
works, teaching in the schools, caring for the sick in the
hospitals and provided refuge centres for the homeless.

The Lwówians considered that the most beautiful place of
worship in the city was the Bernadine Church of St Andrew,
which was part of the Franciscan monastery. Dating back to
the 17th century with its splendid facade, it possessed Italian
and Flemish influence in its design and could compete in
architectural prestige with places of worship anywhere in the
world. It was here that Jania particularly loved to attend the
Christmas Eve Midnight Mass conducted by the monks at
which the students from the Lwów University choir sang carols
to exquisitely played music.

Around the Square were delightful restaurants and cafés, the
most famous of these was Zaleski patisserie and a restaurant by
the name of Roma and Warszawa. The Lwów cafés were
influenced by the skills of Austrian bakers from Vienna, serving
the most elaborate gateaux and pastries from sparkling glass
displays to accompany their speciality of selected fine freshly
roasted coffees and creamy topped cappuccino served in
delicate bone china. Smart waiters and waitresses, dressed
formally in black and white, graciously served their clients both
inside and those seated on the canopied terraces outside. These
splendid coffee houses and restaurants were the places to meet
friends and enjoy what was then considered luxurious
indulgencies of wealthy society.

Most restaurants served delicious doughnuts filled with
many varieties of confitures, including rose petal jam. Lwów
was particularly famous for its doughnuts which were
produced in the city's specialist bakeries and exported by air
throughout Europe in the 1930's. Such was their quality, that it
was customary etiquette for courting young men to present
their girlfriends with a box of doughnuts when they called to

18

visit, or beautifully boxed chocolates with various soft centres which Lwów's own chocolate factory was famous for manufacturing. Such gifts would also be accompanied by flowers to impress and bewitch the girl of their dreams.

On the corner of Number 12 Ulica Kopernika (*Copernicus Street)* was a famous chemist by the name of Pod Złotą Gwiazdą (*Under the Gold Star)* which had been built in 1823. In the middle of the nineteenth century it employed a pharmacist by the name of Ignacy Lukasiewicz, who became interested in rock oil which his Jewish tenant brought from a town called Drohobycz. The Jew was interested into the possibilities of converting this oil into commercially profitable medication. However, the pharmacist saw alternative possibilities of using the oil, which was in fact camfin and later known as paraffin, as a source of fuel, and so it followed that a new form of lighting was invented using paraffin, which at that time was very revolutionary. This was used from July 1853 to illuminate one of the early hospitals in Lwów. The initiative quickly took off and paraffin lamps were installed in Vienna, Berlin and the United States and this expanded to every corner of the globe. The pharmacist did not make a fortune as he invested his money into national and community improvements. However, people that followed in the trade of paraffin made enormous fortunes.

On the far side beyond the square stood The Grand Hotel which when it was built in 1893, had excited the public as the first building in the city to have electricity. This was used by the upper classes and visiting businessmen. Its luxurious accommodation and excellent cuisine attracted wealthy customers from other parts of Poland and merchants from overseas. Particularly impressive were the ornate ceilings and stained glass windows which formed part of the entrance halls. The vast semi-circular dining room was decorated in cream and gold with matching curtains and drapes around its vast windows, through which the guests could view what was going on in the busy streets of Lwów while they enjoyed good food and entertaining piano music. The hotel exhibited paintings of local artists which were displayed in its entrance hall and many lounge areas which provided facilities of viewing of contemporary art work.

The town square was filled with elegant shops and tall department stores where one could purchase designer hats and evening gowns as well as beautiful coats and suits of the latest fashion. During the bitterly cold Polish winters, with temperatures plummeting down to -40°C, everyone wore fur coats, hats and gloves and so the retail outlets for these were abundant and the choice of garments enormous. There were several tableware shops, displaying expensive fine crystal glasses, ornate silver cutlery and elegant bone china dinner services to grace the tables of prestigious Lwów houses. Most housewives took pride in the quality of the glassware and china which their household possessed and they invested in good tableware and silver for entertaining visitors. The aristocracy in turn, took this to a different level and wined and dined their guests in most lavish style in an attempt to raise their profile in society.

Jania often polished the silver and washed the expensive variety of crystal glasses at Lubomirski Palace with the help of the parlour maids when they were expecting to host a dinner party for guests. It was a major task to clean such a large collection of ornate table candelabras, cutlery, plate chargers and trays to a shine thus enhancing the presentation of the table set in the huge dining room. As a professional, she was proud to see the fine food prepared by her being carried on sparkling silver and offered to guests by the household waiters dressed in black and red. As she handed dishes to the waiters, she often cast a glance at the guests enjoying the gastronomic delights, reflected in the gilt edged wall mirrors and lit by several huge sparkling crystal candelabras suspended along the length of the table from gold chains. Their smiling faces as they savoured her variety of dishes, whilst exchanging conversation, confirmed in her mind that she was made for this line of work.

In one of the wings of the palace there was an enormous library with a magnificent collection of books. These had been chosen with great taste and covered novels and poetry by famous Polish writers and plays as well as history and arts. The Count had heard about Jania's love of literature and had warmly invited her to use the library in her free time, a privilege which she accepted gratefully and with much joy. On her days off in lieu of evening work, she would often go to the library and select a novel or poetry book to immerse herself in and relax after a busy day in the kitchens. On the other hand, sometimes she wanted to find out details on geographical subjects or historical facts and she would research through books to find answers and in doing so, learn and retain valuable knowledge, thus building upon her education. This self learning proved worthwhile, as her in-depth knowledge was evident when holding conversations in society. She could recall historical and political events as well geographical details eloquently. She also showed great knowledge of Polish literature and could make reference to these in detail from the books she had read in the elegant easy chairs of the wood panelled library of the palace, or in her own room when she had borrowed books to take away.

Although Jania enjoyed time to relax, she made sure it was productive time, well spent. The two things she loved most were to read and to embroider. She was extremely skilled at needlecraft, both in sewing garments and embroidery which she found relaxing and creative. It gave her time to escape from the busy life of gastronomy duties and the opportunity for quiet reflection to plan her daily schedules while decorating a tablecloth or pillowcase with intricate designs.

Lwów was an attractive city to live in with a rich variety of culture, wealth of entertainment and mixture of society. Jania was glad to be part of all this and was proud to contribute her skills to this vast metropolis. She was valued and respected by her employers and the prestigious household to which she now belonged. She had formed a close circle of friends both through the local churches which she attended on Sundays and religious holy days and also the theatre and opera house which she occasionally visited on her weekends off work.

The magnificent white building of Lwów Opera House, built between 1897 and 1900, stood in the centre of the city. The main façade was richly decorated with carvings some of which depicted "the joys and sorrows of life" others symbolised Comedy and Tragedy. The topmost pillars had bronze figures of Drama, Fame and Music. The entrance hall distinguished itself by its magnificent wide curved staircase carpeted in rich red and finished with carved gold banisters leading to the upstairs seating and galleries. The walls were mirrored and on these hung famous paintings in heavy ornate gold frames. The vast circular ceiling was decorated with gold, plaster carvings and richly coloured frescos. All these surroundings, added to the atmosphere of glamour to a night out at the opera on the stage of which appeared famous stars such as the Italian Caruso and the Polish Jan Kiepura. Jania loved the music and exquisite singing and attended these performances as often as she could, having read about the details of the play or opera beforehand in the palace library.

Miss Jania was well known by the retail owners and businesses in the city. The butchers knew Jania as a local chef and welcomed her as a valuable customer who ordered large quantities of meat for the Lubomirski Palace. She visited the upmarket butchers to select specific cuts of meat including venison, hare, rabbit, geese and ducks and these were brought by the shop delivery boys to her kitchens as required. On days when the Countess planned to entertain female friends to afternoon tea, Jania would visit the confectioner at Zaleski's patisserie to personally select and order gateaux and exquisitely fancy cakes for the occasion to be delivered to the palace in good time before the arrival of the society ladies. Some of these cakes had preserved fruit set on top and others were saturated in rum or brandy and decorated with beautiful designs in dark chocolate. Particularly attractive were the individually refrigerated cheesecakes which had fresh fruit set on top. The fruit had previously been set in a clear jelly in round bottomed bowls and when set firm, the cheese mixture would be set on top. When all was set and turned out of the containers, the cakes appeared like sparkling glass domes containing strawberries, raspberries and cherries.

The ladies outfitters and department stores were always pleased to advise Jania with selections of appropriate garments from their collections. She chose smart suits in navy, black or brown wool for the winter and cream or blue linen for the summer with matching gloves, shoes, bags and hats with white or cream silk blouses for church and formal functions. She had chosen a few elegant gowns in taffeta and velvet in colours of green, burgundy and black with evening jackets or stoles to wear over them for the evening opera, concerts or theatre outings which she loved to attend. Sometimes she would get complementary tickets from her employer as a bonus for her hard work.

Jania frequently visited Fryzura Dama, the popular hairdressing salon where she had her short ash blond hair permed twice a year and then every week set in the latest 1920's style with waves and curls. The skilled hairdressers advised on the style to suit her slim face and created a neat and smart look with which she felt comfortable in her workplace.

Several of the Lwów banks knew her as she regularly completed housekeeping transactions for the palace kitchens. She was responsible for a small budget out of which she would pay cash to the visiting service providers such as the chimney sweep, who annually cleaned the many palace chimneys, the window cleaners who kept the huge windows sparkling clean and the delivery boys from the local grocers shops and stores, who brought her orders for the kitchen on bicycles or carts.

The staff employed in the palace constituted of a team of three cooks who worked under Jania's supervision and guidance in the kitchens on the basement floor. There were two maids who cleaned the rooms, made the beds and made up the fires on cold winter days to supplement the central heating and did the washing. Two waiters were on staff to serve food at mealtimes in the dining hall. The butler assisted the male members of the family with organisation of their diaries of official engagements, sorted their dressing and travelling arrangements and took responsibility of the servants below. A tall, well spoken and strikingly handsome footman answered the door to visitors and helped them out of their carriages into the entrance hall, especially if they had baggage to bring. He would also receive post and deliveries which were made to the household and undertake errands such as sending letters and parcels and sometimes oversee parking of vehicles for visitors who came in automobiles. He was sharp to detect anything that went on and was a source of information on events which happened in the city.

The Lubomirski family consisted of the Count and Countess and their four children, three sons and one daughter along with the Count's elderly parents all resided in the palace. There were various family members who sometimes visited from residences in the countryside to take the opportunity to enjoy some of the high life of the city. The children had a nanny who looked after them, took them on outings to the beautiful Stryjski and Łyczakowski parks and supervised their play in the nursery and in the palace gardens. Once they were of school age, a governess was employed and additionally, visiting tutors came to conduct lessons so the children were educated at home by selected specialists.

One day, in 1925, Jania heard the Countess mentioning that they would be considering a vacancy for a ladies maid to assist her daughter Lucia who had turned sixteen. As a growing young lady, Lucia would need the help of a female companion for social engagements and shopping trips. The lady's maid would assist with her wardrobe, be responsible for ensuring that the expensive gowns of different fabrics and matching accessories would have the proper cleaning and pressing to enhance their appearance and preserve their quality.

On hearing this, Jania politely asked whether they would consider her sister Tonia, who had just turned twenty. The Countess was very keen at the idea, as she had been pleased with the way Jania had settled into the establishment so admirably and was so impressed with her work and the way she carefully managed the kitchen staff and had a flair for putting the finishing touches to enhance the most elaborate events. She was sure that Jania's sister would be equally good and wanted to meet her if she was interested in the position.

Jania immediately wrote to her sister Tonia to encourage her to seize this opportunity and come away from the family village of Waniów to live with her in Lwów and work at the palace in this new role. Tonia was still living at home helping her parents with work on their land and smallholding. She had helped to raise her younger sister Julia who was born in 1909, but Julia was now sixteen and capable of taking responsibility to help her parents with the work.

Tonia's prospects of her future in the village were bleak, as at the age of twenty she was not even engaged and it did not look as though she would ever marry and have a husband to financially support her. She did have some income from employment in the local manor house as a maid. She was a very attractive young woman, tall and well built with long thick dark blond hair which she platted and arranged around the top of her head like a crown around her oval face. She was also a young woman of spirit and confidence who was able to think independently and organise herself and others even in difficult situations. However, like Jania, she too had been prevented by her father Jan Hunka from following her quest for love and she had decided not to marry any man unless she loved him.

She had received many propositions of marriage from young men in the village which she had turned down over the years, but had only been utterly and completely in love when she was eighteen with a young man who lived in the neighbourhood, Jędrzek Dolecki. He was a strikingly handsome, tall and charismatic young man with charm and charisma. As far as he was concerned, she too was the love of his life and he desperately wanted to marry her. However, her father forbade the marriage and considered that Jędrzek was from a financially poor family and would not be able to support his daughter adequately. Jędrzek tried to persuade Tonia to elope with him and promised he would work hard and give her a good life with him. How could it not work out when they both knew they were meant for each other? However, although Tonia was sure Jędrzek was right for her and she was completely in love, coming from a strong Catholic upbringing, she could not go against the wishes of her father. If she married without his blessing, she would be disowned by her family and more importantly the Church. No amount of her tears or pleading on her knees would move Jan Hunka to conceding and she, like Jania, vowed that if she could not marry Jędrzek, she would never marry anyone in her life.

Two years passed since she had been forced to turn down his final proposition of marriage down. Jędrzek's family finally persuaded him to marry another girl in the village by the name of Kunda. He did so but with a heavy heart, as he knew he would never love anyone in the way he had loved his Tonia. He had experienced in his heart the passion that would have secured a happy marriage and realised that he was settling for second best. Tonia wept bitterly on the day of the wedding when the whole village went to the church to celebrate the marriage and the reception. It should have been her standing that sunny morning by Jędrzek's side whilst they exchanged their wedding vows at the altar of God and she should have been dancing the first dance in his arms as his bride at the evening reception. Her heart broke at the thought that Jędrzek would now be lost to her forever, but she held together and bravely went to the ceremony along with all the other friends and family. Their families were after all long standing neighbours in the Waniów community and it would not be considered proper to stay away from the wedding day. She felt she should try and look happy for the newlyweds, after all, Kunda seemed to love him and he would have a caring wife to look after him. She resigned herself to this outcome and there was nothing anyone could do to change the situation.

A few months after Jęndrzek and Kunda's wedding, Tonia received the letter from Jania in Lwów. The opportunity of work in the city was too good to miss and it would give her a fresh start by leaving the village. Lwów would help her to forget Jęndrzek and his new wife and the pain of seeing them in the neighbourhood. The money would allow her to help her parents, as Jania had done for years, by regularly sending some money home to pay for the running of the smallholding and building improvement costs. She would be working with Jania and they got on so well as sisters and best friends. Jania had been working in Lwów and living away from home for six years now and Tonia missed her older sister's wisdom and the calm way in which she could solve problems and provide advice and good counselling. She knew that under Jania's guidance, she would learn and be given an opportunity to improve her own standard of living to a higher level than would ever be possible in the village, where the only way of earning money was to work on the land.

Tonia discussed the proposition with her parents and although Maria and Jan would be sad to see her go, they could see that this was a fine opportunity to make her way in the world. Notification of an interview in Lwów had arrived and Jan took her early one June morning in the horse and trap to the little railway station at Ostrów to see her off. He wished her a safe journey as she slammed shut the door of the steam train and waved. She was excited at the prospect of the trip to the city and what it might hold for her. She had dressed appropriately for the occasion in a smart navy blue suit over a crisp white blouse with lace edged collar, complete with a navy blue hat with upswept brim which suited her oval shaped face. Jania had arranged to meet her at Lwów railway station and planned to introduce her to the Countess at Lubormirski Palace in the hope that they would offer her the position of Lady's Maid.

Lwów had a very large railway station which had been opened in 1904 as a state of the art building to reflect the city's status and rank. It had four platforms which were covered with an enormous glass dome and had richly decorated vestibules and veneered kiosks. There were many restaurants designed for different classes of passengers The underground passages linking the platforms were the first of their kind in Poland. From the main entrance, electric trams transported passengers into the city and the surrounding areas. At the entrance of the station was a huge canopy for shelter of passengers waiting for carriages and automobiles. The outside of the building was a pure cream colour with magnificent carvings, figures and pillars which added to its magnificent appearance. Finally, it was set off with the vast shiny glass dome and this gave it a stately look such as would befit a theatre or even a palace. In the forecourt, a magnificent fountain threw its clear sparkling waters from two huge tiered dishes and could be seen from a distance. The road leading to the railway from the city was a very long tree-lined boulevard with grass verges and ornate colourful flower beds ending with the sight in the distance of the splendid cream facia of the station building itself.

When the station was built at the turn of the century, it was possible for the first time to visit Budapest, Vienna or Kraków in a matter of hours, travelling on the Luxtorpeda train which operated from the Lwów station in addition to the existing steam trains. The Luxtorpeda consisted of a single first class only rail car with a pair of internal combustion engines, enabling it to reach very high speeds to transport passengers quickly.

Tonia's journey took over an hour and when her train slowly pulled into Lwów station and she alighted down its steps onto the vastly long platform, she could see Jania waiving in the distance coming to meet her. They were delighted to see each other and hurriedly exchanged greetings and news. There were many trains arriving and departing on the various platforms of this enormous prestigiously designed station. Although Jania was now used to the busy pace of this large city, it took Tonia a little time to adjust, having arrived from the quiet village of Waniów, where the pace of life was much more tranquil and there was not so much to take in.

They walked across the station forecourt to the trams and took the circular one which travelled through the city centre. It was a ten minute ride along Kopernika Street, past the Grand Hotel and Lwów University and then onto the Market Square, where they alighted. Within a few minutes walking, they were at the palace where the Countess was expecting them and she greeted Tonia with a warm smile as if she had known her for ages and enquired about her journey of that morning. Jania left them and proceeded to the kitchens where she had a function to cook for the next day.

When they eventually sat down in the drawing room over a lemon tea, the Countess outlined the role of the job which included looking after her daughter Lucia and Tonia felt that this would be ideal for her with her organisational skills and eye for detail. She had brought an impressive letter of recommendation with her from the manor house in Bełz, where she had been in service for a year. It was settled, the Countess decided that Jania's sister would be well suited and was confident that the pair of them would make an excellent contribution to the household staff. Tonia agreed to start in one month, which would allow her time to make arrangements with her family in Waniów and move to Lwów.

The butler was asked to show her around the palace and introduce her to Lucia in the wing which she occupied. Lucia was a graceful young girl with a face like a china doll and long black hair tied up with blue ribbons which matched the colour of her eyes. She was charming, bright and bubbly and Tonia liked her instantly.

Later in the day, Tonia told Jania the good news of her appointment and the warm welcome which she had received by all whom she had met that day. Between them, they agreed that Jania would come to Waniów at the end of June to spend a week of her well earned vacation with the family. During the first week in July, she would take Tonia back to Lwów to start her new job in the role of lady's maid and her new life in the city.

CHAPTER TWO

A New Life Together and a Missing Bride

It did not take Tonia long to settle into her new role as lady's maid to Lucia. Her organisational skills and eye for detail and perfection were put to good use and she soon mastered all her tasks and became familiar with her surroundings. She was a cheerful young woman with wisdom and common sense, who could take things in her stride and solve problems by facing them with courage. Her new role kept her busy and gave her a new status and purpose in life. Her service to the family was appreciated and with Jania's gastronomic skills, which she continued to upgrade, the two sisters were valued for their combined contributions to the household.

Tonia enjoyed looking after Lucia's extensive wardrobe which involved many gowns to press, clean or alter in readiness for her society balls and engagements. The laces, satins, velvets and crinolines all needed different type of care and handling to keep them crisp and crease free. She was sufficiently skilled at hairdressing to style Lucia's long hair into beautiful curls or pin and sweep it up into an elegant evening style with sparkling diamond pins for the theatre and dances. There were a number of trips which the young lady was to undertake and Tonia was kept busy with the packing preparations for these. Whilst travelling, garments had to be layered with tissues to avoid creases and hats would be packed in special boxes to keep their shape.

She knew that she had come a long way from her life in the country and she was determined to work hard and make her new life a success. The wages which she was paid were very generous and now both her and Jania were earning a considerable amount together. They sent a sum of money every month to their mother in Waniów, who in 1929 had become widowed but nevertheless had her cottage to upkeep and the smallholding with arable land and livestock to manage. Julia their youngest sister was now twenty, a strong fit young woman, and she was able to help her mother in these tasks. The two women made their living by growing produce to sell whilst also benefitting from a healthy diet of their own fresh food.

The livelihood of the village people depended on the proportion of land which they owned and the skills they had to grow their own crops. The work was relentless as each season brought different farming tasks to be done such as ploughing, sowing, planting and harvesting. Those who did not work on the land, set up small businesses such as blacksmiths, thatchers, bakers and carpenters. Families were generally very large with eight children being quite common, thus the wealth of the household was secured by many sons to work on the land or in the family business. Neighbours all helped each other in a community spirit, particularly at harvest time. All the village inhabitants were well acquainted and many were related by marriages between families, very often arranged according to proportion of land available as the wedding dowry.

One day, whilst Julia and her mother were working in the farm garden, a group of passing gypsies stopped to purchase eggs from the farm's hens. During the purchase, the gypsy woman insisted on reading Julia's palm and told her that she would be travelling to many distant lands and some day living in countries far away. Julia dismissed this with laughter, as she had not even travelled to any large city in Poland in her lifetime let alone overseas. She could not imagine ever wanting or needing to make a journey abroad and in any case, who would believe stories told by some travelling gypsy?

Tonia's and Jania's earnings enabled them to purchase elegant wardrobes which reflected their image as employees of such a prestigious household. Their accommodation and meals were included as part of their jobs and they shared a very large, comfortably furnished room with bathroom on the upper floor of one of the palace wings. Although their jobs were very demanding, the remuneration was good and there was much to see and do in the city during free time. They both enjoyed the theatre and opera on evenings off work and saw the famous Polish tenor Jan Kiepura on several occasions when he visited to sing in the grand Lwów Opera House. Sometimes they were fortunate to receive discounted or complimentary tickets from the Countess and having taken the opportunity to listen to good music as often as they could, they both became knowledgeable of the story line of famous operas and the music linked to the performances. Jania introduced her sister to the literature collection of the palace library and they now frequently borrowed famous literary works to read and discuss.

During afternoons off in lieu of late duties, they would go shopping, book an appointment together at their favourite hairdressing salon or simply stroll in one of the Lwów parks and later enjoy a coffee in one of the restaurants. Łyczakowski and Stryjski Parks were a particular favourite, where the tall mature trees attracted many kinds of birds whose singing was a joy to listen to. Occasionally on summer days they would sit by the cool fountains and enjoy watching the elegantly dressed Lwówians promenading beside the long rows of expertly tended colourful flower beds, the scent of which floated on the warm breeze, while the children played on the lawns.

Sometimes they would take a longer walk up Piekarska Street and step from Świętego Pawła Street into the coolness of the beautiful and enchanting Łyczakowski Cemetery. This was known as the wooded netherworld of wonders and extended over 40 hectares of parkland which had been designed by the head of Lwów University Botanical Gardens. The magnificent memorials and tombs which stood there, some as large as houses, represented elite and famous people. Poets, composers and writers, professors and historians as well as noteworthy politicians were commemorated with each tombstone trying to better the other with size, colour and ornate carvings. On the far and higher side of the cemetery, were military graves depicted by simple white crosses and these were known as Orlęta (*Eaglets*), representing the many young soldiers who gave their life in defending Lwów during the conflict of 1918-19 between Poland and Ukraine. The cemetery was a magnificent park along which inlaid networks of paths meandered through rows of hundreds of tall trees and flowering shrubs. A wide variety of birdlife resided in these trees, so when one walked through the grounds, the bird song was different at the turning of each corner. There were teams of dedicated gardeners employed to keep the area looking beautiful throughout the year. On hot summer days, it was possible to get away from the hustle and bustle of the city by seeking sanctuary and tranquillity in the cool shade provided by the trees which refreshed those who took their walk around these grounds. During the autumn and winter months, the squirrels, rabbits and muntjac deer could be seen scampering amongst the foliage.

On Sundays, Tonia would be busy helping Lucia to dress in her Sunday best for church. Jania and her team had much preparation in the kitchen with cooking of the breakfast and midday meals, as after their mid-morning worship at one of the city's churches, the Lubomirski family would gather to enjoy Sunday lunch together and later some Sunday afternoon engagement or visit to relatives. Occasionally, guests or relatives from the countryside would visit for the weekend.

Tonia and Jania would either go very early for mass in the nearby Latin Cathedral before commencement of their work, or sometimes they would go for an evening service to worship after their duties were finished. In the summer, they enjoyed attending a Sunday evening benediction, when the walk to the church would be in the warm setting sun and the smell of the church incense mingled with the scent of the roses which drifted through the window from the church grounds. Being very devote Catholics, they attended mass every Sunday and on Holy Days of the Church calendar. As their services were required on Saturdays and Sundays, they would have a day in lieu off in the week which they could spend as they pleased and they tried to use this time in the best possible way.

In May 1929 Julia, who had just turned 20 years old, wrote to her sisters to say that in June she would be getting married to a young man in the village by the name of Adam Bielanski and she hoped that they would be able to get some time off to attend the ceremony. Tonia and Jania were very happy for her, as they knew the boy in question who was both charming, extremely handsome and a good carpenter by trade. Tonia wrote back to say that they would arrange to take their holiday leave for the wedding and would buy her a wedding gown and veil in Lwów and bring it with them in time for the wedding.

However, they were surprised at Julia's decision as she had for some time been courting another boy in the village by the name of Antek Zatorski, which from the start had not met with her parents approval. They had never given her a reason for their disapproval and there was no question in this case of financial instability. Later, when her father died, Julia's mother stood by this decision. Antek was one of nine children of a comparatively well off village family, who had originally moved to Waniów from Kraków. The Zatorski family owned a large property set off with a veranda overlooking the front. It stood well back off the main road, its long driveway to the house set with flowering cherry trees on either side and behind it was a large orchard with many varieties of fruit trees. The smallholding had livestock including several well groomed horses. Antek had always had a passion for horses and kept them in pristine condition. They were able to make a substantial amount of money from rearing young foals which they took to Bełz to sell for a good price. Antek's father and five brothers were all skilled carpenters and builders and thus the family income was good.

The wedding was arranged for the end of June and Tonia Jania made their way to Lwów's railway station to catch the train to Waniów three days before the wedding. They were eager to hear about the arrangements and help their mother with the cooking of the wedding feast for the many wedding guests. All village neighbours attended most weddings that took place as they all knew each other, being either related by marriage, by descent or by the close proximity of their houses. It was not uncommon to host one hundred guests at a wedding, christening or funeral.

When they arrived in their village home in Waniów, they were greeted not by a happy bride-to-be but by a downcast Julia. As they had suspected, the marriage she was about to enter, was arranged by their mother as a suitably fitting match. When the beautiful gown and veil brought from the Lwów department store was unwrapped, Julia merely looked sideways at it and acknowledged it as if her fate was now destined. Everybody was busy with the flurry of celebration preparations as there was much to be done, the food to be cooked, church flowers to be arranged, the village orchestra to be invited to play at the reception and clothes to press. Julia's mother dampened down her youngest daughter's doubts by assuring her that it was pre-wedding nerves and all would be well. On the night before the wedding, Tonia and Jania noticed that their younger sister was deep in thought and rather quiet. Everyone went to bed early in anticipation of the busy morning ahead, the day of the wedding.

When the wedding day dawned, it was apparent that the bride was nowhere to be found. Tonia and Jania searched the stables and outhouses and neighbours formed a search party to look through and around the village but to no avail. Everyone was anxious as the time set for the wedding approached nearer and the preparations were almost completed in the hope that she would turn up. The beautiful dress and veil from Lwów was hanging in Julia's bedroom awaiting her arrival and the bouquet of fresh roses, sweet smelling lily-of the-valley and asparagus fern, which Tonia had picked and carefully arranged and tied with pink ribbons, lay beside it.

The church where the wedding ceremony was to take place was in the nearby town of Bełz, which lay about four miles from the village and was a journey made every Sunday by all the village families either on foot or in traps pulled by horses. As this was a wedding celebration, the horses and traps were decorated with ribbons and flowers to help the festivities. The groom and guests arrived in the church at Bełz to the organ's gentle music in the hope that Julia would appear saying she had been delayed somewhere. Julia however did not arrive at all. The groom wept bitterly, comforted by the priest, as he realised that he had been jilted at the altar and he was heartbroken that the marriage would not take place. How could she have done this to him? Where was she?

On the night before the wedding, Julia had negative thoughts about the whole idea of marriage to Adam as she knew that she was in fact in love with Antek and they had been seeing each other for some time. She knew that if she went through with this for the sake of her family, she would regret it for the rest of her life. She was a Catholic and there would be no turning back once she was joined in matrimony at the altar of God in church. Unable to sleep with these thoughts going around in her head, she got up well before dawn and quickly dressed then left the house. She ran until she could run no more and headed for the forest about three miles from the village. She knew the forest well as she had regularly picked mushrooms, berries and firewood here since she was a child. She found a huge tree, part of which was eroded, and this provided a reasonably warm alcove in which to shelter. She sat there and fell asleep to be woken by the dawn chorus of the birds a few hours later on what should have been her wedding day. There she decided to stay until well into the evening when she hoped all the searching and anger which she had caused in the village had subsided and her mother, sisters and Adam would forgive her for causing such embarrassment and scandal, which they eventually did.

In her mind she knew that she had made the right decision and nothing would have persuaded her to change her mind. Antek had heard about the fiasco, but realised that Julia had boycotted the arranged marriage because she in fact loved him. He felt the same way and was delighted and admired her courage. They decided that they would continue seeing each other and bide their time in the hope that Julia's mother would eventually yield and give her blessing to their marriage.

As for Adam, a year later, he married another girl in the village and they were a happy couple, who prospered and went on to have several children.

CHAPTER THREE

A Death and a Wedding

In 1930 Lucia had turned twenty-one and had been busy attending society balls and events for two years, during which time she had the opportunity to enjoy herself, get involved in charity functions, travel and meet many people. Through her circle of friends she had been introduced to a very eligible and wealthy young man, Alexander Potocki, with whom she had found much in common and they had fallen in love. He was the son of a high ranking military officer from Kraków. They had been courting for a year and finally their engagement was officially announced in the new year with a wedding planned for the summer.

Jania and her team would be in charge of organising the wedding breakfast and reception which would be held at the palace following the wedding ceremony in Lwów's Latin Cathedral. There was much preparation and excitement and Jania rose to the opportunity of this grand culinary challenge. Guests would be arriving from all parts of Poland as well as Vienna and Budapest and some would stay at the palace following the wedding. The elaborate three-tiered wedding cake, to be decorated with fresh flowers, was ordered from Zaleski patisserie, but everything else would be prepared by the palace cooks. There were many things to order for delivery and Jania would arrange all this with the help of the city's shopkeepers.

Tonia would have a busy time also, as there were dressmakers arriving to measure and design the bride's wedding gown and outfits for her five bridesmaids. Lucia's mother and grandmother were busy selecting outfits in the largest Lwów department store where the service and attention was second to none and they could take their time and be offered guidance about the colour schemes and accessories which would best compliment the outfits. Lucia had visited the department stores and chosen many outfits to wear for her four week honeymoon which the young newlyweds would spend visiting Venice, Florence and Rome.

Lucia had asked Tonia to help her choose and order all the flowers, as having been looked after by her for four years, she trusted Tonia's judgement implicitly. Tonia knew she would miss Lucia now that she would move away to start her new married life. She had seen her grow up during the last few years from a delightful young girl into a confident young woman.

The staff of the palace would all have roles to play in making the day a success. The footman would look after the arrival and the luggage of the many guests, and the butler would sort out the ordering of the wines, champagne and cigars. There would be extra waiters employed for the wedding reception to assist with serving the many dishes and clearing up. Everyone was involved in the preparations for the big day.

The day of the July wedding turned out to be a beautiful one and all arrangements had gone to plan. Jania's banquet was prepared with meticulous detail and no effort was spared with the preparation and presentation of the food. This had been the biggest reception she had been involved in organising and although it had been hard work, it had been worth the effort to make Lucia's day a memorable one.

The palace was filled with the smell of the many varieties of flowers which decorated every room. The entire household awaited Lucia in the grand entrance hall and the whole team of palace servants stood in line to see the breathtaking sight of her beauty, as she descended the wide red carpeted staircase, wearing a delicate white lace dress on her way to start a new life as a young wife. There was not a dry eye in the room at that moment, especially Tonia, who had helped Lucia to dress that morning for the last time and prepared her for the wedding.

Shortly after returning from their honeymoon, Lucia and Alexander moved to Kraków to set up their new home and with Lucia gone, Tonia was no longer required as her lady's maid and started to look for another position in Lwów. Jania had served the Lubomirski family for eleven years and also felt it was time to move on and so the two sisters agreed that they would try and find another job where they could work together as they had done for the past five years. They got on very well, agreed on everything and enjoyed each other's company. Jania being the eldest, had always provided good advice and wisdom and Tonia sought inspiration from her sister's knowledge and guidance and this harmony allowed them to prosper and grow as elegant people.

An attractive position, to their mutual agreement, did indeed come up at the family residence of Professor Henryk Halban who lived at 38 Kochanowskiego in Lwów. The Halban family needed a chef and assistant for their kitchens, as they often entertained guests from elite society of the world of education. Medical representatives from all over the world would visit the professor in connection with his work at the Lwów University and they stayed at his residence to discuss and assist with his research.

Henryk Halban was a world renowned doctor of neurology and psychiatry and became a professor at University of Lwów in 1905 and later a deacon of its Medical Department. He was born in 1870 and studied medicine in the Jagielonian University in Kraków and later in Vienna, trained as a neurologist. In the mid 19th century, when neurology emerged as a medical speciality, Poland was divided between three occupying powers and eradicated from the map of Europe. Young medical practitioners had to train in foreign neurology centres including Berlin, Petersburg, Paris and Vienna. The first two departments of neurology and psychiatry were established in 1905 by Jan Piltz in Kraków and by Henryk Halban in Lwów. It was not until 1920 that one was established in Warsaw. In those days, every well-known neurologist was concerned with the entire brain as was every psychiatrist and neuropathologist at the same time.

During the period between the two World Wars, Lwów was an active academic centre where approximately 20% of Poland's students were concentrated. A very innovatory pilot scheme was started in Lwów to create an academic system of health care for the university students of the city between 1925 and 1932. Following its success, this became a basis to create similar undertakings in other academic centres. Professor Halban was instrumental in pioneering this health care system for students in Lwów. He was always concerned with welfare and support for young people, particularly the scout movement and those who were gifted and attended higher education, and the young people were immensely grateful to him.

The Halban household consisted of the professor and his wife and their grown up children. Their elegant three-storey apartments were situated in a beautiful tree-lined road in the centre of the city, within convenient walking distance of the university. The building was made of light coloured stone and decorated around the top with carvings. The windows overlooking the front were tall and some of them opened onto balconies with elaborately decorated wrought iron railings. The balconies were filled with colourful pots of pink geraniums and purple and lilac fuchsias. The double front doors made of heavy dark oak opened into a large entrance hall with doors leading to the downstairs quarters. The large kitchen windows at the back of the building overlooked a large courtyard garden with tall mature trees providing shade in the summer and a pleasant relaxation area away from the hustle and bustle of the main city street at the front. It was here that Jania soon established a herb garden which she tended and used the produce to enhance her dishes.

Jania and Tonia were pleased with the good standard of accommodation which was provided at the residence of the Halban family. Their large well-furnished bedroom overlooked the city, with a balcony on which Jania planted a variety of sweet smelling roses in pots. They enjoyed the new more intimate family household compared to their previous employment. As before, they were situated within walking distance of the opera house, shopping areas and parks and they were able to enjoy relaxation time around a busy schedule of gastronomy. The Halban family were a joy to work for and they appreciated their valuable skills and welcomed them as part of their family. The Professor's wife was a kind, elegant and well educated woman in her late fifties and treated them like her own daughters.

"Come, come my children, I have something to tell you." She would say and gather them together when there was some news to convey.

Jania was in charge of the kitchens and Tonia was the housemaid. Jania's gastronomy skills were once again greatly valued within a very prestigious household and she felt she had made a good choice of venue in which to offer her culinary talents.

One day, the Professor was given a young dachshund as a gift by a university colleague. However the dog did not take to anyone in the house except Jania and it soon became her pet which she named Ace. The dog came everywhere with her when she went about her business in the city and he became acquainted with all the traders whom Jania visited, such as the butcher who would make him gifts of bones and scraps. If Ace had been given something to eat which was not to his liking, he would immediately find the nearest tea towel or dish cloth, pull it off its hook and cover his bowl, tapping it firmly down with his nose, in the hope that nobody would see his rejected dinner and scold him. Although dachshunds are by design long dogs, Ace was exceptionally long and very much the picture of a "sausage dog". One day, whilst walking Ace, a group of young male students from the university passed Jania and one of them politely asked,

"Excuse me madam, what price is that dog per metre?"

When Jania had been a chef at the Halban's house for about a year, the Professor sent her on a course in Jewish cooking as he was planning to host an important delegation of rabbis to a business dinner one evening and was aware that their diet would be of a special nature. During the evening, he hoped to seal a financial deal for a university project. Jania spent a few days learning all the particular ways of cooking Jewish dishes, including soups, fish and deserts. She chose and ordered the ingredients with care from the local suppliers and prepared the impressive feast to welcome the very special guests. On the day of the event, some of the delegates walked from the city synagogues, others had come further afield and arrived in automobiles or by train to Lwów railway station.

The large dining room was set out beautifully and the food which she had cooked with great care had turned out to be a very delicious feast. The rabbis were so greatly impressed with the way their special dishes had been prepared, that after their meal, they requested to see the chef in order that they could convey their gratitude and thanks. Jania was called in from the kitchens to meet them and, smoothing her white crisply starched apron, she entered the dining hall to be greeted by all the rabbis rising to their feet and applauding to express their appreciation of the spectacular effort on her part. She graciously thanked them and treasured this moment for the rest of her life.

In 1933, Professor Halban was elected as rector of the Lwów University, which was a position of the highest honour, but which he was unfortunately not able to take up because of a sudden and serious illness. Tragically, on 13th December of that year, the age of 63, he died. The family was devastated by his death and there was official mourning in the city of Lwów, in particular at the university where had taught and helped so many students. All who were connected with him in medical research felt a great loss of a man with so much drive, skill and knowledge who had pioneered many initiatives. Jania and Tonia grieved but felt privileged to have been part of the household of such a worthy person. They busied themselves preparing food for the reception of the many family members and business acquaintances who had attended that sad winter's day just before Christmas.

The funeral service took place in the Latin Cathedral of Lwów, with great pomp and ceremony as was befitting of a man of such important standing, not only of the city, but renowned in the world of medicine. Mourners from many parts of Europe travelled to attend the service. As his internment was to be at the beautiful Łyczakowski Cemetery, the burial place of noteworthy Lwówians, the students insisted on bearing his coffin themselves to his final resting place. This was an arduous walk some way out of the city centre and up a steep hill on a bitterly cold winter day. As he was an important figure in the world of medical science, his death was widely announced in the Polish press and also reported in the British Medical Journal in 1934.

In 1935, both sisters had been in the Halban employment for five years and Mrs Halban advised them to take advantage of the new medical healthcare system which was set up and available to Lwów citizens from 1933. They heeded her wise counsel and visited the community healthcare centre with copies of passport size photographs and were each issued with a small black book in which were entered their personal details, address and current employer, who now were the widow of Henryk Halban and his son Rean Halban. The system provided healthcare insurance for people who were in employment and it also extended to cover their families and dependants. Prior to visiting the doctor to seek health advice, the book had to be signed by the employer, confirming address of employment and residence, which certified that the patient was working and therefore contributed to the insurance fund directly from their wages. This scheme entitled the patient to receive free medical care and prescriptions and also served as a useful and important form of identification. In the villages, such as Waniów where their mother sister Julia lived, there was no such medical insurance and the services of a doctor were prohibitively expensive. Thus people from the country resorted to home remedies and treatments using herbs and potions. The blacksmith would fix a broken leg or take out a tooth and the elder woman of the village regularly delivered many babies.

Following the Professor's death, the work in the kitchens decreased in the Halban residence as there was not so many large gatherings to cater for. Jania and Tonia envisaged that, at some time in the not too distant future, they might be made redundant and therefore decided to look around to see what alternative there might be available in the city.

Tonia did not have long to wait, as she heard through an acquaintance that a position of housekeeper was available at the house of Doctor Jadwiga Kornella at 21 Ossolinskich, which was situated only a few minutes walk from the Halban's residence and so she would not be far from Jania. The sisters agreed that this was the best move and the role of housekeeper would suit Tonia as she did not have the chef skills of her sister who would be looking to apply for a catering position. After a visit to Doctor Kornella's house for an interview, taking with her supporting reference letters from the Halban's house, she was offered the job which she accepted.

The Halban family were sorry to see her go, but wished her well and asked her to visit often. Jania helped her to move into the new accommodation with the knowledge that they could still enjoy their leisure time together and therefore socially not much would change.

Tonia immediately fitted in well with the doctor's household. Jadwiga Kornella was a beautiful young woman in her early thirties, who specialised in urology and worked at one of the Lwów hospital clinics. She was not married and lived with her elderly mother who, because of her age and Alzheimer's, needed assistance, care and companionship during the day whilst her daughter was working. Doctor Kornella occasionally received private patients for consultation in one of the large downstairs rooms of the residence and linked to this there were many telephone calls coming in during the day. Tonia answered the calls, took messages and made appointments for patients.

The property, which the doctor had inherited from her aunt, was a large impressive cream-painted three-storey residence which stood on the end of a tree-lined road. It overlooked the Ossolinski art gallery and ornamental gardens. Its tall sash windows had magnificent views over the city and one of the large end windows, which spanned the corner of the street, had a semi circular balcony designed in wrought iron. The tall double front doors, which were ornately carved in dark oak, were finished off with windows at the top allowing the light to come into the entrance hall from where doors led left and right into the downstairs accommodation. Through a second door facing the street, one entered into a lovely courtyard garden at the back of the residence which had a number of tall mature oak trees providing a cool sanctuary in the summer and attracted birds all the year around. The kitchen, dining room and upstairs bathroom overlooked this area and large cream-painted French doors opened from the dining room allowing direct access into the garden across a stone patio where quiet sanctuary from the busy street could be enjoyed.

Doctor Kornella was a kind, clever and elegant woman with a round angelic face encircled by short wavy light brown hair neatly styled with a fashionable perm. Her eyes were deep velvet blue against a flawless ivory complexion. She was an independent young woman full of confidence and courage, always decisive in her actions and recognised as a very caring and much respected doctor of Lwów. She was academically gifted and as a girl had always dreamed of becoming a doctor. She worked hard to win a university place to study medicine in a world of the 1920s, at a time when women were relatively few in the field of medicine.

Tonia's job included shopping, as she could get to the stores during opening times more conveniently than Jadwiga who sometimes worked long hours if an emergency arose at the hospital. Many of the smaller Lwów shops which Tonia visited were owned and run by Jewish families and so she knew them all well and they always talked to her. One day when she was buying some groceries, the Jewish lady behind the counter remarked, "What a pretty young woman you are Miss."

However Tonia, although being very beautiful and well proportioned, aspired as most young women to be slimmer and replied, "Oh, get away. Look, I am too fat and need to lose weight."

The Jewish shopkeeper laughed and jokingly added, "Just remember Miss, that by the time a fat person has thinned, the thin person is long dead!"

Tonia remembered and recalled this conversation many times during treacherous years that lay ahead of her, of which she was thankfully completely unaware whilst in the shop that particular morning in her beloved city.

Tonia enjoyed her work and life at Doctor Kornella's household and she was able to see Jania every few days when they could meet to catch up on news and discuss any problems. Whenever they could, they would attend a concert or opera at the weekend and, when she was not on duty, Jadwiga and her mother accompanied them and the four women enjoyed each other's company immensely, taking time to relax, socialise and listen to good quality music.

That same year, Jania found a position as chef at the house of Professor Stefanowicz, who lived at 23 Nabielaka near the Abrahamowicz Institution of Education opposite Wulecki Heights. The long street called Nabielaka was the residential area for many professors and scientists from the University of Lwów as well as doctors and other intellectuals. This was situated within walking distance from Jadwiga Kornellas residence and so the sisters were still able to visit each other and spend their leisure time together. The new job was certainly a successful move on her part.

In the summer, they would travel home on the train from the city of Lwów to the village of Ostrów, which had the nearest railway station to Waniów. From there, they would either walk or be collected by one of the Waniów neighbours by horse and trap to travel the few kilometres to their village home to stay with their mother and sister. There they would spend time with relatives and all their friends where they were now considered as well off smart city ladies. They appreciated the change to a quieter pace of life of the countryside which helped them unwind. The tranquillity of the cottage surrounded by fields of corn, livestock and fresh air were all a healthy retreat from the city.

Their mother Maria was a very knowledgeable gardener and grew many varieties of plants and flowers in the garden surrounding the house. The house itself was covered with rambling roses of beautiful colours which gave out an aromatic perfume. She was a most excellent cook and fine baker and had raised four healthy children on her excellent cuisine, all of which was prepared from home grown produce tended by her. She was skilled at hairdressing and the village lads all came to her for hair cuts before any village dances or festivals so they would look smart. Being a devoted Catholic, Maria did much for the local church, supporting poor children by sewing clothes, and helping the choir with her wonderful singing voice. Her fine tailoring and embroidery skills were used to make clothes for her husband Jan and all their children and her skills and care helped them all to survive two historically treacherous periods in Poland of World War I and the Polish-Soviet War of 1919.

Life in Waniów village was very community orientated and on warm evenings, after working hard on the land all day, neighbours would visit each other, gathering on their verandas to socialise, eat and sing to the accompaniment of music played by the young men on instruments which they had carved and mastered themselves. On Saturday evenings, the farm owners took turns in making available their barns and outhouses for dances to take place. When there were village weddings, the nearest church was situated in the town of Bełz, about three kilometres distance from Waniów. The whole village would be invited and they helped with the cooking and then enjoyed the dancing accompanied by music from the local boys and drinking the locally brewed beers and vodka. Sundays, would be devoted to attending church not only for worship but also to network and meet fellow villagers which kept everyone in touch with what was going on and provided mutual support.

The residents of the village were an extremely close community, so everyone knew everybody from generation to generation. They all helped each other with the work on the land, in particular sharing the work involved with harvesting. Each household would help in the gathering of the crops of their neighbours and thus everyone benefited from having this help reciprocated and as a result prospered and developed their lands. The young people usually chose partners from their own village and therefore married people whom they had known from childhood. This sometimes caused problems, as the young men objected to boys from other villages arriving to attend dances and as a result of these disputes, fights often broke out in defence of their local girls. There was also much matchmaking from the parents and village elders, which unfortunately in many cases, stemmed around the amount of land and dowry that came with a prospective son-in-law or daughter-in-law rather than their suitability or any feelings on the part of the young couple themselves. There were instances where weddings were arranged completely by the parents of both families and the bride did not meet the groom until the day of the wedding, which is why pictures in some Polish folklore books around the turn of the century, depict "the bride on her wedding day" crying whilst being dressed and prepared for her wedding by the older women of the village.

There were several very young girls as young as sixteen married off in Waniów but one case comes to mind where a local man's wife had died leaving him with six children of varying ages, amongst these were two teenage sons. As there was a large house to upkeep, younger children to look after and the land and livestock to tend to, the widower could not manage without the help of a woman to look after the home. One of his neighbours had a fifteen year old daughter and a mutual agreement was made to marry her off to the widower's eighteen year old son. However, because the bride was under age, the groom was not permitted to consummate the marriage until she was sixteen. However, she took up her role as the woman of the house and they eventually became a happily married couple within the large family home.

In the summer of 1937, Julia wrote to her sisters to inform them that their mother Maria was very ill. They immediately took advantage of her healthcare insurance system to arrange medical care for their mother. A doctor from the nearby town of Bełz was called and he regularly visited and administered medication but her illness was terminal. Tonia and Jania had their work in the city and their money was now needed for the extra medical care which was required because of the complications of Maria's prolonged illness.

Most of the caring for their mother was now left to Julia who was at home and as Maria's condition worsened, she was bedridden for a whole year and towards the end even needed regular turning to relieve her pain. Although neighbours and friends did help out, Julia found this extremely difficult whilst she was now running the smallholding with its livestock and working on the land. She would return from the fields to hear her mother calling in pain for help to be turned. The local Catholic priest came every few days to give her spiritual comfort and prayers as she fought the illness and the pain courageously.

Julia had been courting Antek Zatorski for many years and seeing her in such a desperate situation, he was only too pleased to help her and she looked to him for support to survive in the difficult situation she was facing on her own.

Finally, on the morning of 22nd April 1938, Maria Hunka, from the house of Kraus, died peacefully at the age of sixty with Julia at her bedside, leaving her earthly suffering behind. Tonia and Jania were informed and they travelled to the village to make preparations for the burial and attend the funeral. On a bright May morning, the whole village turned out for her funeral to mourn her passing. Dozens of children ran behind the funeral procession for they knew Maria as the kind lady who often gave them her homemade cakes and threw handfuls of sweets to them. The three sisters held each other for support and comfort as they buried their beloved mother.

Maria had left no will concerning her estate, which was originally in the name of herself and her late husband Jan, and so the property and smallholding would by law automatically be divided between her three surviving daughters. However, Jania and Tonia were now living in Lwów and had no need of the house. They sensed that with their mother's passing, Julia would eventually marry Antek Zatorski and the couple would need the property to make a home for themselves and their future family. So they agreed to seek the advice of a notary in Bełz to enable each to officially reject their third share of the inheritance, thus allowing the property to pass legally into Julia as sole owner.

Julia was delighted at their generous gesture and confirmed that she and Antek indeed wanted to get married that year. They were both now twenty-nine years old and together they could manage the estate admirably and prosper. They would have a fine start as a newly married couple with an established smallholding and Antek's skills of agriculture, animal husbandry and horse breeding.

The wedding dress from Lwów, which had been packed away for so long from the previous arranged wedding which she had refused to be forced into, was this time unwrapped with excitement and worn with great joy by Julia as she was finally marrying the man she had loved all these years. This time it was not arranged, it was her choice and they had both waited for this moment. Tonia and Jania were thrilled to see their sister so happy and settled and were now confident that she would be well looked after by Antek, while they in turn had their work and each other in the city.

The wedding took place on a bright and crisp day of 30th October 1938, a few days before all Saints Day, in the church in Bełz. The village turned out to attend the ceremony and although Julia only had her two sisters as her entire family; she felt that she was now part of a very large family and would not be on her own any longer. Antek's relatives consisted of parents, grandparents and eight brothers and sisters and their partners, who were all delighted for them both. At the reception, there was no music or dancing, as Julia and her sisters were still within the Polish customary period of one year's mourning following their mother's death. Jania and Tonia had prepared a huge feast with the help of neighbours as there were many people to cater for that day and the celebrations were enjoyed by everyone.

The newlyweds were very happy and both prospered working in harmony on the land, sowing and harvesting crops with the help of the sturdy working horses which Antek had reared from foals and had brought with him from his parent's household to the new marital home. They bought fine milking cows and a variety of pigs and bred these to sell. The mares had healthy foals which they sold for a handsome price and within one year they had enough money to extend their house and build on new barns and stables. They hoped to start a family as they were both now thirty years of age.

In August 1939, Julia discovered that she was pregnant and they announced that they were to become proud parents in May of the following year. Their friends, neighbours and family were delighted for them. Tonia and Jania were thrilled for their sister and in the weeks following the news, busied themselves with knitting and sewing in their spare time. They visited some of the Lwów stores to purchase items for the new baby and were looking forward to becoming aunties.

Amid the celebrations, it was difficult to ignore the storm clouds which were gathering around Europe. There had been signs that a war might break out, but it seemed unbelievable that they should go through another major conflict having already survived the Great War only twenty years ago as children. However, from past experience, Polish citizens were always wary of their past history and of the threats and conflicts which had taken place several times as a result of being geographically situated between two powerful and aggressive countries.

Antek had completed his three-year period of compulsory military service in 1927 when he was eighteen years of age. He had been an extremely fit young man and with his love and skill of horse handling, had been accepted into the cavalry. The cavalry soldiers were hand-picked for their physical fitness and stamina and it was not easy to meet the high requirements expected for entry. He knew now that if a war broke out, he would be called up along with his brothers, friends and neighbours to fight.

At this time, Poland was not appropriately equipped for war in terms of weapons and machinery. The Polish government had levied taxes from its citizens, who had for years willingly denied themselves comforts in order to fund the budget for vital defence of the nation, and were led to believe that Poland was sufficiently armed. However, the money which had been given by the taxpayers in good faith had not been used efficiently by the government to arm the country adequately.

Additionally, Poland had been forced by Britain and France to delay modernisation of her weapons in case it was interpreted as aggressive behaviour. As a consequence, when on 1ˢᵗ September 1939 Germany invaded Poland on three fronts, the Germans had 2,600 tanks against 180 Polish and over 2,000 aircraft against 420 Polish. The Polish anti-tank guns were at the time the best in the world, the capabilities of which the Germans had under estimated. Polish navy and air force were well trained, but when the country's defences collapsed, the Polish Navy and Air Force escaped and reorganised itself abroad, including the British Isles, where they offered their services to Britain as allied forces to fight Germany.

Doctor Jadwiga Kornella

Tonia aged 31 and Jania aged 38 in Lwów
(Photos from 1936/1937 medical insurance documents)

CHAPTER FOUR

The Outbreak of World War II in Poland and the Siege of Lwów

On 1st September 1939, 1.8 million German troops invaded Poland with Blitzkrieg tactics which had never been seen before and caught Poland completely off-guard. From the air, German planes bombed defenceless towns and early attempts by the Germans to capture Warsaw on 8th September were repulsed, but finally by 14th September, Warsaw was surrounded. leading to the siege of the Polish capital which lasted until 27th September. The Polish Armed Forces put up a desperate fight for their country, falling back on successive lines of defence. The Polish defence plan was based primarily on a coalition war in accordance with the terms of the French and British alliances in force. It had been agreed that Poland should fight a defensive campaign for only two weeks and therefore Poland saw its role as one of carrying out a delaying tactic to hold the German advance, which would give time for the French army to attack in the west. Meanwhile, French and British bombers were to strike at military targets within Germany itself. However, although Britain and France declared war on Germany on 3rd September, there was no practical help offered to Poland. Whilst Poland was reeling under the onslaught of the German attack, the guns on the western front remained silent.

In the meantime, on 1st September, Antek, along with his brothers and neighbours from Waniów, was drafted into the army. However, when Poland's defences collapsed, the soldiers were all released and sent home. When all the men returned to the village, Antek was not amongst them and Julia was worried about his safety as he did not appear for several weeks. As there was talk of arrests and killings, she feared that should the worst have happened, she would be left on her own with a war on, a smallholding to run and a baby on the way.

One afternoon, as Julia was working in the fields finishing harvest, she saw in the distance a figure walking through the meadows and waving. It was Antek returning and she was overjoyed and hurried to greet and welcome him. Then she heard that the trains with Polish soldiers and officers setting out to the war front had been turned around and directed by the Soviets into deep Russia. Antek had been detained as a prisoner, but somehow by luck managed to escape and make his way home on foot, keeping under cover of forests until he arrived at his own village. The journey had been very dangerous as he had to avoid being seen in his Polish uniform by invading Russian troops but also the local Ukrainians who, at the outbreak of war, had sided with the Soviets in the hope of evicting the Polish farmers and gaining their wealth and properties for themselves. At every opportunity, they attacked and murdered the Polish occupants of villages on the Eastern Polish borders.

The Polish farmers, who were military settlers in the Eastern Borderlands of Poland, owned properties and smallholdings which they had acquired some twenty years previously as virgin land which they developed, cultivated and built upon. Some of the Polish soldiers, who had fought with Piłsudski in the 1918 Polish-Bolshevik War, had been given land by the government as a reward for courageous service. These land owners had been targeted by the Ukrainians, who burned down or evacuated them from their properties. Many of the local Ukrainians had been employed and earned their living working for the Polish farmers, but were envious of their employers prosperity and took the outbreak of war as an opportunity to covet the fruits of other people's hard labour as easy pickings. Many Polish families would hide at night and sleep in the fields for fear of being murdered in their homes. There were instances where Ukrainians would attack the Polish farmers in their homes, usually under cover of darkness and butcher them or kill people travelling through the forests off the beaten track. Thus familiar Ukrainian neighbours had suddenly turned into deadly enemies.

Antek, Julia and their Waniów neighbours were self reliant for their produce, having gathered a good harvest that summer. They had meat from their own pigs, cows and chickens. In addition, eggs, cheese and milk were plentiful, so they did not feel the shortages as the people in the towns and cities experienced from the very onset of war. The shortages were felt immediately in the shops, as food items were rationed because the army needed the supplies and food was prioritised to sustain the armed forces.

In Lwów, Tonia and Jania soon experienced reductions, and when Tonia went to buy salt for Doctor Kornella's household, there was none to purchase in the stores. She was astounded that in the magnificent city of Lwów, in which the grand shops and department stores stood as she had always remembered them, she could not purchase basic food items. However, she went to visit her friends the Jewish shopkeepers and they had some supplies which they sold to her as a regular customer. The price of all goods had suddenly risen dramatically because of the shortages.

On 1st September, Jania as usual, went to bank some money for Professor Stefanowicz. She noticed that here was panic in the streets and anxiety in people's faces as war had been declared and Germany had invaded Poland. It was the start of a new academic year for the schools and many parents were in the bank to cash money for school fees, uniforms and other expenses relating to their children's' new academic year. As she went inside the grand entrance hall of the city bank with its domed and gold painted ceilings and marble pillars, she noticed that there was a commotion at most of the tills and suddenly customers at the counters were crying, screaming and some tearing at their own hair. Eventually, everyone was behaving as if they had gone completely mad. She looked around and was terrified at what she saw. What had happened to the sophisticated Lwów that she loved and knew so well? What had happened to its citizens? These were after all, still the elegantly dressed, elite people she normally saw about their business in the bank.

It transpired that with the outbreak of war that morning, the banks were no longer releasing cash and the people could not obtain their money from their own bank accounts for their needs. At a time of such crisis, the banks had in fact impounded their savings. Everyone was devastated and in utter despair. The cashiers were apologetic but rather frightened for their own safety at the reaction of their customers. Jania realised how serious the situation already was and went to Jadwiga Kornella's house to tell them what she had witnessed.

At a speed much faster than they ever imagined, Tonia and Jania found themselves in the middle of a third war in their lifetime. They had not considered that Lwów would be threatened so early but the Germans had proceeded with their onslaught with such an incredible pace that Lwów on the far east of Poland was already threatened and the battle for its defence had started. The thunder of the artillery could be heard advancing closer until it was at the outskirts of the city itself. Fires could be seen glowing in the distance against the night sky and in the daytime smoke rising from strategic targets which had been hit. The grand railway station was bombed on 10th September.

Initially, Lwów was not considered in danger of being used in warfare as it was too deep behind the Polish lines. However, Germany's assault on Poland was moving at such a furious pace and with the collapse of Polish reserve, on 7th September, organisation of defence of the city was started. On 12th September, the first German motorised units arrived in the area. The town of Sambor, which lay about 66 kilometres from Lwów, was already captured and the Germans were determined to take the prestigious city of Lwów next and reached the its outskirts. Although the Polish defenders of the city were greatly outflanked, they put up a bloody fight to repel the attacks, helped by local volunteers, cadets, scouts and refugees.

The Germans from their vantage points of the surrounding hills, targeted Lwów's hospitals, churches and strategic buildings in their artillery shelling and destruction. As the thunder of their tanks, vehicles and motor cycles approached the city, the fighting broke out around the railway station and down through the main Grodecka Street with every available fighting person armed and waiting to attack them.

Jadwiga was overwhelmed with casualties brought in to her hospital and other medical points which had been set up as emergencies. Many buildings were turned to rubble and stood smouldering whilst fire-fighters worked around the clock to put the fires out and rescue buried citizens underneath. There eventually was a shortage of water and the buildings burned out of control. The grand shops and department stores were no longer lit in the evenings as blackout regulations were imposed, but in the daytime they were determined to trade as usual, unless they had sustained damage. Some of the churches and monasteries were targeted, resulting in St Elzbieta's Church and the Jesuit and Bernadine monasteries being hit. However the churches which were still standing, were full of people praying for salvation and peace, but it was too late. The ringing of ambulances and fire engines as they raced through the city could be heard day and night highlighting the most recent targets hit. Many houses which had been hit, buried women and children as their structures collapsed resulting in a death toll of about 300 citizens every day.

Tonia and Jania lived in the cellars below the town houses, as did all Lwów citizens, and from day to day the situation became more difficult. They tried to purchase whatever was available and nutritious and relied on their contacts and friends who were shopkeepers to supply produce which was being brought into the city from the countryside on the outskirts of Lwów where owners of smallholdings and farms grew vegetables and kept the city from complete starvation. There was shortage of everything including water and soon the electricity and sewers were not functioning and the smell in the houses was unbearable. Due to electricity supplies being affected it was not possible to bake bread, although flour was still available. The telephones and radio station were damaged which cut the city off from Poland and the rest of the world in its suffering and agony.

Meanwhile, in line with Stalin's and Hitler's secret pact to carve Poland between them, of which the world was not aware, the Soviet armies also invaded Poland from the east, crossing the border east of Lwów on 17th September and marched towards the city. On 19th September, the first Soviet armoured units arrived to the łyczakow area. They completely encircled the city and were joined by the German army from the west.

When the Soviet armies crossed the Eastern borders of Poland, they were met with no opposition as they entered under the false pretence of coming to assist Poland in the fight against Germany. When meeting with opposition from Lwów, they tried to persuade the Polish officers that they had come to the aid of Lwów. The Russian soldiers were too ashamed to admit that they had in fact come as enemies, invaders and allies of Hitler. No one suspected that Poland had in fact been invaded from the east by Russians as well as the Germans. The Germans demanded that Lwów be surrendered to them and sent airplanes over the city to drop propaganda leaflets to target the citizens into submission. This was rejected by the citizens of Lwów, whose motto was *Semper Fidelis* (always faithful), to Poland and in any case, they would not consent to giving away their beloved Lwów to the German invaders, who were a long-standing enemy of all Slavs and with whom Poland was once again at war. To give the city to the Germans would mean that they would inevitably plunder it and then turn the citizens over to the mercy of the Ukrainians who were ready to turn on the Polish.

As the situation now looked hopeless, and to save any further destruction of the city and civilian lives and casualties, General Sikorski saw the tragic situation and decided on 22nd September to sign an act of surrender to the Russians, who seemingly accepted all conditions and terms requested, ceremoniously announcing their assurances that they would allow the privates and NCO's to go home after registration and for the officers to leave Poland and seek refuge in other countries and additionally the citizens would enjoy freedom of movement and safety.

However, on that same afternoon, the Russians broke the act of surrender and the Polish soldiers who had put down their weapons realised that they were in fact prisoners of war of the Red Army who claimed to have come to help. Why were they being persecuted for fighting the Germans? What about the terms of the agreement and the assurances of the Soviets? The Polish then understood that the terms of the agreement was a lie. They realised that they should have learnt from past experience and never trusted any promise made by the Russians.

The Russian soldiers began to arrest Polish officers including many university graduates, policemen, teachers and anyone of authority or social standing and tortured them under interrogation to confess to crimes they had not committed. Following which, they would be sentenced for anything up to ten years and banished to the frozen wastes of Siberia for hard labour in the Gulags. Some 20,000 of these army officers eventually became victims of the terrible crime of the Katyn Massacre in 1940 to which the Russians would not admit their guilt until under pressure in the 1990's.

Lwów had managed to hold off the German advance for a period of ten days of intense blistering fighting. Although ten days does not seem any significant achievement, it has to be considered that at that time, complete nations fell in ten days under the German onslaught. Holland, for example, was taken in only five days. It took the Germans ten days to drive through Holland, Belgium and France and reach Amiens near Paris. It took seven days to break the defences of Yugoslavia. In 1941, it took ten days to reach Dnieper in Russia, and cut through Stalin's impregnable fortifications which had taken him twenty years to build. However, they did not manage to conquer Lwów in ten days and the city would have held out longer had Hitler's Soviet allies not come in great force under the pretence of liberating the city. It was probably the only city that the Germans did not manage to take, despite Hitler's determination to seize Lwów. The city was a jewel of great beauty, elite culture and significant status which would have made a prized trophy for the power-crazed German dictator.

Following courageous fighting on two fronts against both German and Russian attacks, Warsaw surrendered. The Polish government, along with President Władysław Raczkiewicz and Prime Minister General Władysław Sikorski escaped to Britain and France via Rumania and a Polish Government in Exile was formed in London. Soldiers and civilians in their thousands made this journey as well where they would have a chance of reforming into allied forces and contribute to the war effort with their ultimate goal of reclaiming Poland.

Doctor Kornella continued to work tirelessly in the hospitals helping the wounded and dying. Tonia tried hard to keep the household going and purchase food which was becoming ever more scarce. Once the city was under siege, there were many restrictions and Russian soldiers in the streets and in government buildings. Jania now had limited means of catering for Professor Stefanowicz's family, but managed to produce nourishing meals out of what was available. She was fearful for the safety of the professor and his household, as in times of war, educated citizens were generally targeted by invaders, who considered them as a threat.

One evening, when Jadwiga Kornella returned home after an exhausting day in the hospital, she wept as she recalled the day's event to Tonia and her own mother. Somewhere in a wooded area on the outskirts of the Lwów, Polish soldiers had found a twelve-year old Jewish boy whom the Germans had captured in the outskirts of the city. As the child was a Jew, they beat him, bound his hands and then tied him to a tree by his penis, leaving him in the cold autumn night to die. The Polish soldiers had untied him and brought him to the hospital. Jadwiga treated the terrified child whose badly swollen penis had turned black and he was both dehydrated and suffering from hypothermia. He died that night in a hospital full of strangers, away from his family and in a city that was raging in warfare.

At this point, the sisters realised that this was a totally different type of war than they had experienced previously, because now civilians were being targeted directly. Previous wars which they had lived through had involved soldiers fighting at a frontline to settle the outcome, but now the women and children were involved in their homes and each day brought different terrors as Poland was in a desolate situation between two deadly and ruthless enemies with its government and defences gone.

In the villages, the farmers noticed that the soldiers of the invading Soviet army were poorly equipped with ragged uniforms and starved faces as they crossed the border. They plundered crops, livestock and food from the Polish farmers and village peasants as they passed through.

Anyone who had been involved in any kind of community organisation or taken part in debates was in danger of being arrested and detained as were teachers, priests, judges, policemen and local government officials. Once arrested, they would be tortured and detained in the most inhumane conditions with starvation and cold and finally, under the pretext of some crime that a tribunal found them guilty of, they would either be executed or find themselves on cattle trucks bound for Siberia to start a sentence of up to ten years hard labour.

October and November passed in terrible fear and deprivation for the citizens, although they were grateful that the heavy shelling and destruction had subsided. Tonia and Jania would normally have travelled to Waniów to spend Christmas with Julia and Antek in the village, but they did not go because of the fear of travelling from the city at such an unsettled time. Instead, Antek travelled to Lwów to take them a hamper from the family smallholding with home grown vegetables, meat from their own pig, homemade bacon and sausages, flour and mushrooms to enable them to prepare the special Christmas Eve (Wigilia)* supper. He met them at Lwów railway station to hand over the large hamper and the sisters gave him their gifts to take back to Waniów. Early in September, whilst the city shops still had supplies, they had managed to purchase items for the eagerly awaited baby and warm clothes for Julia and for Antek. After exchanging their news and good wishes Antek returned home and related to Julia the bombed destruction which he had witnessed in Lwów, which as yet they had not encountered in the countryside. They were in fear of what might next be in store.

The two sisters spent Christmas Eve with Doctor Kornella and her mother, cooking the traditional supper and sharing it with them. Together they attended midnight mass, praying for God's mercy and safekeeping whilst tearfully singing Polish carols. It was a very subdued Christmas Eve celebration with a very bleak and uncertain year ahead. Little did they all know, or could have imagined, that this would be the last Christmas that they would ever spend in Lwów and the last carols they would ever sing on Polish soil.

* * * *

Christmas Eve in Poland is celebrated as the main and most cherished holy day of the Christmas festivities. It is centred around the family evening dinner which consists of twelve different types of food (in days gone by it used to be twelve courses) to represent the twelve disciples of Jesus. No meat is eaten at this meal as a mark of fasting before the Yuletide celebrations. The supper consists of beetroot soup with wild mushrooms dumplings. This would be followed by a fish dish, the most popular being carp prepared in a variety of ways. Other courses might be a selection of dumplings containing either potatoes, cabbage or wild mushrooms. For desert would be offered yeast pastries, cheesecakes, poppy seed cakes and dried fruit compote. All accompanied by plenty of cherry flavoured vodka!

Family members travel far to be with each other and when the first star appears in the evening sky, the supper is served on a beautifully decorated table, with the best china tableware set on a dazzling white table cloth and in the presence of a festively decorated Christmas tree.

Before the family sit down to eat, they share opłatek *(Christmas wafer), bought from the parish church, which is offered around to everyone individually by the eldest family member and all participants break a piece off and exchange their good wishes for the festive season and for the coming New Year. If for some reason a person is not able to be present at this family gathering, then the* opłatek *is exchanged by posting it to them in a Christmas card. Soldiers on the frontline during a war, for example, would have a parcel from home or a letter with a piece of* opłatek *sent by their mother, which in spirit united them to their loved ones back home and if they were abroad, it reminded them of their Polish identity.*

After the meal, presents are exchanged from under the Christmas tree and opened. Later, everyone goes to church for the midnight mass with carols. In Poland this would have been in sleighs in the deep snow.

The Christmas angel brings children their presents under the tree on Christmas Eve. However, Saint Nicholas comes on the evening of 6th December and leaves them presents under their pillows.

✳ ✳ ✳ ✳

In the new year of 1940, goods in the shops in Lwów were getting scarce and there were serious food shortages. At the beginning of February, Julia wrote to her sisters inviting them to come and collect some smoked meat, as Antek and her were planning to kill one of their large pigs and make smoked sausages and bacon which would make a good and nourishing food supply for the coming months. Tonia and Jania agreed to come to Waniów on 9th February and bring with them an additional empty small suitcase in which to take back the meat products to Lwów, as this would be welcome addition to their now poor variety of diet.

They set off for Lwów railway station early in the morning of 9th February dressed in heavy coats, winter boots and fur hats with change of clothes and shoes in a suitcase. The winter of 1940 was particularly severe with heavy snows and temperatures plummeting to -30°C, but the day was bright and crisp. They took the tram which stopped directly at the railway station and purchased their return tickets to Ostrów, from where Antek would fetch then with horse and trap. The station was busy with anxious looking people making their way up and down the grand staircases with their baggage. Russian soldiers were on guard everywhere and checked the documents of travellers as they entered the station's entrance hall. Tonia and Jania showed them their little black health insurance books with their photographs, dates of birth and addresses which served as sufficient means of identification.

The train pulled slowly into Lwów's exceptionally long elegant station and its steam rose into the enormous glass dome which covered the platform and concourse areas. The two sisters climbed up the steps of the tall train and entered the warm carriage to find some window seats. As the whistle blew, the train moved slowly out of the station, following the huge curve of the rails on its exit into the open countryside. Through the windows Tonia and Jania looked with sadness upon the damaged city of Lwów against its bright blue winter sky.

Gradually, the city disappeared from their view as the train gathered speed taking them on their journey.

They could never have imagined in their wildest dreams that when their feet left Lwów's station platform and ascended onto the train that morning, terrible events were about to unfold, which would take them on a voyage half way around the world and they would never again in their lives be permitted to return to their beloved Lwów.

CHAPTER FIVE

Next Stop: Siberia

On 9th February 1940, Tonia and Jania arrived in Ostrów station. It was mid-afternoon and the temperature was dropping rapidly which indicated a very cold night, as is normal in Eastern Europe in February. By the time Antek met them and transported them to their Waniów village house, it was getting dark and Julia met them with much joy as they had not seen each other that Christmas and she had been very anxious about their safety in Lwów, which had sustained such bombing, invasion and deprivation of food. She had a hot meal prepared to greet them from their winter's journey and together, the sisters helped to put the finishing touches to a hearty family supper which they ate in the cosy cottage with a log fire cheerfully crackling as it threw out its warmth and light, blocking out thoughts of the severe conditions which prevailed outside.

Julia was keeping well, however, now being in her sixth month of pregnancy, she was beginning to find some of the heavier tasks around the smallholding tiring. She had been particularly busy that day making the sausages and helping Antek to cut up and smoke the bacon and meat from the large pig which Józef Dolecki, their good neighbour next door, had helped them to kill the previous day. There was a huge supply of meat which, when hung and smoked, would sustain them through the worst winter months. They had put aside selected cuts for Tonia and Jania to take back to Lwów, where they intended to return in a few days. Tonia and Jania were particularly thankful to be back in the village, as the war did not seem so close here, with no destruction to witness on a daily basis as there had been in their city during the last few months. They had suffered shortages of food but having now eaten a nourishing meal, they realised how deprived the city, which they had come from that morning, had become in such a relatively short space of time. Who would have thought it would come to this? Lwów after all had been a prestigious city of wealth and elegance only five months ago.

After their meal, they sat and talked into the evening on what they had each experienced since the outbreak of the war. It was clear that although there had been no bombing in the village, there were hostilities amongst the Polish residents and the local Ukrainians and some arrests had been made by the Red Army when they had crossed the borders, with internments and disappearance of many local community representatives, army officers, bankers and lawyers. This situation made people wary as to what they discussed, in case someone to whom you voiced your opinion might be an informer, who would promptly report you to the Russians. Even in their own houses, people talked in hushed voices so as not to incriminate themselves and their families. Antek mentioned that he had heard from the local men that an increased amount of goods trains had appeared at some of the local railway stations and these had remained stationary in the sidings for some weeks.

Julia planned to bake a fresh batch of bread the next morning and the three sisters would be busy doing baking most of the day. They would make enough bread and pastries to take some back to Lwów using the cottage wood burning oven which baked the bread to perfection. In preparation, they fetched a sack of Julia's own flour from the cellar and put it into basins in the kitchen to allow it to warm to room temperature in readiness for the next day and ensured there was enough yeast. Having decided on the plan of the next day, they all went to bed and fell asleep after what had been a long exhausting day. They could never have imagined that the supper which they had eaten that evening, would be the last one they would share in their house or indeed their homeland.

In the dead of night at two o'clock, they were suddenly awoken by a violent constant hammering and banging on the door. Antek jumped out of bed and ran to open the door and the sisters, now also awake, could hear several men's voices shouting aggressively. They were all suddenly confronted in their own home by an armed Russian soldier, who had been banging the door with his rifle butt, accompanied by two Ukrainian soldiers, who barged their way into the house shouting angrily.

"Where are your weapons? Hand over any guns if you are storing them in your house."

They proceeded to ransack the house looking for weapons but found none. They threw everything in all directions and within a few minutes, the house had been turned upside down and ransacked. Antek was lined up against a wall with the Russian's rifle pointing at his head whilst the women were ordered to pack the essential contents of the house.

"You are leaving tonight and have one hour to pack your belongings. Hurry, move yourselves." The Russian soldier shouted, pointing the gun aggressively.

Momentarily, Antek went into shock at the sudden commotion as he was in fear for his family, but Julia indicated to him with a frown to pull himself together and not appear vulnerable in the eyes of the aggressors. The four of them proceeded to dress themselves as quickly as they could, bearing in mind that the temperature outside was 30°C below zero. Tonia and Jania tied up pillows and feather quilts with sheets. They packed their small suitcase which they had transported from Lwów with whatever change of clothes they had brought with them. Julia packed all the things which had been gradually accumulated for the baby. She threw as much of the freshly prepared meat as she could into one sack and the flour and ingredients which were out for the planned baking day into another. They fetched some vegetables which were stored in the outhouse and threw those into a container. As they worked in complete panic and terror, the Russian stood in the middle of the room with a watch and shouted with his rifle pointed at them. Julia thinking ahead, fetched a tin containing paraffin to take with them for fuel, but the Russian snatched it out of her hand and mockingly laughed.

"You don't need paraffin where you are going. Why, we now have electricity in Russia, you know!"

Julia scurried about throwing items which she thought would be useful such as cutlery, cooking pots, pans and cups onto the kitchen table which was covered with a large tablecloth, then tying all four corners of the cloth, she secured the contents for the journey.

She reached into a box containing a large sum of money which represented their savings earmarked for their summer project of extending their house. This was snatched from her hand by the Russian and he would not allow her to take it with her, nor family photographs or the picture of Christ and the Virgin Mary which she took from the wall. Meanwhile, Tonia ran out to the barns to get some milk from one of the cows. The temperature that night was so bitterly cold, that as she carried the milk to the house in a container, it froze immediately.

Outside every household in the village and all surrounding villages were experiencing an identical scenario as, in their thousands, people were being evacuated in the night from their homes. There was one armed Russian solder with two Ukrainians in each home as Stalin's terror raged through Eastern Poland that February night. Unsuspecting families were all awakened violently and crying children, screaming babies and frail old people were dressed and prepared for a night journey into the unknown. Terrified mothers had to pack whatever they could whilst the men of the household were held in numb terror under armed guard. Some households consisted of only a mother and many children as the husband happened to be away that night either on business or visiting relatives in another part of Poland and therefore they thought that they would not be taken away. Who after all would take lone women with small children? Nobody at this stage had imagined or experienced the brutal mentality of Stalin and his plans, but they were not spared. In such cases, the fate of these families was doomed as they were being taken away without the protection of the father and the family became split.

Not all the Russian soldiers however were as arrogant as the one that was in charge of Antek and Julia's evacuation. Some of them advised mothers to take plenty of food and warm clothing for the children as they would be travelling a long distance. Some of the soldiers helped to carry the items to the nearby waiting sledges and one soldier in particular suggested that the housewife took her sewing machine which she refused to obey. She thought this would be an insignificant item to take under such circumstances. The soldier however insisted and took the machine himself and put it onto the sledge. In doing so, he saved the life of that whole family because in months to follow, the mother was able to sew whilst in exile during the war and thus earn money to feed her children.

At Dolecki's household next door, the Russian soldier advised them to take their pig. However, Dolecki could not understand how he could possibly take his pig with him, but the soldier insisted and drawing his gun shot the pig and ordered Dolecki to drag and load the dead animal onto the sledge as food supply for his family for the journey.

"You will need that where you're going, comrade," he added.

In some cases, as the houses were being evacuated of their Polish inhabitants, there were local Ukrainians already waiting outside to take possession of the property and its contents. At the sight of this, one forward-thinking Polish housewife, realising that they were being taken into exile, ran back from the waiting sledge into her home, and in her desperation doused its contents with paraffin and set it alight, thus ensuring that the years of work put in by generations of her family was not going to be taken by looters and opportunists who were waiting to benefit from other people's hard toil.

Some households were ordered to harness their own horse and trap, others were loaded onto waiting rows of sledges bound for the station. The same scene was repeated at most stations in the eastern parts of Poland that terrible night. Waniów's nearest railway station was Ostrów and that is where Antek, Julia, Tonia and Jania were heading in the sledge filled with the only belongings which they had mustered the wit to gather together in one hour under such violent harassment. The snow was very deep and people had difficulty in getting around quickly with their belongings, whilst carrying terrified infants. Mothers wrapped their children in duvets against the cold before loading them onto the sledges. There was crying and confusion in the darkness of the frosty winter night and the aggressive shouts of the Russian and Ukrainian voices could be heard above all this mayhem, ordering people out of their homes onto the waiting sledges.

In addition, the farm animals sensed the impeding danger and the cows, horses and pigs shrieked in terror. Most households had dogs which were kept for guarding the smallholdings and these were running, howling and barking trying to defend their families. Then, when the sledges moved off with their victims, their faithful dogs followed howling and running all the way through the thick snow to the station. Before Julia left her cottage, she threw some bread and meat for their dog and shut him in their barn so that he would not become too distraught at seeing them abandoning him.

As the sledges arrived at Ostrów station, they saw long rows of cattle wagons standing on the railway lines and everyone now realised that this was their means of transport for their yet unknown destination. Antek now understood that these were the wagons which the local people had seen recently and nobody had suspected the significance of their standing in the sidings for so long. Under armed Red Army supervision, fifty deportees were ordered to board each wagon with their belongings after which the doors were slammed shut by the Russian soldiers and securely bolted from the outside. There were sixty such wagons to every train and it took most of the night to load the wagons with some three thousand people from the local areas and for the soldiers to check their deportee lists. Each wagon was packed tightly with people and possessions leaving barely room to sit in rows on the floor, leaning against the sides of the wagon.

Finally, in the morning, which was now 10th February, the trains moved off on their journey to the unknown. Their passengers cried helplessly, prayed and finally collectively began singing a familiar hymn which was particularly relevant in their desperate situation:

> Into Your protection, Father in Heaven,
> This gathering of your children, entrust their fate in You.
> O may You bless us. Save us when we're needy
> Shield us from peril, when danger threatens us.

Inside each wagon, there was a cast iron stove bolted to the floor, which gave very little heat against the extreme temperature outside but provided a basic means of cooking for those who had brought food. The toilet facility consisted of a hole cut in the wagon's floorboard which itself let the extreme cold to enter the wagon and these barbaric conditions allowed no privacy, so everyone, especially the young people, were too embarrassed to use this in such a tightly packed accommodation. Eventually, someone had a blanket which they secured to some nails in the wall and this served as a hanging screen to allow the toilet to be used by the occupants with some degree of dignity. There was a small grilled window high up on one wall where the nearest person would peep out and report to their fellow passengers the progress of their transportation.

The faithful dogs which had followed the sledges had waited by the wagons in the frost all night and as the train moved off, they proceeded to run after their families. They could smell the scent of their owners and each animal ran beneath the respective wagon in which their family was now incarcerated. Occasionally the train would stop and they would fall down panting to rest and then they would run when the transport restarted. Their anguished families, although not able to help the animals, could see them through the hole in the floorboard as they ran trying to keep up with the train, until finally they dropped on the railway tracks from exhaustion and presumably died there in the severe temperatures. The children in particular cried desperately at the anguish of their beloved pets. Antek and Julia were thankful that they had locked their dog in the barn thus sparing him such cruelty. They wondered whether the plundering Ukrainians would shoot him when they eventually discovered him in the barn.

After the train had travelled several days, someone could see through the tiny grilled window and announced that they were approaching the Polish border into Russia. This scenario must have occurred in each wagon as, at that moment, the whole train transport as one voice simultaneously burst into the song of the Polish anthem, *"Poland Has Not Yet Perished, Whilst We Are Still Alive."* Following this, everyone cried with despair and then turned to prayer, as it was now clear that they were being exiled from their homeland to Russia, which meant Siberia.

In Antek's wagon, as well as Julia, Tonia and Jania, there were his eight brothers and sisters with their families and children and his elderly frail parents Jan and Katarzyna Zatorski. The Dolecki family, who had been his immediate neighbours, were also in the same wagon and many other Waniów inhabitants who all knew each other as they had all grown up together in the village, inter-married and worked collectively all their lives on the land.

As Dolecki had brought his slaughtered pig on board, he did not have his own space to sit and had no option but to straddle the dead animal for the whole journey, cutting portions of meat off and handing it to the occupants to cook on the stove to eat.

His legs became terribly swollen through lack of movement for such a long period of time and he was clearly in discomfort and pain.

Occasionally, the trains would stop, sometimes for a short while and sometimes for many hours. The station stops were usually made during the night, thus this crime of war, which was unfolding, was not readily witnessed by the local population neither in Poland, nor later during the journey through Russia. Additionally, the trains did not travel near inhabited areas during the daylight hours. During the stops, the escorting guards would unbolt the doors and let out two men from each wagon to fetch buckets of snow which would serve as water for drinking and washing when it was heated on the stove. They also supplied a bucket of cabbage soup per wagon which was in effect clear water in which some cabbage leaves had been boiled. However, on some days when the guards did not open the door at all, this had to last the fifty occupants for two days.

The food which most families had brought with them lasted for the first two weeks, but as the journey took over four weeks in total, starvation and the cold took its toll on infants and the elderly. There were families who had taken little or no food with them as they had either panicked and lost their senses in terror, or had been too busy getting their children dressed and ready for the journey. One woman under the shock and duress of evacuation from her home, managed only to bring a few possessions including a huge dressing table mirror, which was useless to her now and took up much space in the wagon. Such people now relied on their fellow travellers to share what little they had with them to keep them alive. In addition to the inadequate sanitary conditions, lice and fleas tormented the evacuees day and night. The wagons rattled monotonously and relentlessly on their wide-gauge Russian rails, bound for their destination to the depths of Siberia.

Along the journey, there were instances where tracks widened and merged at junctions allowing several cattle wagons to be travelling parallel to each other and at close distance. All these were filled with Polish evacuees in transit for the same destination and it was only then that the prisoners began to realise the magnitude of their situation. Some families, who had not been complete when they were collected from their homes, could hear their relatives calling from other trains travelling parallel to theirs. Women with children in one train could hear their husbands and fathers and crying and shouting to them from another train as in some instances they had been taken from different towns and were now bound for different destinations.

Some women in the wagons were in the late stage of their pregnancy and went into labour amidst the chaos, and other women travelling with them helped to deliver their babies who were now born into a world of imaginable insecurity and danger. The infants survived feeding on their mothers' milk which could only last while food was available for their mothers. Julia was thankful that her baby was not due for another two months. It kicked healthily inside her, oblivious to what was taking place. She consoled herself by thinking optimistically that in two months time, when her baby finally arrived, conditions would improve and it would be born in a more stable environment.

Small infants were dying of starvation and one little girl cradled in her mothers arms asked, "Where are we going to mummy?"

Her mother tried to hide the terrible truth as she could sense that her child was dying and answered, "Don't worry little one, we shall soon arrive home in Poland."

To which the child replied, "When we get home to Poland mummy, will you boil me an egg to eat?" and with that, she died in her mother's arms. At the next stop, she was taken by a guard and thrown into the snow by the railway. Her mother fainted with anguish when the train moved off leaving her dead child in the foreign snow-covered wastelands.

Similarly, during one of the stops, a small two-year old boy saw rocks and boulders across the fields when the doors were opened by the guards. He was starving and asked his mother,

"Look mummy, if we fetched those, perhaps they would be good to cook and eat?"

His mother replied, "Darling, but they are only rocks that you can see."

"I will eat even rocks, if you cook them!" the child assured her. Later that evening, he also died.

The nights were particularly cold as they travelled further into Russia with temperatures outside falling to 40°C below zero. As a result, some of the children who had been sleeping propped up against or near the walls of the wagon, awoke in the morning screaming and crying as their hair had frozen to the walls overnight and when they attempted to move, their hair was torn from their scalps. Parents frantically found knives or scissors to cut the hair off and release their child's agony. At the sight of this tragedy Julia, in a moment of emotional grief, wrote this poem on a scrap of paper which Tonia later found and memorised:

Stalin, O Stalin, what crimes could we have done,
That from our dear homeland, you took us one by one.
When starved and dead you threw us,
into Russia's deepest snows,
Whilst our little children's hair, to those icy wagons froze.

As the wagons rattled along their rails, people continually said collective prayers to their rhythm. Soon the brutal conditions of the journey took their toll on elderly people and small children who became ill with either pneumonia or hypothermia and along with starvation, died during the third week of the journey, including Antek's parents which caused much grief and despair to their family on board. Antek and Julia were thirty-one and thirty years of age respectively. Tonia was thirty-four and Jania was forty-one. They were all healthy and fit people who were managing to somehow endure the cold and through their faith and prayer, kept up their spirits and supported each other. On the night of the evacuation, even with a Bolshevik's rifle pointing at their heads, the four of them had collectively found the strength and wit, to take with them plenty of food, appropriately warm clothing, footwear and bedding. However, with the length of such a journey, even their food was starting to diminish at an alarming rate.

People taken from their homes that night, had genuinely thought that their exile would only be temporary. They did not envisage the war lasting long and believed they would return to Poland to their own homes in the near future and resume their lives when peace was restored.

When the trains stopped at stations and the wagons were opened by the guards, the soldiers collected anyone who had died on the journey and disposed of the dead bodies by throwing them by the railway tracks onto the snow. The grief of the relatives remaining in the wagons at the sight of their loved ones being left in such a manner was unbearable. They were all strong Catholics who expected to bury their relatives with respect, in the presence of a priest and on consecrated ground. At seeing this, some mothers did not admit that their babies or children had died and clung onto their dead little corpses in the wagon lest they too should become cast out and abandoned in the snowy wastelands of Russia.

The trains passed through Kiev into Moscow, Chelyabinsk, Omsk, and Novosibirsk crossing the Urals on the Trans-Siberian railway through Krasnoyarsk, arriving in Sośva in the first week of March. The temperatures were plummeting to minus forty when the wagons came to a halt in Sośva, as the trains went no further. The guards then unbolted the doors to finally order the prisoners out under armed guard.

"Everyone out! The train goes no further. Hurry, hurry!" they shouted.

After four weeks of continuous travelling, well in excess of two thousand miles since leaving Poland on 10th February in such conditions, everyone who had managed to survive the long journey, was starved, ill and exhausted and could barely stand. When they scrambled down from the wagons, they were almost up to their waist in snow and the children shrieked in terror having been plunged into its icy depths. They came out straight into unbearably cold frost and a howling snow blizzard which took their breath away. Within a few minutes in these conditions their ears and noses became purple with cold and everyone shivered uncontrollably whilst the frost stabbed at their bodies like knives. The guards checked that everyone was out of the wagons and those who were too sick to stand had to be carried.

All prisoners from the wagons were formed into lines and marched under armed guard to nearby school buildings where they were allocated into rooms. Although the rooms were each packed with many people, they allowed slightly more movement than had been possible in the wagons. At least it was a little warmer in the school building and there was a cauldron of boiling water (*kipyatok)* available for tea. Here they had to wait for three days for their onward transport to arrive. During this time, they were able to rest and sleep in what space they could find on the floor, and recover a little from the horrendous train journey. The guards provided a small quantity of bread per person, which was the first bread some of the travellers had seen for weeks.

On the third day, names of families who were on the Soviet's list to travel further were called out by the Russian guards. However, with so many hundreds of people to process and the disorganisation and chaos that prevailed, this process took several days. Antek's family was not called out until the fourth day, which meant that part of their room was cleared by people who were taken away and this left space for those remaining, enabling them to walk and stretch their legs.

Finally, on the morning of day four, they heard their names being read out and they discovered that they were with the same group of people with whom they had shared their wagon. They hurriedly took their belongings outside where rows of horse-drawn sledges were lined up waiting to take them further on their journey, this time to an appointed work camp, which would be a further journey of thirty miles. They were told to put their possessions onto the sledges and women and children would make their onward journey travelling in these. However, the men were ordered to march behind under armed guard through snow which was half a metre deep. The sledges were driven by old Cossacks who were thickly wrapped in either sheepskin or long fur coats, fur hats, gloves and boots against the extreme mid-winter Siberian temperatures. Their beards and moustaches were covered in frost as they drove the sledges calling orders to their horses.

They travelled for three days, passing over rough frozen snow-covered fields and moors where the wind chills brought the temperatures down to unbearable levels. Visibility was obscured by snow swirling in the howling wind which lashed the icy flakes into people's eyes like daggers. Many of the men, who were both exhausted and sick, fell in the snow as they walked trying to keep up with their families on the sledges. Those who were still alive were piled onto the nearest sledge, but those who died were simply left behind. Mothers travelling on the sledges tightly held their babies and children wrapped in whatever they had to protect them from the elements of the brutal climate. The three sisters covered themselves with the feather duvets which they had brought with them and huddled close together on their sledge. Antek, trudging behind their sledges, could no longer feel his ears due to the frost. Suddenly, one of the Russian guards walking beside him noticed that Antek's ears had turned white and grabbing a handful of snow, proceeded to briskly rub them.

"Your ears are frost bitten. You need to rub them with snow, otherwise you will lose them." he said

This method was indeed effective and the Russian, having knowledge and experience of such a harsh climate, advised Antek well, otherwise he could have lost his ears to the frost.

In the early evening of the fourth day, they could see that they were entering a pine forest planted in rows of trees which reached high into the sky and stretched as far as the eye could see into the distance. As they entered the forest, the density of the trees gave a little more shelter from the severe frost than the open fields had up to now. Suddenly, in the distance they could see row upon row of wooden barracks, which were the living quarters of the workers. They had at last arrived exhausted and starved at their destination of the labour camp in the Urals by the name of Chary, situated in the province of Sverdlovsk in the district of Syrov.

Late into the evening, all the prisoner's names were read out by the camp commandant assisted by officers in charge following which, families were allocated by the guards to their respective barracks. This took many hours as there were many hundreds of prisoners to accommodate. Each room, measuring four by three metres contained eight people. Antek, Julia, Tonia and Jania were accommodated with Antek's married sister Elza, her husband Mietek Kraj and their two-year old son Roman. Each barrack contained eight wooden bunks for sleeping and a rough wooden table with two benches. There was also a small stove in the corner for cooking.

When they entered the barrack, they were completely exhausted from the journey and each immediately selected a sleeping bunk in order to rest. In an effort to thaw from the severe frosts which they had endured for so long, they wrapped themselves into the bedclothes which they had brought with them from home. They were all by now extremely hungry, but in their exhausted state could only think of sleep and await their fate which would be revealed in the morning. The night was very uncomfortable as the barrack was freezing cold with no heating and its cracked windows let in the howling wind. Even worse, all barracks were also infested with lice and cockroaches which attacked the sleeping prisoners from all sides as soon as they lay down on the bunks, even dropping on them from the ceiling and making them scratch until their limbs developed bleeding wounds.

Having committed no crime whatsoever, they were now starting their lives as prisoners in the gulags, sentenced to an indefinite and unspecified period of hard labour, intended for extermination in the most harsh and brutal environment of the frozen wastelands of Siberia. Jania and Tonia recalled the days of their beautiful life in their beloved Lwów and wondered what was happening in that city which was now lost to them at the other side of the world.

* * * * * *

Stalin's treatment of Poland during World War II was one of the most atrocious series of crimes against humanity of the 20th century perpetrated by the Soviets. From winter 1940 to June 1941 the Soviets carried out four massive ethnic cleansing programmes, deporting over 1,300,000 Polish citizens, who were taken into the depths of Siberia, Kazakhstan and as far as Asiatic Russia for hard labour. The first transport left on 10th February 1940 with 200,000 men, women and children taken in 110 cattle trains. The second transport went on 18th April 1940 with some 320,000 civilians, taken in 160 cattle trains. The third in June and July, with 240,000 deportees each month, and finally on 4th June 1941 with 300,000. Only 7% of those exiled actually survived. During the twenty months of Soviet occupation, Poland lost 1,700,000 of its inhabitants.

These crimes were concealed to the world and even today are not common knowledge, unlike the crimes committed by the Nazis, which were dealt with post-war at the Nuremberg Trials. Nobody has ever been held accountable to answer for the lives of those who perished as a result of these deportations from Poland at the hands of the Soviets during World War II.

Due to Poland falling under the so called 'protection' of Russia after the war, until Solidarity's victory when she regained her freedom and independence from Communism in 1990, the crimes of Stalin's ethnic cleansing were suppressed.

The post-war generation of Polish children, who grew up in Poland under Communist rule and Russia's dictatorship, were oblivious of this holocaust in Poland at the hands of the Soviets and had never heard about the mass evacuations of Polish citizens to the Gulags in Siberia. Post war history lessons taught Polish children that the Russians had entered Poland in 1940 to liberate it. Although the war crimes of Germany were freely published in books and shown in films, it was not until 1990, that the Soviets eventually acknowledged their guilt of the massacre of the 22,000 Polish officers and intellectuals at Katyn Forest at the hands of the NKVD under the signed orders of Stalin in 1940.

For example, a book entitled 'An Outline History of Poland' printed as late as 1986 in Polish, German and English, covers the events of World War II and writes about German atrocities but makes no mention whatsoever to the ethnic cleansing carried out by the Red Army in the Eastern borders of Poland or evacuations of those citizens to Siberia. Interestingly though, it refers to a Polish army being formed in the Soviet Union in 1942, but fails to explain the circumstances by which these prospective soldiers had found themselves in Russia in the first place!

CHAPTER SIX

Life in the Gulags

Next morning at six o'clock, after a very cold and uncomfortable night, the prisoners were woken and marched into a large hall for a roll call and addressed by Ivan, the Camp Commandant. Dressed in his Russian military uniform, with long heavy coat and fur hat, he stood on some wooden boxes in order to be seen and heard by so many hundreds of recently transported prisoners gathered there and proceeded to read out information and instructions on the camp's expectations and regime.

"You are in Chary, a work camp in the Soviet Union." He bellowed through a sound system. "Today, you will all be allocated jobs according to your specialist knowledge. So, if you have a particular trade, you must report this and appropriate work will be given to you using these skills. If you do not have a trade, you will be allocated to work in the forest felling trees or collecting sap for production of rubber. You will be paid an allowance in roubles and given a ration of 200 grams of bread and some soup every day provided of course that you have achieved your daily targets of productivity. Therefore, if you don't work, you don't eat!"

He warned everyone that although they would not be working under armed guard, it would be futile to try and escape for their own safety, pointing out that the camp's geographical position was situated in dangerous a zone which in itself was a deterrent to prisoners escaping, and those who had attempted escape, had lost their lives either in the thick woods or surrounding marshes.

"Escape from here would highly dangerous for you as we are many hundreds of kilometres from anywhere, situated in taiga coniferous forests lying between tundra and steppe and the temperatures here can drop to minus fifty degrees. If you get lost, you will freeze to death in a few hours. It is very easy to lose yourself in these surrounding forests as they are thick and in addition they are inhabited by bears and wolves. Some areas lead to stretches of quagmires and swamps and those who have tried to cross these in the past have sunk in the mud and perished. Once a month, you will be allowed to travel to another neighbouring village for shopping, but you will have to ask for a permit to travel which will specify where you are permitted to visit. If you are found outside the designated area without a pass, or if you overstay your permitted time, you will be punished by imprisonment."

At the end of his speech he added mockingly, "You have to think of yourselves as Russians now comrades, as Poland no longer exists and you had better get used to it."

At this point, he flipped his left hand palm upwards and tapping it firmly with the index finger of his right hand and laughing loudly he added,

"It is as likely that Poland will ever exist upon the world map again, as hair growing here on the palm of my hand!"

Everyone would have to work and there were many areas of trade needed. Women in late stage of pregnancy and mothers with babies and children up to the age of two were exempt from work and could stay and look after their children. However, women with children over two years old had to work all day and take their infants to a nursery (sadek) provided, where the children would be cared for and fed. Their mothers would collect them in the evening after their day's work. Older children were found places in schools with local Russian children and those over the age of twelve, worked alongside the adults in the forests or timber yards.

When the three sisters and Antek finally arrived at the front of the queue in the barrack intended as an office for allocation of work, Julia was exempt from work as she was now seven months pregnant. Antek was given the task of tree felling, as his agricultural skills were not considered a trade that would be useful here in the forest area. Tonia similarly was assigned to work with the men and women in the forests. Jania's chef skills however, were considered highly valuable and she was assigned to the nursery kitchen working with three Russian girls, Klava, Stacha and Ania, who were established cooks in the kitchens of the nursery school, preparing meals for both Polish and Russian children whose mothers were out working during the day.

It took many hours to issue so many people with appropriate uniforms. Jania was given a white starched overall and hat to wear in the kitchen and sent to the nursery to meet her new working colleagues. The nursery school looked after some fifty children who ranged between two and six years of age. Klava, Stacha and Ania welcomed her and showed her the kitchens and the work that needed doing. Jania discovered that the ingredients which they could obtain were limited and variety was unpredictable as the world was at war. However, with their cooking skills and Jania's flair and resourcefulness, they endeavoured to do their best with what was available to prepare hot meals for the little ones and the staff caring for them. Jania found all three girls to be good colleagues and they formed a cheerful and supportive working team, who always looked on the bright side and enjoyed a joke and laugh to brighten the day. Jania found that there was always a little soup or broth left over at the end of the day, which she could take back to their barrack to give to Julia who needed nourishment in the last few months of her pregnancy.

At the nursery there was a dining area which also served as a morning meeting place where the children were taught Russian songs and nursery rhymes. There was also a play room for the little ones to amuse themselves with basic handmade wooden toys, picture books and puzzles and other things that people had either donated or made. On one wall hung a large portrait of Stalin and on the other there was one of Lenin. One room was dedicated as a quiet area where they would sleep and rest on small camp beds after lunch. Mothers had to start off for work in the morning at seven o'clock and so the youngsters' day also began very early and did not end until they were collected at five or six o'clock in the evening.

Only Russian was spoken at the schools and so the Polish children began a life of hearing and learning Russian more than their native language, as they only saw their mothers for a short time in the evenings when they were collected. This resulted in children not being able to communicate with their own parents, who spoke only Polish. However, the adults gradually learned Russian, having to work and live alongside the Russians, who were on the whole kind and extremely sympathetic that the Polish people had suffered such a fate at the hands of their government. They themselves did not have much, but were prepared to share whatever they had. The Russian soldiers in charge of the prisoners, although strict, were not permitted to hit them or physically abuse them and would face punishment from their superiors if they had done so.

Tonia, Antek, Elza and Mietek having all been assigned to work in the forest, worked alongside Russian and Polish colleagues. Some of these were from Waniów village and they were formed into working teams with equal proportion of men and women in each one. One of the girls in Tonia's team was Kunda, the wife of Jędrzek Dolecki the man whom Tonia had loved and wanted to marry so many years ago in 1923. The women knew each other and were close friends, supporting each other in their difficult place of work.

The eight-hour working day in the snow covered forest was very long and hard and the bitter cold winter took its toll on people who were not used to working outside. The workers were allowed a few minutes break during the day for a *zakurka,* which was a smoking break. Many people who had never smoked, started doing so in order to avail themselves of a few moments rest from their toil. There was also a short lunch break to allow them to eat some bread and thin soup.

Tonia and Kunda worked as a pair felling the pine trees, using large heavy saws with two hand grips requiring one person at each end. They then dragged the logs onto the platform of the saw mill for the men to cut these into smaller logs, strip the bark and pile up for storage. In the spring, when the river thawed, the logs would be rolled into the rapidly flowing river to be transported along to the next processing destination.

Each working team was supervised by a Russian foreman who checked everyone's *norma,* which was a fixed target set for all jobs and checked at the end of the day. If the target had been met, two hundred grams of bread and some watery cabbage soup was rationed per person in the communal eating barrack in the evening when they returned from the day's work in the forest. They were also paid in roubles, calculated on the daily productivity. These targets were set at an unachievable level and many people who were sick or not used to such hard labour went hungry and died of starvation and exhaustion. All prisoners between the ages of fifteen and seventy worked in the open in all weathers with the proviso that when occasionally the temperatures plummeted below -50° degrees, they were not required to go to work outside. They worked together, supporting and helping each other in order to meet their individual targets and thus have some chance of survival. In Tonia's team the foreman was Vladimir, who was a cheerful man who helped the workers as much as he could and they liked him.

The food was inadequate and poor to sustain people labouring such long hours in freezing conditions. There had been only a few days of respite when the prisoners had not been required to report for work owing to the temperature dropping below -50°. The starvation and cold caused the prisoners to become ill and many contacted tuberculosis and died or were taken to the local hospital where conditions were scarcely better and medication, when available, was inadequate. Dysentery and typhoid started to reap the lives of the young and old but during the severe freezing temperatures, it was not possible to bury the dead bodies as the ground was frozen solid and impossible to dig. The corpses were temporarily buried in shallow graves in the snow for a few months to wait for the thaw in the spring when they could be reburied in the earth.

Drinking water was acquired by collecting snow, melting it and boiling it. There were no facilities for washing, as the standards of hygiene in this remote part of the world were extremely low. Additionally, the war caused shortages of basic commodities such as soap, which prevented any chance of improvement. People washed their clothes in the frozen rivers, after breaking the ice, in the hope that this might kill the lice in the garments, but these seemed to survive even when people tried to bury infested clothes in the snow. Sleeping conditions were fearfully infested with lice and other vermin which bit and tortured their victims all night and caused open wounds which would not heal.

One day, Tonia went to wash clothes in the nearby river and as she stooped down at the river bank she was horrified to see legs and arms of corpses protruding out of the muddy bank and bobbing about in the river. She realised that at some stage during the winter, the dead had been buried near the river where it had been soft enough to dig graves in the mud, but as the water eroded the bank, the limbs of the dead were washed out rotting and polluting the river. As she gazed down the length of the meandering river, she could see dead limbs visible along its bank and she almost vomited in disgust and desperation at the unimaginable nightmare in which they now found themselves.

Meanwhile, Julia awaited her baby and tried as best as she could to housekeep for the family. If she was able to obtain or buy some ingredients, there was a two-ring stove in the barrack where she could cook some potatoes or soup. She was busy trying to keep their living quarters clean and free of lice, bedbugs and cockroaches with the intention that when everyone returned in the evening to the barrack, after their gruelling day in the forest, they could at least sleep and rest without being bitten all night. As was the practice in the camp, Julia asked the Camp Commandant for some quick lime which she spread thoroughly on the walls and sleeping perches in an attempt to kill the vermin. From time to time the bedding would have to be taken outside and scalded with boiling water which, although this technique gave some respite for a short while, it did not prevent the lice from returning and quickly multiplying and so the process had to be repeated regularly. This was a ritual which all prisoners living in the barracks followed in their desperate fight with the vermin infested accommodation.

While working in the nursery school, Jania befriended a four-year old Polish boy by the name of Marek, who called her Aunty Jania (*Ciocia Jania*) and often came and talked to her. Later, when he got to know her better, he would confide his worries and anxieties to her as he missed his mother who was working such long hours every day. His father had died of dysentery in the cattle truck on the way to Russia and at such a tender age, he felt he was now the man responsible for looking after his mother. While she worked, Jania would listen to all he had to say and try to give him advice if he asked her to help. His comments showed evidence that although he was only a small child, he had the spirit of Polish patriotism in him and realised that the war had struck a bitter blow at his country and the Russian system was trying to squeeze their Polish identity out of the children at school.

"Aunty Jania," he whispered one day with his little finger to his lips, "they make us sing stupid songs of allegiance in front of Lenin's portrait every day. I have found a way of fooling them into thinking I am singing what they teach us, but I have changed the words."

His little eyes lit up with a smile. "Instead of singing 'We Honour You Our Lenin', I sing 'We Honour You Our Yelen." and at that, he giggled and so did Jania. (He had transposed Lenin for Yelen, which in Polish means reindeer, and so just to show them that he would not show allegiance to a Russian dictator, he sung in honour of a reindeer instead!).

Some time after that, the Camp Commandant came striding into the communal eating block where the workers ate in the evening. He looked furious and stood on a chair to shout his angry announcement.

"A criminal offence has taken place." he shouted with his face red and angry. "Someone has scratched out the eyes on the portrait of our Lenin which hangs in the school dining hall. This is wilful damage and when I find the perpetrator, they will be severely punished. If any such damage occurs again to the camp property, I will halve all bread rations for two days."

A few days afterwards, Marek came to Jania in the kitchen whilst she was washing up after lunch and whispered,

"Aunty Jania, it was me that scratched Lenin's eyes out. Look what these bandits have done to us. They have taken us from Poland and our home to this terrible place and my mummy has to work in the forest such long hours in the cold."

Jania was horrified as she understood the consequences this could bring. She looked at Marek severely and waving her finger at him to show that she was very serious replied,

"Marek, you must never do such a thing ever again. Don't you realise, if they found out that you were responsible, your mummy could go to prison for goodness knows how long, and who would look after you then?"

At this Marek hung his head and realised that this could mean big trouble, but Aunty Jania assured him that his secret was safe with her.

A few months later, Jania noticed that Marek had not attended the nursery for a few days and she learnt that he had he became ill with pneumonia and, as medical help was scarce, he had sadly died. She missed him terribly as they had befriended each other in such grim circumstances and shared conversations where he had confided his worries and anxieties to her. She cried for the brave little patriotic boy who resented being taken away from Poland and refused to comply with the communist regime imposed on his young life.

His heartbroken mother buried him herself in a corner of the pine forest amongst the graves of hundreds of prisoners as people were dying every day. Parents buried their dead children, sometimes tragically losing three or more. Orphaned children buried their parents, subsequently relying on the eldest brother or sister to look after the siblings left in the middle of such devastation and deprivation. The camp rules specified that when someone died, only two relatives could attend the funeral so that not too much time was taken out of their busy work schedule.

Antek lost many more members of his family through typhoid, dysentery, malnutrition or exertion in the felling of timber. His sister Elza, a young woman in her twenties, died of tuberculosis and shortly after, her husband Mietek died of dysentery, leaving their small son Roman an orphan. He was taken by the local orphanage which was managed by Russian and Polish staff. It was considered that he would have the best possible chance of survival, as in the orphanage, food was available and the children had heated accommodation with some form of hygiene provided by the staff who ran the establishment. Tragically, there were now hundreds of children who found themselves without families and were taken into care.

In March, Tonia was assigned to different work in the forest, this time collecting resin from the trees. She was part of a team of women who worked their way along rows of trees from dawn until dusk, fastening cans onto the tree trunks. They then had to make slits with knives in the bark from which the sap would flow during the day into the attached cans. The following day they returned to collect and empty the cans into larger containers which they carried with them. Once the big containers were full, these were delivered to a central point where they would be weighed to ascertain that the daily targets were met. This was particularly gruelling work as the sap was thick and terribly sticky and however carefully it was transferred, some always spilt onto the workers overalls which then became hardened, heavy and uncomfortable. Additionally, in the extreme cold temperatures, the sap covered clothes froze. One of the girls in Tonia's sap collecting team was Kunda Dolecka, who in May contacted typhoid and collapsed and died whilst at work in the forest where they later buried her.

One evening at the end of May, on her way from a day's work in the forest, to the communal dining barrack, Tonia stopped in her tracks and, with her heart pounding, stared at a woman approaching her. At first, she thought she had must have made a mistake, for the figure that she thought she recognised, looked thin and pale. She realised that the woman was having difficulty identifying her also, as she too had lost a great deal of weight and the poverty, hunger and three months hard labour had aged her by years. She had also cut off her once beautiful long thick platted hair, to eliminate some of the lice. She suddenly recognised that she was looking at Doctor Jadwiga Kornella, her employer and best friend from her beloved city of Lwów. The two women ran towards each other and embraced crying with joy at finding one another and also in despair at the circumstances which they now found themselves in. Each one remembered their lives which they had once enjoyed in Lwów and which now seemed a lifetime away, almost like a fairytale dream.

Whilst they ate their meagre supper of stale bread and thin cabbage soup, Jadwiga recalled how worried she had been when Tonia had not returned to her employment as housekeeper in February and had made enquiries as to what had happened. She finally learned of the deportations from Waniów and the surrounding villages and had guessed the unimaginable, that Tonia and Jania had been taken to Siberia. She herself had been taken in a cattle truck by the Soviets in the

April deportations whilst visiting a relative in a village. She had arrived that week at the camp where she was now also assigned to work collecting resin.

Jadwiga now found herself working in the forest while her skills as a doctor were not utilised and she was determined to do something about it. She confided in Tonia that in the morning, she was planning to see Ivan, the camp commandant. Tonia could see that Jadwiga still had her character of spirit and courage but warned her to be very careful as it was all too easy to find oneself in prison here or simply to disappear without a trace.

According to her plans, Jadwiga instead of going to the forest to work in the morning, made her way to the commandant's office and knocked loudly on the office door. When invited, she walked in decisively and found Ivan sitting in a large room behind a veneered desk reading some documents, overlooked by a portrait of Stalin behind him. On the desk, stood a cut glass ink bottle with a carved silver top and beside it lay a quill pen. On the other side of the desk, in a metal tray lay an assortment of rubber stamps and an ink pad. Finally, he looked up and peered over his gold rimmed spectacles at the pretty young woman standing in front of him with a serious but intelligent looking face.

"What can I do for you?" he asked calmly, trying to recollect the new prisoner's name. "You are ...... Kornella, are you not?"

"I am Doctor Kornella," she replied firmly, "I have come to ask why it is that I have been assigned to work in the forest collecting resin, when as a qualified doctor of many years practice, my medical skills could be used helping the sick and dying in the hospital which you have here?"

"We have enough of our doctors here already and there is no vacancy at the hospital," he explained. "You do realise that you should have started your shift an hour ago. There is a penalty for arriving late for work you know." he added, looking at his watch and resuming reading the document on his desk.

Jadwiga wanted her professional status to be recognised and calculated that if she allowed the Russian to brush her off at this point, she might never get another chance and her assertiveness snapped into action. In a moment of anger, and her determination to make him see sense, she made a lightening move over the top of his desk and grabbing the ink bottle banged it sharply on the desk top, spilling some of its contents onto the commandant's beautifully polished desk. Her heart skipped a beat as momentarily, she thought that this impetuous act would now certainly cost her life or at least imprisonment.

"Now look here," she blurted out with her face flushed. "I am a qualified doctor. There is a war on and you send me to the forest collecting damned sap from the trees? There are people dying here like flies of diseases and there is an epidemic of typhoid which will soon be affecting your own people as well as the prisoners. You can't have too many doctors at a time like this. Yes, you do have a hospital, but they are struggling to keep up with the sick and the pharmacy has barely any medicines. I have medical contacts and maybe I could arrange for supplies to be sent through."

The commandant was taken aback at the outburst of this beautiful young Polish woman and he could see the determination in her blue eyes which sparkled with anger.

"Kornella, Kornella," he replied slowly shaking his head, trying to appear unperturbed and leaning back in his chair, "calm yourself down. I can understand that you are keen to carry on in your profession as a physician. If you genuinely think you can make a difference, leave it with me and maybe I will see what can be done."

A few days later, whilst working in the forest, Jadwiga was asked to report for work to the hospital where she set about tightening hygiene procedures to combat the diseases and strived to obtain some additional provisions of medication with the help of her professional contacts through the Red Cross. She worked relentlessly in the profession she loved being a dedicated and highly respected doctor. She knew that she could make a difference and help to save lives but also thanked God that having being released from working in the forest, she now might also have a better chance to survive herself.

The severe winter frosts and snow lasted until the middle of April. Finally, spring arrived in May and Julia's baby was due any day. As the time approached, Tonia was getting anxious as there was hardly any medical care and several women had died in childbirth in the local primitive hospital having just been left to give birth on their own and encountered complications. She managed to secure the best help she could from an elderly local Russian woman who was a self taught midwife having delivered numerous babies in her lifetime. Jędrzek Dolecki, who was a carpenter by trade, brought over a wooden cradle which he had carved as a gift for Julia and Antek's baby and they made this ready for the baby's arrival with whatever blankets they could find.

On 8th May, 1940, Julia went into labour and with the help of the Russian midwife, a strong and healthy baby boy, Ireniusz Zatorski, arrived into the world oblivious of the present turmoil. They were all delighted at the arrival of the baby and with the coming of the spring, the weather improved reducing the severe temperatures which would have been hard for a newborn baby to endure. Keeping the baby's clothes and nappies clean was easier now as the river was no longer frozen. He was a happy baby who smiled and was content with whatever little was available as long as he had his family around to love and care for him and keep him safe.

The lice and bugs and cockroaches were particularly difficult in the barrack and they would crawl into the cradle to bite the poor tiny infant making him scream in pain. Tonia, in her resourcefulness, came upon the idea of putting each of the cradle's legs into a small tin filled with a little paraffin to deter them from climbing up and although this worked for a while, the lice changed their tactics and climbed up the wall and dropped on the baby's cradle from the ceiling so Julia had to keep a close watch all the time.

Meanwhile, whilst peeling potatoes in the nursery kitchen one day, Jania noticed that these were quite old and were starting to sprout. After cooking the potatoes for the children's lunch, she decided to try and carefully bury just the peelings in the earth in an area outside the school kitchen. She noticed that the earth here was very rich and dark and thought it was worth a try. Her colleagues who witnessed this laughed at her efforts and thought she had completely lost her senses, but she was determined to try. There was nothing to lose, the peelings would normally be thrown out however, if her idea worked, they might have fresh potatoes later in the summer. During the months that followed, she checked and to her amazement green leaves appeared and with her constant care and attention, these developed into healthy bushes. In August, she proudly went and dug up several bushes to provide the children and staff with fresh, tasty potatoes for their meal and was able to take some home to cook for her sisters also. Thereafter, they had a constant supply through to the autumn.

As the summer months came, the fields and forests of Siberia became quite enchanting and beautiful in the warm sun with the multitude of lovely scented flowers and shrubs that blossomed everywhere. Fortunately, there were abundant varieties of mushrooms and berries growing in the forests which the prisoners collected to supplement their diet. They also dried these to preserve and store them for food for the winter months to come. There were however many occasions when people became lost in the depths of the deep forests in their endeavour to collect this free supply of nutrition. Some eventually found their way back to the work camps by simple navigation skills such as observing which side of the tree trunks were moss covered and thus gauging where north lay or listening for the sound the flow of the river leading closer to their camp. However it was quite common for people to disappear and perish in such vast expanses of forestation or be eaten by hungry bears or other wild animals who inhabited these terrains.

For those who laboured in the forests collecting resin, the summer months now brought a different problem in the form of terrible plagues of mosquitoes, which were so dense that one could barely see anything beyond these dancing clouds. The insects bit them as they worked, making their skin react with sores and wounds. So, with the sticky resin from the trees on their overalls and the insects, life was again unbearable and typhoid deaths multiplied rapidly.

Those prisoners, who had worked in the timber yards over the winter, were now set the task of taking all the logs and sending them to float down the fast flowing rivers which had finally thawed to allow for their transportation. In order for these to be carried by the current, men and women took turns to stand on the moving logs to manoeuvre them with their feet away from the river bank into the direction of the river's flow to stop them jamming. This was an extremely dangerous task and many people lost their lives or sustained terrible injuries falling off the logs into the fast flowing current and being crushed by the logs flowing at a fast speed.

The summer nights in Siberia were very short, so it was difficult to sleep in the light and people would get up for work tired through lack of a good night's rest. Children however, found the long daylight hours to their advantage as they could play outside longer, long past their normal bedtime.

The warm weather allowed people to live different lives after the harsh conditions of the winter months so in the evening after work, the prisoners would gather to talk, sing or listen to someone playing a musical instrument. They also arranged prayer meetings, especially in May which was traditionally dedicated to the adoration of the Blessed Virgin. These however had to be conducted in complete secrecy, as any form of worship was strictly forbidden and considered a punishable offence. Any bibles, holy pictures or icons were confiscated if discovered by the soldiers.

It was now at last possible to give proper burials to many of those who had died in the winter months, as the ground had thawed, making digging graves easier. Some had been buried temporarily in the snow for five months awaiting the thaw of summer. As there was no priest to conduct the customary religious proceedings for funerals, and grieving relatives, having been brought up strict Catholics, found this very difficult to come to terms with but did the best they could under the circumstances to give their loved ones dignified burials.

The summer passed by and when autumn came it once again turned cold. The war was now having more effect on supplies reaching these distant parts of the world and creating great shortages. Although there were a few small shops near the camp where prisoners could purchase basic supplies with ration coupons or the few roubles which they earned for their labour, these shops seemed to stock random items. One day there might be a delivery of sweets and that was all that was available and another day perhaps pearl barley, buckwheat or *dzugara* a type of millet. There were towns further afield to where prisoners could make their way by hitching lifts from Russian peasants in horse drawn carts or local trains, provided they were granted a travel permit. There they could take whatever they had of their possessions to see if they could exchange them for food or other basic provisions.

In October, baby Ireniusz became ill with bronchitis and Julia took him to the Russian doctor who gave him what medication was available and although recovery took several weeks, he eventually got better. It was difficult to purchase suitable food and milk for the baby but it was possible to barter with local Soviet peasant women who, although were not particularly interested in money, would sell things for items which were in short supply. Tonia and Jania sold their gold rings, earrings and necklace for milk and cereals and Julia and Antek sold their wedding rings in exchange for some *lepyoshki* (flat bread which the Russian peasant women baked in their clay ovens). They sold whatever they could spare including some blankets. One of the local Russian women advised Tonia not to give a whole blanket for a jug of milk as this could be cut into four pieces and the Russian peasants would give her a jug of milk for each piece. Following their advice, this was exactly what she did in order to get as much as possible to keep Ireniusz alive at all costs.

December came and with it a very sad Christmas with little food and no time allowed off work. They celebrated the traditional Polish Christmas Eve supper in the best possible way they could in the very poor circumstances. Jania and Tonia had collected and dried mushrooms in the summer so they were able to cook some mushroom soup. They managed to purchase some flour and used this to bake some bread, using one of the local women's oven, which they used for the traditional breaking of bread and exchanging of wishes. Tears filled their eyes as they recollected previous Christmas Eve suppers in their homeland, enjoying good health and surrounded by love in the midst of their families. Their fate in the coming New Year of 1941 was unknown and they could only hope and pray to God their Father to protect them and redeem them from this hostile land and eventually return them home to Poland.

The New Year did not bode well as towards the end of January, Julia became gravely ill with tuberculosis. Tonia, fearful for her sister's life, went to see the camp commandant and pleaded that he arrange for Julia to be taken to hospital which he agreed and organised, taking into consideration that she had a small child to bring up. When a sledge pulled by mules arrived to take Julia to hospital, she wanted to take baby Ireniusz with her, but because of the seriousness of her condition and in the confusion of the transportation by the Russian sledge driver, they would not allow her to take him and she left him in the care of her sisters.

At this point, Antek was desperately worried about his wife's health and indeed about the chances of any of them surviving these conditions. A year had gone by with no hope or chances of change in their circumstances. He had endured enough of the Russian regime, cold, hunger and deprivation and his thoughts turned to their home farm and his beloved horses and everything they had strived for which he had been forced to abandon. One day, he fell into great depression and he refused point blank to go to work for the Russians in their timber yard, resulting in his imprisonment for several months. Whilst in prison, he also contacted tuberculosis but he was not sent away to a hospital. Instead, he received care from an in-house doctor who was in charge of medical care in the prison.

In the meantime, Tonia and Jania were both left with baby Ireniusz to look after. Tonia was allowed by the Camp Commandant to stay in the barrack and take care of the baby and this thankfully spared her from working further in the forest during the winter months. Jania still cooked at the nursery and was able to bring a little food home, being paid in ration coupons and roubles. In February, whilst fetching a bucket of snow for drinking water in temperatures of -40°, Tonia slipped and fell heavily on thick ice and broke her wrist. The excruciating pain made it very difficult to care for a nine month old baby as there were nappies to wash either in the frozen icy river or by carrying and heating snow over a stove to provide hot water.

Finally, Jania became ill with typhoid and was delirious for many days. Tonia now had the responsibility for looking after a small baby and a seriously sick sister to care for having the use of only one hand. She soldiered on with determination to keep them all alive and help them to recovery. She was also concerned as to how Julia was, as the sisters knew nothing of her progress in the hospital, being too unwell and preoccupied to make the journey to visit her. Towards the end of February, temperatures plummeted to -50° and little Ireniusz became very ill again with bronchitis. Throughout March, Tonia fought hard to keep him warm and fed as best she could but she knew that she was loosing her battle as the baby now had pneumonia and was having difficulty with breathing. As there was no medical help, the situation became hopeless.

On the morning of 20th March, Tonia found the baby sleeping peacefully in his cradle, but on examining more closely, she was devastated when she realised that little Ireniusz had died. He had only been given ten months in this world and these were months of life in the gulags, enduring great deprivation caused by the war and the deportation of his family at the hands of Stalin and the Red Army. She wept and prayed over him as did Jania who had recovered from her bout of typhoid which had left her weak and unsteady.

Tonia informed the camp commandant requesting that Antek be notified in prison of his baby's death and he was given compassionate release in order to bury his infant. Tonia found a pale blue silk blouse of hers which was the only thing she could find suitable and she dressed Ireniusz's little body in this and he looked angelic and peaceful laid in the little pine coffin which Jędrzek Dolecki had made with great care.

Antek himself had the task of digging the small grave for his own baby and he was beside himself with grief wondering why God had forgotten them all in their hour of need. Tonia helped him to bury the infant and they marked his grave with a cross using pebbles and stones which they collected and they put in place a wooden plaque showing his name and the period of his short life 8th May, 1940 - 20th March, 1941.

Towards the end of March Jania, having made good recovery, was back at the nursery school but had not been granted leave to attend the burial. Julia, on the other hand, whilst in the hospital and recovering from tuberculosis, had not been told of her baby's death but by chance on day overheard someone at the hospital saying that the Zatorski boy had died. At this news, she was so overcome with grief causing the terrible fever, which she suffered during her illness, to return and this delayed her full recovery for several more weeks. When she eventually returned to the camp barrack, she visited her baby's grave to weep and pray for him, as there was nothing else that could possibly be done. She knew she was not the only mother who had lost her child to this war as small coffins being carried for burial were a daily occurrence. Infants and children were dying every day and some parents had tragically lost their entire family of three or four children whom they themselves had to bury side by side in the hostile Soviet earth, somewhere in the forest.

Following his release from prison, Antek resumed his work at the timber yard and Tonia had to go back to the resin collecting in the forest. As Julia no longer had a baby to look after, she was also designated to work in the forest with Tonia.

Tonia and Jędrzek Dolecki, who was now a widower, had resumed their former romance and he supported and helped her as much as he could, even amidst the tragic circumstances in which they now found themselves. They were very much in love as in their youth and this kept their determination and spirits up thus enabling them to endure the hardships in the hope that one day they might be free.

"If God allows us to get out of this hell one day," he promised her, "I will look after you for the rest of my life. We were meant for each other all those years ago, Tonia."

On 30 July, 1941 the prisoners were all called to assemble by Ivan the camp commandant and they wondered what had happened and what the meeting was about. He looked pleased as he started to deliver his announcement which unbeknown to the prisoners, and out of the blue, would at last bring a turning point to their lives.

"The Germans have attacked Russia and the Soviet Union is now at war with Germany. An amnesty has been granted to all prisoners and you are free to leave and travel wherever you want to. We shall issue you with permits as soon as we can, which will give you freedom of movement and you will be able to leave. You are now free people! Of course, if you wish to stay on here to live and work as free people, you can do so and you have our assurance that the conditions will improve and payments for work will be raised."*

The prisoners' initial reaction was one of disbelief and then there was a triumphant uproar. People cried with joy and hugged each other and praised God for his mercy in answering their prayers. Other cried at the realisation that although they had witnessed this long-awaited moment, their dead children, parents or other loved ones had not been given the chance to see this joyous day.

On hearing this news, Tonia's foreman Vladimir, ran over grinning and hugging her shouting, "Tonia, you are now free people. I am so pleased for you all."

As she turned, Tonia met Jędrzek Dolecki running towards her and they ran into each other's arms and kissed. In his joy and elation at the news of their amnesty, he proposed to her and she accepted with all her heart, as she had never stopped loving him. They knew that somehow, somewhere, some time, they would eventually be married. They were both free to do so now, without fear or restrictions or relying on parental consent. However they both knew that there was a war to fight before that moment could come, but at least they were no longer in captivity as slaves. They were free Polish people and nothing could stand in the way of their deep love for one another and for now, they would plan their dreams upon this.

All Polish people of course wanted to leave as quickly as possible, but it was not so straight forward, as the Camp Commandant's official discharge had to be obtained, along with travel permits and the relevant documents to verify the amnesty. There were thousands of people to process and the Russians were in no particular hurry to release their cheap labour force. However, the attitude of the Russians authorities towards the Polish people greatly improved after the announcement of the amnesty.

The camp conditions thereafter, did improve slightly and people's spirits were raised with their new status of freedom. The camp commandant encouraged everyone to grow things and collectively, the Polish families set up vegetable patches which they did successfully as many of them were farmers with many years experience. Old potatoes were cut through and planted and onion sets were bartered for or bought from the Russian peasants. They managed to grow cabbages and beetroots, and along with the mushrooms and berries from the forest, their diet improved gradually.

People were advised to travel south on their exit from Siberia, as there were rumours that the Polish Army would be forming 'somewhere in the south of Russia' and so anyone who wanted to join these allied forces, would have to make their own way there somehow, but this represented a journey of thousands of miles. Young people could also join the cadets and thus acquire improved conditions with food and medical care under the protection of the Polish Army. Everyone who signed up to join the armed forces, would be entitled to better conditions for their family and dependants and this represented hope for survival and an opportunity to serve abroad thus a possibility to travel out of Russia.

Whilst the weather was warm, Antek, Julia, Tonia and Jania decided to stay and work in the hope of finding out more information before travelling south in the autumn to avoid having to live and work outside through a third severe Siberian winter. As they lived and worked together, they managed to buy some food and ate mostly their own grown produce, thus saving their roubles from their wages to cover any future transport and food expenses which they would have to cover during the duration for their journey to the south. During the warm summer months, Tonia had managed to grow some tobacco in a plot at the back of their barrack and the leaves had been dried and stored with a view to exchanging it for whatever they needed along the way. Tobacco was scarce and in great demand, thus one could use it as a currency to purchase things more readily than with roubles.

In November, Antek was called to the Commandant's office to be issued with the long awaited papers confirming his family's free status and permits for them all to travel (*udostoverenye*). The office also paid out some outstanding roubles owed for their work in the forests. They thanked God for his mercy and took the decision to leave before the weather became more severe, although it was already cold and snowing.

After packing the few belongings which they possessed onto a sledge, along with a few potatoes, some dried bread, mushrooms and berries to sustain them on their journey south, they made preparations to go. Jania notified the nursery that she would be leaving and Klava, Stacha and Ania her colleagues in the kitchen, cried when they heard they would be losing her. They had become very good friends and had worked as a happy team, despite the difficult conditions caused by the war. Jania was sorry to be leaving them behind and they asked one of the school workers, who happened to have a camera, to take a couple photographs of them together as a souvenir. He developed the pictures himself in time for Jania's to take away on her journey.

Before they left, they all went to pray at Ireniusz's grave and say their last goodbyes. They were distraught at having to leave him behind in the Siberian forest. Julia picked up a few of the small stones from the top of his grave and placed them in her bag as it was the only memento of her child's life which she could take with her. She would never be able to visit the grave again and these few pebbles represented all that was left of the son whom she carried all the way from Poland on that tragic evacuation journey and who provided so much joy and love in the ten months of his short life with them.

Finally, on 4th November, 1941, after over one and a half years in the gulags of Siberia, they were relieved to set off and the four of them left their barrack and work camp Chary, on another journey into the unknown. They went with confidence and hope in their hearts, as they considered that their newfound freedom and release from the work camp would surely mean better prospects and chances of survival. This journey would not be easy, as they had to make their way back to Sośva railway station, where they had disembarked in March 1940, which was about thirty miles on foot through dangerous and isolated terrain. Although it was early November, there was already snow on the ground and the frosty temperatures were severe.

Many other families were also leaving before the winter set in and others had already travelled south as soon as they had received their permission documents. All prisoners from the gulags and deportees were heading south, firstly because the weather would be much warmer and secondly because there were rumours that a Polish army was shortly to be formed "somewhere in the southern regions of Russia".

The route initially took them through the thick pine forests where for one year and nine months they had toiled, froze, starved and watched hundreds of people, including members of their family and friends die. Then they crossed over open bleak, snow-covered countryside which the cold winter wind swept over, chilling them to the bone. Their route then took them through the dense forests of those surroundings which were particularly dangerous as these were inhabited by boars, wolves, and brown bears. Here, at this time of the year, was an additional danger from polar bears, who hunted in these forests. When the sea ice freezes and expands in the winter, reaching the continents of Eurasia and Canada, polar bears often migrate south from their ice fields in the High Arctic to find better feeding grounds.

After they had walked all the day in the snow and frost, it was getting dusky and they came across what appeared to them a very severe problem. In order to cut many miles off their journey and the effort of unnecessary distance of walking, they would have to cross a river so wide, that its far bank was barely visible from where they stood. As it was frozen, their only option was to walk over it in order to get across. Antek went ahead along the river bank to see if there was a possibility of finding a narrow crossing in the distance. As Tonia attempted to step onto the ice, it began to creak and cracks appeared under her foot. Julia tried further up the river with the same terrifying result. In their desperation and terror, the women began to cry in panic and discuss tactics of overcoming this new obstacle.

Suddenly, they saw a tall young Russian man in a large fur hat, sheepskin coat and boots approaching them over the ice from the other side of the river. He was walking quickly on the ice, seemingly without difficulty. When he came closer to them, he could see that they were all troubled and in distress.

"Ladies, what is the trouble? Why are you all crying?" he asked, looking most concerned.

They explained that they wanted to cross the river in order to cut their journey, but were afraid that the ice would not hold them as it was creaking under their feet when they attempted to put their weight on it and none of the sisters could swim.

Grabbing the rope of the sledge from Tonia's hand, the Russian instructed them to spread out so as not to walk close together and thus to distribute their weight across the ice.

"Don't worry. You will be safe. Follow me as quickly as you can and don't stop," he said confidently. He then proceeded to march back across the river from where he had come, pulling their sledge behind him and encouraging them to follow him. Antek returned to join them having not found any easy crossing further up the bank and proceeded to follow the Russian's instructions.

"Like this, watch me. One, two, one two, left, right, left, right," he shouted like an officer in charge of army training manoeuvres.

They had no choice but to obey his orders and walked as he instructed. They did not dare to look right or left but kept their eyes straight ahead on the Russian who, not only had taken command of all their earthly belongings on the sledge, but clearly was not at all concerned about the safety of the ice underfoot. Although the ice did creak somewhat, it did manage to bear their weight and following the Russian, they eventually reached the other side of the river and thanked him with all their hearts for his help and interest in their plight. When they bid their farewells, he smiled and turned to cross the river again to complete his initial journey.

* * * * * *

At the start of World War II, Germany and Russia, as allies, had an agreement to dismember and share Poland between them. However, when Germany attacked her Soviet ally (Operation Barbarossa) on 22nd June 1941, they were at war. As a result, the Sikorski-Mayski agreement was signed in London on 30th July 1941 between Polish Prime Minister General Sikorski, British Foreign Secretary Antony Eden, Winston Churchill and the Soviet ambassador to the United Kingdom Ivan Mayski. This demanded that all Polish prisoners who were held captive within Russians territories in the labour camps, be released with the intention that they would form a Polish army and join allied forces in order to defeat Germany. It also specifically insisted that wives, children and dependents of these soldiers also be released from the Soviet territories under the protection of the armed forces. However, some camp commandants did not bother to announce the news of the amnesty and the prisoners remained in the camps working for years. Indeed, after a certain period of time had elapsed, they were forced to become Russian citizens, losing their right to leave and remained in the Soviet Union for ever.

Women prisoners working in the forest, supervised
by the Russian foreman (far right)

Chapter Seven

Next Stop: Uzbekistan

Arriving in Sośva, they found the whole district and station terribly overcrowded with thousands of people struggling to carry their belongings, some with crying children and others with sick elderly relatives all of whom were travelling south out of Siberia. It was rumoured that the Polish army would be forming in Tashkent in Uzbekistan. When the amnesty had been declared, a Polish Embassy was established in Buzuluk which was situated in the south of Russia and several outposts were created in the remote areas of Russia where deported families could obtain help and advice.

Some people who had managed to reach Sośva were either too sick or weak from starvation and lay dying where they fallen. Just like Antek and his family, they all looked lost, ragged, emaciated and covered with mosquito bites, having gone through the work camps. Some had no shoes as these had worn out and fallen apart over time, so they had improvised by wrapping their feet with old rags or even cut up pieces of rubber tyres and secured these in place with string in order to keep their feet protected. Hundreds of refugees were sitting on the ground as they had been delayed at Sośva for days, waiting for a train to arrive in a system of transport which was very slow and notoriously unpredictable.

Antek left the women to look after their sledge with their possessions on it and went in search of information. Although it took several hours, he managed to purchase tickets to travel with some of the roubles they had between them and obtained directions for their further travel. They would need to head for Tashkent travelling south via Zlatoust, Chelyabinsk and crossing Kazakhstan.

There was a delay of several days for the train and they made themselves as comfortable as possible at the station to wait, taking turns to sleep so that one of them would look after their belongings. It was all too common for possessions to be stolen in the night, as all the ex-gulag prisoners who were now escaping, were desperate for clothes, shoes and food and people were trying to save themselves and their families from starvation and frost bite at all costs.

Towards the end of the fourth day, at daybreak, a heavy black locomotive, pulling a very old train, appeared in the distance and slowly drew into the station. Everyone on the platform rose to their feet, some with excited energy and others with the last ounce of strength they could muster up in their body. The guards checked the tickets carefully before allowing passengers on board, as many people who had not been able to purchase a ticket were hopeful of barging their way onto the train to make their long-awaited escape. As there was such a volume of people waiting to travel, this procedure took quite a while with arguments and confusion between the desperate refugees and the overwhelmed railway personnel.

Antek and the three sisters gathered their belongings carefully and having their tickets checked, climbed up to board the train. They thanked God that the day which they had many a time prayed for, had at last arrived and they were soon to be on their way south, as far as possible from their life of bondage. Although the train was old and dirty, it was a passenger train and an improvement from the cattle truck in which they had arrived in February 1940. The conditions were cramped to bursting point as far more tickets had been sold than the train could accommodate, but everyone was prepared to endure the discomfort with a view to imminent salvation.

On leaving Sośva, the journey to reach Tashkent in Uzbekistan lasted for two months. The distance amounted to approximately 1,400 miles and, in between travelling, necessitated many days of waiting at remote stations for connecting trains to board for their onward journey. Sometimes they boarded passenger trains but when these were not readily available, they would scramble onto goods wagons, just to ensure they kept on the move towards their destination. All means of transport was filthy and crowded with war refugees and deportees in their thousands, the majority of whom were sick and many dying on route whilst making their way south. In the middle of all this, Christmas came and went but they had no way of celebrating it, except to share some dry bread to exchange their customary Christmas Eve wishes and they all wished for each one of them to survive and for their journey to eventually take them out of Russia.

They used their hard earned roubles sparingly to buy basic food when their own supplies had eventually run out. Sometimes they exchanged possessions with the locals to acquire whatever was available to eat in villages or at stations where their trains stopped.

The Russian system of railways was very erratic and sometimes trains left earlier than scheduled, whilst at other times, they would make a stop at a station or indeed somewhere in the countryside for hours. This caused many tragic situations to occur, as those making their journey south were hungry most of the time and whilst their train stopped at a station, they took advantage to disembark and quickly buy some food for their families. There were many incidents where a parent went in search of food or milk for their children or indeed where children were sent off to quickly run and purchase something on the platform and whilst they were paying, the train would unexpectedly move off and families were separated, in some cases for ever. Having survived the trails of the Siberian labour camps, they were now left abandoned to perish somewhere else in Russia. However, in rare cases, if they were lucky, a later train might allow them to catch up to reunite with their families.

A particularly terrible and unfortunate incident happened one frosty winter morning. A teenage girl, whose parents had both died in the labour camps of Siberia, was travelling south with three younger siblings who were now her responsibility. At one of the stations, she jumped out to buy them some hot potatoes which she saw traders cooking on the platform. Suddenly, she heard the guard's whistle being blown behind her and saw her train moving off with her siblings inside. She began running to catch the moving train and the passengers inside were encouraging her to hurry to make sure she got on. When she jumped onto the ice covered footplate, her foot slipped off and she was dragged beneath the wheels of the train which severed both her legs. The train increased speed, leaving her to die screaming on the rails whilst hearing her brother and sisters crying in terror inside the train which disappeared with them into the distance. There was no question of the train stopping or any help available, as these were times of war in a hostile land.

Unfortunately, just as Antek and the sisters were about to reach their destination, the train was halted abruptly and soldiers boarded the train announcing that Tashkent was overcrowded to bursting point with refugees. The train could therefore take its civilian passengers no further, since it was required to transport soldiers for the army. Therefore, only men and young boys, who were travelling to Tashkent with intentions of enlisting, could continue with their journey.

At this point, Antek saw his opportunity, realising that joining up would mean he could eventually have some chance of saving his wife and sisters-in-law. The three sisters would now be considered as family of a soldier, if he included them on his records as military dependants. As a soldier in the allied forces, he would have means of finding the movements of his family through the Red Cross and army information points, but unfortunately they would now be left to look after themselves. Many of the men who joined up for service were leaving their wives and several children behind in these hostile terrains in the hope of eventually tracking them down whilst in active service. There was no other way, and so they said their desperately tearful farewells and Antek took leave of them. None of them knew when, where or indeed if, they were ever likely to meet again.

Widows left with children to care for, whose husbands had died in the labour camps, had no way of escaping from Russia without someone in the army registering them as their dependents. Many women therefore, in an attempt to save themselves and their children, had to resort to living with men who agreed to pretend to be their husbands in order that they would be considered eligible for leaving.

Meanwhile, Julia, Tonia and Jania along with other refugees were transferred to army trucks and were taken to neighbouring Uzbekistan, some 68 miles in distance, to Fergana. There, one very cold winter evening in the middle of January, the sisters found themselves in the outskirts of a town to spend a freezing winter night under the stars. Fortunately, they had with them their life-saving goose feather quilts and pillows, under the protection of which, they slept in the open and were kept relatively warm. In the morning when they awoke, they heard rustling and crackling and discovered that the surface of their quilts had frozen overnight and as they moved at daybreak, the crispy ice cracked on the quilt covers.

They were left in a very uncertain state, as ongoing transport and entry into Tashkent seemed unavailable for an unspecified length of time. Their only option now for survival was to go to the villages and work on the Uzbek collective farms which paid in food rather than money. They managed to hitch a lift in a cart with an Uzbek farmer who took them to a collective farm. There, they were able to work in the spring of 1941 on farms and then on cotton picking plantations in the hot summer months. The winter months in the south were much warmer than they had previously experienced. However, when the work became scarce, starvation set in and poverty and deprivation was very severe in these parts. Everyone lived in barbaric conditions in primitive mud huts, sleeping on the beaten earth covered with straw with no doors, windows, heating or sanitation. Once again, typhoid harvested the already malnourished and sick deportees, and people died in their thousands. Communal graves in Uzbekistan could barely keep up with the numbers of people dying every day.

Eventually, there was no work and nothing to eat whatsoever, and the sisters spent their waking hours simply walking around, scanning the ground on the lookout for anything which could possibly be pliable enough to cook and eat. Sometimes they resorted to cooking the empty husks from the cotton fields, which even when cooked were quite tough. One day, a group of men caught a dog which they killed and ate in their desperation for food, even though the animal was scrawny from starvation like themselves.

One morning, Julia was walking past a small Uzbek bread shop and saw the baker cutting loaves, for which she had no money to purchase even a roll. She noticed crumbs of crusts falling off the chopping board onto the table. She had not eaten bread for months and in her hunger, she crept up quietly to catch the falling crumbs into the palm of her hand. Suddenly, the Uzbek shouted and struck the bread knife down onto the table, intending to cut her fingers off, but she managed to snatch her hand away in time. She realised that there was no sympathy or pity to be expected for a foreigner in a strange and hostile land in times of war.

As time went on with these conditions of shortage and deprivation, all three sisters simultaneously became ill with typhoid and could do nothing but lie on the mud hut floor awaiting death. They were so thin by now, that when they slept on the straw, the bones of their emaciated limbs knocked together sounding like wooden dolls. Tonia, being a little stronger than the others, went out every few days to collect some water for them to drink. However, typhoid had made her so weak and dizzy that she could only get along by crawling on all fours, making every effort to hold her head upright. If by chance she looked down, her head would fall forward making her fall down prostrate. Julia was the most seriously ill with dysentery and was taken to hospital in Kitabu in an oxen drawn cart, this being the common means of transport in these Uzbek regions. As Tonia and Jania were very sick, they were not able to visit her and had no idea when she would be released.

As if by miraculous good fortune, Tonia and Jania discovered that although there was no food, and nothing grew in the barren soil as it was winter, every few days tiny leaves of some kind of grasses appeared through the snow and these were tender to eat when boiled and so they picked these leaves early in the morning. Then, melting some snow and boiling the water, they cooked the leaves to make a kind of hot tea and ate the boiled leaves just to keep their stomachs from completely shrinking. They were barely palatable as no other ingredient was available to flavour or add nourishment, but this alone kept them alive for weeks. However, in the mud hut next to theirs, were three Polish men who were also starving and Jania and Tonia encouraged them to eat the cooked leaves in order save themselves from dying. The men persevered but were unable to eat the leaf broth which made them vomit and within a few weeks, all three died of starvation. Jania and Tonia realised that their only hope was to keep up their newfound diet of leaves in order to survive on a day to day basis.

Meanwhile, Julia remained in hospital for some weeks and when she was released, the hospital staff simply pushed her out of the door and told her to go home, but where was that? She had arrived at the hospital very ill and almost unconscious so had taken no notice of the directions. Coming out of the hospital, she walked in a daze with nowhere to go. She was now completely disorientated and had no idea where the mud hut with her sisters was sited or the name of the area where they had been living in this remote wilderness. All around there were

Uzbeks hurrying with their donkeys and mules which carried goods piled high in baskets on their backs in the barren countryside.

Around her and spreading into the distance, she could see large looming black mountains which looked threatening against the evening sky as it was getting dusky. She had never felt so alone and forsaken in all her life and the enormity of her situation suddenly hit her. She was in the middle of remote Uzbekistan during a war, completely alone with no knowledge of where her hut and sisters were. She had no money and possessed only what she stood up in. She approached a square where there were some empty market stalls, as the traders had by now packed up and gone home, and she lay down on one of the stalls to sleep. She lay crying and prayed for death as she could see no other way forward.

Suddenly, she heard a female voice speaking to her and as she opened her eyes, she saw a large Uzbek woman wrapped in a red shawl standing over her in the evening sunset.

"What is the matter? Why are you crying lady?" the woman gently asked in Russian.

Julia was surprised that anyone should take any notice of a lone shabby woman crying, as after all, there were hundreds of people crying every day in such times of deprivation and tragedy.

"I am lost," she replied in Polish. "I have come out of hospital today and I don't know where to go. I have two sisters living somewhere not far from here, but I have no idea where."

The Uzbek woman thought for a while and suddenly, as if recollecting some detail, got hold of Julia's arm and helped her to her feet.

"I know of two sisters who live together in my village," she said. "Come with me and I will take you there. You never know, maybe they happen to be your own sisters."

Julia did not hold out much hope that she should be saved by such a coincidence, but it was the only option she had left and she walked with the Uzbek woman through several villages which all looked alike as the houses were all primitive mud huts. Finally, she recognised her surroundings and realised that the woman had indeed brought her to the right hut, wherein she found Tonia and Jania, both lying on the floor recovering from typhoid. She thanked the woman for her great kindness and lay down beside her sisters on the straw to rest. They were overjoyed at being reunited and thanked God that the three of them had survived this far. All Jania and Tonia had to offer Julia was the tea made from the boiled leaves, but she was grateful for that and just thankful that they were together again.

One day, whilst on their daily search for something to eat, they came across a sack behind a shed and opening it, discovered that it was full of salt. They had not seen salt for over two years and no proper food for months so in their starved condition, they fell upon the contents of the sack and ate the salt in handfuls. They then took some in a cloth so that they could flavour their grass tea to make it more palatable and use the salt as currency for obtaining food. Another day, they saw a cart of yellowed oil cakes made from cotton seed intended for cattle feed and they stole a few to eat. Although these were not appetizing, nonetheless they stopped the hunger pangs for a while. Thus they managed most days to share some item which was remotely edible and sustain them. Sometimes they would find something and other times they would beg the local Uzbeks or exchange one of their possessions such as a headscarf for some *lepyoshki*, flat breads which the Uzbek women baked in their clay ovens. Tonia and Jania sold their gold earrings and Julia sold her twenty-two carat gold ring in order to buy food. One could only think of surviving one day at a time and be prepared to take risks to achieve that.

At the beginning of March 1942, the sisters heard from some soldiers and a Red Cross information point, that transport might be available from Tashkent to take them out of Uzbekistan. However, they would have to reach the nearest railway station which would mean travelling by foot for two days. The news was that the Polish army were ready to evacuate Polish citizens from Russia into Persia. Julia made enquiries about Antek and finally was relieved to hear the news that he was safe and had managed to join the Polish army which would be evacuating out of Russia into Persia shortly. He had registered her and her sisters as his dependants and they would be eligible to join the evacuation transport. Tonia enquired about Jędrzek Dolecki, and to her relief, he too had managed to join up and was safe. Those refugees who had husbands, sons or daughters in the armed forces, would have the opportunity to join the evacuation but would have to make their own way to the port of Krasnovodsk to make their escape over the Caspian Sea. Jania, Tonia and Julia packed the few belongings which they still had and set off on foot to the railway station in order to travel onto Tashkent from where they could proceed with their journey to the port.

Eventually they arrived at a station where they understood that they would be able to, at some point soon, board a train to take them from Uzbekistan across Turkmenistan, which was the route leading to the port of Krasnovodsk, where the Polish army were organising the evacuations of their personnel and civilians to Persia. After showing their travel passes, they managed to purchase the necessary tickets and waited until the next day, sheltering at the station which was full of people travelling in the same direction. A very old passenger train arrived early in the morning and this was already very full but they were grateful to find a place on the floor where they sat for the journey. This part of their journey covered a distance of some 1,200 miles and took two weeks in utterly cramped and poorly sanitised conditions.

As it was almost impossible to find food, most refugees travelling on the train were starving and sick with typhoid, dysentery or tuberculosis. On the floor of one of the wagons, lay a mother very seriously ill, surrounded by her six small children who were all ragged and crying. Having managed to keep her children alive through the years in the gulags, she now could no longer do anything for them whilst they cried with hunger. When the train stopped at a station, a young Russian soldier who was passing by on the platform, heard the children crying pitifully and putting his head through one of the windows asked, "Why are these children crying so much?"

"Their mother is very sick and they are starving," replied the passengers.

On hearing that, he went out of sight, but returned within a short while carrying a brown paper bag which he passed through the train window.

"Please give these to the crying children and their sick mother," he asked one of the passengers and went on his way.

The bag contained seven beautiful white bread rolls. Nobody knew where he could possibly have bought or acquired these, as it was almost impossible to buy any kind of bread at that time. This act of kindness was greatly appreciated by the children's mother, as it gave them all a chance to survive a while longer.

Antek's sister had died of tuberculosis leaving behind her husband and two small daughters aged ten and six. Tragically, her husband was later also taken very ill with dysentery and after a few days with no medical attention, realised that he was going to die and leave his two small girls behind alone in these hostile surroundings. In his desperation to save his precious children, he warned them to expect his imminent death, giving them specific orders of what they were supposed to do when he had finally departed this world.

He pinned their release documents and travel permit to the eldest daughter's coat and instructed them both to leave at once when he was dead and find the main road and walk along it. Hopefully, there might be a possibility that army personnel travelling along would pick them up and enable them to complete their journey south and hopefully out of Russia.

The two girls did not have long to wait, as next day they saw that their father was indeed dead, as he had predicted. Although they were terrified and mourned his death, they put their faith in his carefully explained instructions and did exactly as he had told them. They collected their coats, hats and warm clothes and holding hands they said their last farewell to their beloved father's dead body and went to find the main road, along which they walked for some hours.

Eventually, they heard the noise of a truck behind them on the road. This slowed down, as Polish soldiers were travelling inside and were concerned to see two little girls walking on their own. Speaking to the girls, they realised these were Polish orphans, and took them in the truck heading for Krasnovodsk. They were placed in the care of the orphanage, where they were looked after and eventually evacuated out of Russia to Persia.

For the thousands of people making their tremendously long journey south using trains, the only way to buy food or drink was to leave the train whilst it was standing at a station. The timing of these stops was never easy to estimate and it was a gamble like a game of Russian roulette as to whether you would get something to eat and return to the train in time to continue your journey. One afternoon, during their two-week journey to reach the port of Krasnovodsk, such a tragedy struck the sisters, when their train had stopped for some while at a large station called Ashkhabad, where Tonia decided to dismount to see whether she could purchase some milk which was being sold on the platform. Taking her small round wicker pannier and purse with roubles, she dismounted from the wagon and began walking briskly to the far side of the platform to purchase milk for them. Just as she had finished paying, she heard a train whistle and to her horror, realised that it was her transport starting off. She turned and began running to catch up before the train gathered any speed. Although before the war she was a very fast runner, her legs now were swollen and painful, following her bouts of typhoid and the cramped travelling conditions. She suddenly realised she could not move them as fast as she used to and she could not speed up despite her efforts. She tried to increase her pace and at least attempt to jump onto the back footplate and grab the rear bars of the last carriage, but the train gathered speed suddenly and she could hear Jania and Julia screaming and crying at the sight of her being left behind.

There was nothing she could do and she felt as if she was experiencing the worst nightmare possible from which she could not wake up. She watched helplessly as the train disappeared into the horizon and with the terror of her situation closing in on her, she collapsed in desperation on the platform somewhere in the middle of Turkmenistan.

On the moving train, Julia and Jania were beside themselves. Jania had been particularly close to Tonia, as they had been together constantly for so many years. They had worked together, spent their leisure time together and in recent years, supported each other through terrible illnesses and misfortunes. Their strong bond had helped them to survive and together they could hope for a better future. Now her beloved sister Tonia was lost for ever and she felt there was no point in living. She became hysterical and tried to throw whatever was left of their belongings out of the train window. As far as she was concerned, she had no more need for possessions and was ready to give up on life. Julia had to restrain her, calm her down and they sat and cried and prayed that somehow God in his mercy would spare Tonia. They could not believe that just as it seemed the long awaited salvation and escape from Russia was almost in their grasp, only a few days away, Tonia should be left to die in some desolate part of the world. Could God really be so uncaring?

The train travelled another few days with very few stops until it finally reached the port of Krasnovodsk which was packed with many thousands of refugees all waiting to make their passage over the Caspian Sea to Persia. Here there were Polish army personnel trying to organise the crowds. Those civilians who were eligible for embarkation waited to have their identification documents checked. Although Jania possessed an identity booklet, which originated from Lwów and proved very useful, Julia did not have such a document but had to give Antek's name and army details in order to be accepted for the crossing. The procedures took several days in order to process so many people, many of whom had their documents lost or destroyed in the turmoil of war.

Finally, Julia and Jania boarded the ship for Persia and thanked and praised God that the day which they had so long awaited had finally arrived. They were at last leaving the country of their bondage and were now under the care of the Polish army where they would have a better chance of survival. In what should have been a joyous moment, their hearts were heavy. They were leaving Russia, but their sister was lost somewhere in its vastness. They wished with all their hearts that Tonia was here to sail away with them to freedom.

Meanwhile, what had become of Tonia at Ashkhabad railway station, where she tragically became detached from her sisters? God was indeed looking after her and had sent a guardian angel in the form of a kind elderly Jewish man, who came across her on the platform where she had collapsed crying. Seeing her in such a distraught state, he bent over her and touching her gently on the shoulder and enquired what the trouble was. She looked up and saw a tall orthodox Jew, dressed in a long black coat and wearing a tall black hat from under which hung two side curls which framed his neatly bearded face. He had kind blue eyes which looked sympathetically at her through his gold-rimmed spectacles. He carried a briefcase in one hand and some books under his arm.

"I have become detached from my transport which is heading for Krasnovodsk with my two sisters." She told him. "I am now left here all alone and there is nothing more left for me now but to die."

He took great pity on her and felt he could not leave without somehow helping her.

"Have you any money with you, madam?" he asked.

"Yes, I have quite a few roubles," she replied.

"Do you have a platform ticket?" he enquired. "If you have a ticket to enter the station, you will be able to buy yourself hot tea and some bread in the station foyer."

She did not possess a ticket and would therefore not be permitted to re-enter the station. He pondered hard for a moment trying to devise a plan and then, having thought of an idea, proceeded to explain.

"Go and stand by the platform fence, with your hands behind your back," he instructed carefully in a whisper. "I will go into the foyer itself using my ticket and then pass this to you through the gaps in the fence. Use my ticket to get into the foyer and when you are in there, buy yourself some hot drink and food. In the meantime, I will make enquiries to establish whether there will be an alternative train to enable you to catch up with your transport."

She was overcome with gratitude at his concern, as he now represented her only hope for survival. Quickly she did exactly as he had instructed. Standing by the fence with her hands behind her, she felt the precious ticket being slipped into her fingers from the other side of the fence and using that, she entered the large station foyer. There in a kiosk she saw hot tea being served and lovely white bread rolls which she had not seen or tasted for over a year. Using her roubles she purchased a cup of hot black tea which she drank with great delight, as she had not drunk tea for many months. Having come across such a golden opportunity, she thought of her sisters and bought several rolls, immediately eating one and realising that she had forgotten the taste of bread. In order to hold on to her will to survive, she had to keep hope in her heart that she might somehow, somewhere be reunited with Jania and Julia and when that moment came, she would bring them some bread. She placed the remaining rolls in her pannier, thinking how pleased her sisters would be to eat them.

Some while passed and she suddenly saw the Jew hurrying towards her smiling.

"I have good news for you, lady," he said. "I have just found out that there will be a train at ten o'clock tonight which will stop briefly at this station. However, it will not arrive at this platform, because it is not officially scheduled to pick up passengers, but it will make its stop over on the eighth track and you must try at all costs to board this. The train will be carrying Polish soldiers who are travelling to Krasnovodsk for the crossing to Persia. I must now leave you and I wish you good luck and may God go with you. I'm sure everything will be alright," he added nodding and smiling.

Tonia could not thank him enough for his trouble and kindness and went to wait until the evening in the warmth of a waiting room at the station. Looking at the layout of the railway lines, she could see that they stretched over very many tracks across into the distance and guessed that this station must have been a major junction point. The only way for her to reach the eighth track would be to walk cross all the other tracks to reach it. When evening came and she saw the station clock saying half past nine, she decided to make her way over to the designated place where the train was due to stop.

It was the middle of March and still quite cold. There had been heavy rain which left the tracks very wet and in between the rails, there were huge puddles of dirty muddy water which had collected with the rainfall. Although the station and its platform were lit, once she started to cross the tracks away from the platform, it was difficult to see in the dark and so she counted to make sure she would place herself near the correct track. Some rails she managed to balance on as she counted and crossed them. However, sometimes her foot would slip on the wet rail and she would overbalance falling between the rails into the cold water up to her ankles. When at last she had calculated that she was on the eighth track, she stood and waited, straining her eyes in the darkness to see if she could see any sign of an approaching train.

Suddenly, in the distance, there appeared tiny bright lights flickering and she guessed these belonged to a locomotive. Then she heard the thundering noise of the train getting closer and slowing down as it approached the track by which she stood. The locomotive looked enormous as it stopped to a halt near her with a deafening hiss of steam which shot across the tracks. She was overcome by its gigantic size with its wheels higher than her head and she felt dwarfed as she stood on the ground beside it.

Looking up, she recognised Polish army uniforms as the windows began to open and soldiers and officers looked out to see where they had stopped. One of the Polish officers caught sight of her standing by the track, lit up by the train lamps and she quickly approached him waving her arms to attract attention.

"Hello officer, I am Polish," she shouted up to him. "I am on my way to Krasnovodsk to sail with the Polish evacuees but became detached from my transport. I have been told that it would be possible to board this train to catch up my family who have gone ahead. Please can you help me sir?"

"Oh, we have a Polish lady," the officer shouted with joy. "Come on aboard quickly madam."

Opening the door, he stretched out his hands to her and grabbing them, she felt herself being pulled up to board the tall train which was filled to bursting point with Polish soldiers all on their way to the port. Some were singing national songs, others were smoking and playing cards. The officer escorted her to a compartment occupied by some women where there was a vacant seat and as he left her, she thanked him sincerely.

As she sat down, she looked around and recognised that the women travelling with her were all gypsies who were escaping for the port to avoid persecution. They were dressed in fineries and wore much gold jewellery, probably representing their wealth which they were taking with them. When they saw how wet and muddy she was and heard her tragic story, they took pity on her and offered some clean clothes and a hot drink. She was able to clean her muddy garments in the warm bathroom on the train and relished the chance to wash herself with hot running water, which she had not access to for over a year. Her clothes dried out in the heated train compartment and she had not felt such warmth and comfort since life in Lwów. She ate another roll which she still had in her pannier so she was no longer hungry. All she now needed was to find her sisters and with that thought in her head, she fell asleep.

When her train eventually arrived in Krasnovodsk, she saw thousands of people waiting for their documents to be checked for the passage. In her pannier, she had her identity booklet which had been arranged in Lwów before the war and this was sufficient. She informed the officials that she was the sister-in-law of Antoni Zatorski who was already enlisted as serving in the Polish army. It was verified that Antek had entered her on his list of his dependants and she was passed as eligible for boarding and evacuation from Russia.

As she boarded the ship, she realised that there were thousands of people packed on board and she was glad that she was leaving Russia after all the ordeals which she had gone through. It was 24th March 1942 and the journey would take two days to reach Pahlavi in Persia. The Soviet ship they sailed in was overloaded beyond its capacity and there was a serious lack of drinking water and little sanitation, although there was provision of dried bread. Many civilians lay on the decks where they fell as most were very sick or recovering from malaria, typhoid or other diseases and of course starvation. At this point only a small proportion of the 1.5 million Polish citizens taken to Siberia at the beginning of the war remained alive to make this journey.

As the ship started to sail, Tonia walked on the decks and thanked God that she had been so miraculously spared and saved by the Jewish man. She had never before travelled on a ship and she was curious to see her whereabouts. As she looked up the length of one of the decks, what she suddenly saw, made her heart skip a beat. She could not believe her eyes for a moment, as coming towards her, she recognised a thin skeleton figure which was her sister Jania. They ran towards each other, crying, laughing and hugging at the same time. They could not believe their good fortune that amongst so many thousands of refugees and in such chaos, they had managed to find each other again. When Jania took her sister to find Julia, the three of them were overwhelmed with happiness and considered that God was watching over them for a purpose. They had been granted at last what they had begged God for in their prayers for the past two years – to survive and escape from Russia together and He had at last answered their prayers. They learnt that Antek had also sailed in an earlier ship to Persia ahead of them. They gave thanks to God for his mercy and care and sailed on to freedom hardly daring to believe that it was reality.

At this point, from the time of leaving Chary labour camp in Siberia, the sisters had on their own crossed the distance of three states of one of the largest countries in the world, namely Soviet Russia. This alone, spanned approximately 2,500 miles, which they completed by travelling on foot and using whatever forms of dilapidated rail travel they were able to board, legally or illegally.

* * * * * *

On 22nd June 1941 Germany invaded its ally, the USSR and on 30th July the Polish Government in exile in London signed the Polish-Soviet Sikorski-Mayski Agreement which specified the release of all deportees from Russia. This made it possible for the formation of the Polish army which would be operationally subordinated to the Soviet High Command, whilst under the control of the Polish Government. However, Russia took every opportunity to sabotage the smooth running of any operations in terms of providing adequate food, shelter and training facilities for the Polish soldiers.

When rumours spread that Stalin was prepared to release them from Russia, these former prisoners of the gulags made a desperate journey southwards by whatever means possible and often on foot. Sometimes this represented thousands of miles according to where they had been held in the Soviet camps. It was an exodus of biblical proportions. Sometimes on this journey, dying parents in their desperation, would give their children away to total strangers or place them in orphanages in the hope that they could thus save them.

General Anders was in command of the evacuation of these soldiers and their families which was conducted in two large-scale evacuations in March and August 1942. During this operation, a total of 115,000 soldiers and civilians were transferred to Persia, which represented less than 7% of all Polish citizens who had been forcibly deported to Russia following the Soviet invasion of Eastern Poland in 1939. However, in 1943, the exit routes were sealed off by Stalin, as a result of the breakdown of diplomatic relations between Poland and Russia following the revelation of the Katyn massacres. This situation left many people stranded in remote Russian territories for ever, after being forced to take on Soviet citizenship.

CHAPTER EIGHT

Next Stop: Persia

The crossing of the Caspian Sea to Persia took two days in extremely cramped conditions and passengers seriously suffered through lack of drinking water and inadequate sanitation provisions. The Soviet ships in which they sailed were cargo ships, comprising of filthy oil tankers and coal carriers, which were all loaded beyond their capacity. Many people suffered with dysentery, and as there was only one toilet on most vessels, it meant when one had visited the toilet, it was necessary to re-join the queue again. Nonetheless, any type of vessels available, which could serve as a means of escape, was considered a bonus. People were rejoicing having made their exit from Russia at last and heading for warmer climates to a completely unknown land but hopefully a better future.

For almost one million Polish citizens released from the gulags of Siberia, Persia now stood as a beacon lighting the road to freedom, but only 115,000 were fortunate to make the escape. A majority of men and young boys took the opportunity to join the allied forces in action for the Middle East. Women and children remained as guests of the Persian government for up to three years until other countries could open their borders and offer them temporary refuge.

On 26th March 1942, the three sisters found themselves in Persia arriving at the port of Pahlavi. Exhausted by hard labour, prolonged starvation and disease, and barely resembling human beings, they disembarked, clutching their few scruffy belongings in their hands. Here, along the warm welcoming sandy shores of Persia, they joined thousands of people in an emotional gesture of thanksgiving. All those arriving knelt down together immediately to kiss the welcoming Persian soil and give thanks to God for their salvation from slavery.

They instantly noticed the warmer climate and all the civilian refugees transported arriving onto the beaches of Persia and were soon looked after by the Polish and British armed forces, the Persian government and the Red Cross with provision of food and drink. Persia had to make great efforts to accommodate all the refugees, as their country was suddenly flooded with far greater numbers of immigrants than they had ever anticipated. A vast amount of facilities had to be set up at a very short notice to cater for such an influx of refugees and bathhouses, latrines, disinfectant booths, laundries and many more amenities had to be provided.

During that spring in Persia, Easter arrived in early April and was joyously celebrated with masses conducted in the open fields. Everyone wept with emotion as these were the first masses which these devout Catholics had been given the opportunity to attend since leaving Poland. People joyously sang their traditional Polish Easter Day hymn. However, on this occasion, the words which express rejoicing at the resurrection of Christ, presented a different meaning to those who had arrived from the Gulags:

A happy day has dawned for us today,
One which we have all been waiting for.
Upon this day Christ rose from the dead,
Alleluia, Alleluia.

The Persian traders learned that hard boiled eggs were customary for Polish people to eat at Easter time and sold these on the beaches. (As eggs represent new life, on Easter Sunday morning, it is a Polish tradition for families and friends to share wedges of hard boiled eggs, which have been previously blessed in church, exchanging their mutual good wishes, rather in the same way that the wafer is shared on Christmas Eve. Having quickly learned the word for eggs in Polish, the Persians came around with their baskets filled with hard boiled eggs calling, "Yajka, yajka!"

Religious services always ended with the old Polish hymn which asks God for the protection and freedom of Poland. Singing this hymn brought out much emotion in the Polish refugees, as Poland was now helpless, completely overpowered by invading forces and the people in exile were all too far from their homeland to be of assistance. At this point in time, nobody knew if and when the words of the song would indeed become reality and bring freedom to Poland:

O God, who for such countless ages past,
Surrounded Poland, in lustre of power and glory.
You shrouded her, with the shield of your protection,
Against disasters, which threatened to crush her.
Before your altars, we bring our beseeching,
Grant that our nation, be returned to freedom.

Accommodation was provided by the Persian army, who hastily erected some 2,000 tents on fields and on beaches. Rows of tents, for several miles, housed thousands of people who had escaped Russia and were now refugees in exile. The numbers of refugees arriving from Russia were far in excess of the numbers expected and Persia was overwhelmed with housing and hosting the arrivals. The army set up field kitchens to feed everyone and there was some medical care provided by army doctors and volunteers in the hospital.

Unfortunately, here immediately arose a problem, as many people who had arrived from Russia were starved and emaciated and not having seen food for so long, were suddenly confronted with plentiful supplies. Rich army food such as lamb, corned beef and fatty soup was distributed by British soldiers which, when eaten in large quantities and too quickly, resulted in people becoming ill and many died as a result. Children and the elderly, had to be looked after by the field hospitals under the care of the army medicals, as their food intake had to be monitored to allow their digestive systems to readjust to normal eating. Sadly, many of those arriving, who were already suffering from illness and diseases, met their death within a few months. Freedom had come too late for them and the local cemetery in Pahlavi quickly filled up with Polish graves.

The condition of those who had escaped Russia was so appalling, that on arrival, they initially had to undergo a period of quarantine in Pahlavi, in order to stop the spread of infectious diseases which they had brought with them. Survivors of the Soviet gulags arrived suffering from tuberculosis, typhoid, scarlet fever, dysentery, diphtheria and smallpox. They were taken to baths and through a disinfectant and delousing process. Men and women had their hair completely shaved off and their ragged and filthy clothes burned in order to destroy the lice which had lived on them for two years. All suitcases, bags and bundles with belongings had to be given up to be burned also, to ensure diseases and parasites were eliminated.

There were supplies of clean underwear, clothes, sheets and blankets handed out to everyone by the Red Cross, which had been donated by various charities around the world, including generous contributions from America. The sheer comfort of having fresh clothes on a clean body, even though most people were covered in sores, scabs and flea bites made them feel instantly better. The warmth of the sun, fresh sea air and decent meals, were a luxury which the sisters had not experienced for two years and they slowly started to recover, although it took many months as they were still weak and frail following their ordeals.

The Persians were very kind and generous to the immigrants who had arrived in huge numbers in such a short time into their country and unoccupied houses were requisitioned in the city for accommodation. The Shah of Persia extended his welcome to all those arriving and offered his country's hospitality. He also offered the facility of his own palace and swimming pool as did other organisations which had large buildings to offer. Some beautiful palaces were offered as temporary accommodation to house schools and academies for the Polish children and young people in exile. Orphanages were set up in Isfahan to look after children whose parents had died in Russia or who had become detached from their families in their journey south. Some of the Polish children learnt Farsi and for many years after, Isfahan became known as the city of Polish children.

Those refugees who had no passports or suitable identification, had to be provided with documents and temporary passports to enable them to be recorded and accounted for and also to enable them to travel in the future. Jania and Tonia queued up with the crowds for most of a day to get their documentation organised in the offices set up for this purpose. It was 17th June, 1942 and it was Tonia's thirty-seventh birthday and the happiest she had known for several years. Through the army post, she had received a lovely birthday card from Jędrzek Dolecki with a romantic poem which he had composed and written down for her in his usual exquisitely stylish copperplate handwriting.

Julia did not accompany them, as she was recovering from malaria and had to be hospitalised for a few days. However, she too eventually received her Polish temporary passport on 22nd June stamped by the Vice Consul from the Polish Embassy in Teheran. All three sisters had to line up for their passport photographs to be taken and saw their own image in print for the first time in two years. Their hair was shorn off and they could see themselves as pitiful convicts, who had been starved within an inch of death and resembling skeletons. It took many months to erase the damage which the Soviet gulag camps had imprinted on them. However, with the warm climate, nourishing food and feeling of reasonable security and safety, they began to restore their dignity, health and original beauty.

Two years of living in destitution imposed by the Soviet gulags had not prepared them for the sight of shops filled with goods and facilities for bathing and cleanliness. It was like a dream come true. They walked by the sea and enjoyed the sun and fresh air to regain their health and strength. Fresh exotic fruit such as they had never seen, apricots, dates and pomegranates were plentiful to buy and these vitamins helped them to regain their strength gradually. The three sisters had never been exposed to such hot climate as they experienced whilst living in Persia and soon developed a deep tan which they never had before. Julia, having a slightly darker complexion than her sisters, was the most tanned which complemented her shiny black hair. When their hair finally grew back, they were again three striking looking women.

Tonia received letters from Jędrzek Dolecki who was also now in the Polish forces along with his two nephews and his brother Józef. His letter was full of plans for their future which hopefully would come with the end of the war. He wrote to her whenever he could and included romantic poems, assuring her of his love and fidelity until they met again when peace would eventually be restored.

There were only 10 doctors and 25 nurses in the whole of Pahlavi at this time. Polish priests who themselves had escaped from prisons in Siberia, were at hand to comfort the sick, bury the dying with religious ceremony, conduct masses, teach the children and provide spiritual support. This was a great joy to everyone, as during their gulag existence in Russia, praying was forbidden and being strong Catholics, they had missed the services of priests and opportunity to worship whilst held captive on Soviet territory.

Shortly after their arrival, Julia did some searches through the Red Cross information point which resulted in accessing details about her husband's whereabouts. Antek in the meantime had heard that evacuations of civilians to Persia had taken place and hoped that Julia and her sisters were amongst those who had arrived. On checking with the army information officials, he was notified that his wife and sisters-in-law had boarded the ship in Krasnovodsk and were on the sailing lists. It was possible to trace which camp they were in and send communication through the army postal system. He wrote to assure the women that they would now be safe under the protection and care of the armed forces so it would be easier to trace their whereabouts via military records and they would be able to receive mail. Additionally, Antek would now be able to send some of his soldier's allowance to financially support his wife and her sisters.

When the Polish Army was created in Russia in the autumn of 1941, it consisted solely of men who had somehow by God's grace survived Siberia's slave labour camps along with diseases and starvation for almost two years. Although they were all keen to join the forces to defeat the Germans and avenge the invasion and destruction of Poland, they were unfit for action and needed time to recoup from the terrible ordeals which they had endured whilst prisoners in the gulags. They also had to complete intense military training before they could be sent onto the battlefields.

During the creation of the new Polish Army in Russia by General Tokaczewski, it was decided that it should form an integral part of the Polish Republic with its soldiers swearing allegiance to Poland. Its operational matters would come under Soviet High Command for the purpose of defeating Germany, which was now the common enemy. Polish units were to be subject to Polish military discipline, equipped to standards current with the Polish forces already fighting in Great Britain and fed and supplied with standards in the Soviet Army. This was to be financially covered by a system of Soviet and British Lend-Lease Credits.

The Commander of this army was to be nominated, with Russia's agreement, by the exiled Polish Government based in

London. This responsibility was set on the shoulders of General Władysław Anders', who himself had recently been released from the Lubyanka prison in Moscow, and he took command on 18th August, 1941. Thereafter it was known as 'The Anders' Army' and by October 1941, this already numbered 41,000 men who had managed to make their way out of gulag captivity from widespread and most remote parts of Asiatic Russia in order to join the Polish army at all costs "somewhere in the south". Additionally, this figure was outnumbered by civilians who followed the army's route in the hope of thus making their escape from bondage in the Soviet lands. The initial assembly points for the new army recruitment was between Volga and the Urals, with Headquarters sited in Buzuluk (east of Kuibyshev) and other centres were at Totskoye, Kotlubanka and Tatishchevo near Saratov. Antek had managed to travel long distances and finally made his way to one of these points to be recruited into the newly formed Polish Army.

Unfortunately, when severe winter weather came, there were severe problems with supplies and weapons sufficient for only one or two divisions had been promised. The men of the newly formed Polish Army, based initially in Russia, were housed under canvas tents in temperatures of -35°. Until the shipment of British uniforms arrived, half the soldiers had no boots. They were pleased with the issue of British uniforms which replaced the rags which they had enlisted in, following their release from the Soviet labour camps. However, the Russian government was in no hurry to supply adequate food or medical care and so hunger, typhus and dysentery once again set in. Therefore, in order to save the lives of these prospective soldiers and to enable them to make a recovery, undergo training and be incorporated into the allied forces, General Anders felt that there was no option but to remove them from Soviet territories into the Middle East via Persia. It took five weeks to complete this evacuation in the most appalling conditions. As a result of Anders' leadership, in the spring of

1942, gulag survivors, both soldiers and civilians, found their long-awaited salvation and sanctuary on the shores of Persia.

Few people today, even those knowledgeable about World War II, know of the history of Anders' and his army, although British Prime Minister, Harold Macmillan referred to it as one of the greatest fighting units in World War II, winning battle after battle against Germany's finest soldiers and opening the road to Rome for the Allies. Sadly, its contributions were completely ignored by Western historians, so you would be hard pressed to find information recorded in history books. However, this was no coincidence, as a deliberate decision was made by Western powers to suppress this part of the history of the Second World War, because it would unavoidably flag up the crimes of the Soviets, namely the Katyn massacres and the deportations and suffering of one and a half million Polish citizens in Siberia, the publicising of which might offend Josef Stalin.

Antek had sailed to Persia with the men of this contingent, who like many other soldiers had arrived in Persia where they at last received nourishment, medical attention, uniforms and a short time to recoup, following which, a fleet of lorries took the soldiers to Teheran on their long journey south. Like many other Polish soldiers, they were on their way to Palestine and Egypt, where they would be re-grouped in accordance with British Army organisation. Those coming with Anders' Army from Russia, would eventually be incorporated into the Polish Second Corps. After completion of military training, Antek was assigned to the 3rd Carpathian Rifle Division.

On this journey through Persia an unexpected and amusing event took place, which amid the unimaginable turmoil and deprivation of war, gave the soldiers warm happy memories which would stay with them for the rest of their lives. During the passage south from Persia to Palestine, when the convoys of trucks stopped at a remote mountain village near Hamadan for a rest break, the Polish soldiers from the 22nd Transport Company came across a small hungry native boy, carrying a dirty old sack and they offered to share with him some of their rations of corned beef.

Whilst the lad was busy eating, the soldiers noticed that the sack which he had put on the ground was moving and from it emerged strange squeaks. When questioned, the boy tried to explain in his native tongue what it was that he carried. Unfortunately however, none of the men spoke any Persian, so they could not understand the mysteries within the moving sack. On investigating its contents, the soldiers were astonished to find inside a tiny bedraggled and hungry-looking brown bear cub. They finally learned from the boy, by using signs and gesticulations, that he had found the bear abandoned in a cave in some nearby mountains, after the mother had been shot and killed by hunters. He would not be able to keep it himself and because the cub was so young and had not yet been weaned, it would undoubtedly die if someone did not take it into care.

The soldiers were filled with compassion at the situation of this helpless orphaned creature, as they were at that time experiencing what it was to be orphaned and homeless themselves. They decided that there was no option but to keep the bear, collectively paying the delighted boy in some Persian money, chocolate, an army pen knife and some corned beef. They then took turns to feed the cub, who was still suckling, by mixing their army rationed condensed milk with warm water and feeding this to the bear in a vodka bottle through an improvised teat made of a piece of cloth. Unanimously they agreed to give him a Polish name of Wojtek, and thus the Second Corps acquired its mascot in the shape of a brown bear.

As Wojtek was so very young, the soldiers secretly took it in turns to look after him but were anxious that army regulations might refuse permission to keep him. He slept in their tents at night, cuddling up to the soldier who had undertaken to be his main carer and surrogate mother. He travelled in the lorries on the long four-day journey to Palestine, over the Persian mountains, across the desert of Iraq, arriving in the lush countryside at the River Jordan. Finally, when they stopped at

Ghedera, the soldiers had to seek permission from the Commanding Officer and authorities to adopt Wojtek as their official mascot, which was seen as a morale boosting incentive and it was approved.

It was taken into account that most of these men had survived unimaginable conditions in the gulags and unlike soldiers going to fight in other countries, they had not left their wives and children at home or indeed in their own country. Most of them had left their dependant families (in some cases children in the care of orphanages) in the middle of hostile terrains in the care of fate and God. They would have little to take joy in and it had been a long time since they had cause to smile. The bear cub would provide a distraction from their personal troubles and losses and so the 'care bear' was approved and officially entered on the army lists as a new recruit.

In the care of the soldiers, he grew rapidly into a large brown bear who loved to play fight and wrestle with the men. When given a mouth organ he would attempt to sit and play it, likewise drinking beer from a bottle, having observed the soldiers' technique beforehand. As his appetite grew in line with his huge stature, he would often sneak extra food from the army warehouse and on one occasion came across an enormous catering size tin of marmalade in the stores, which he managed to open and devour. Unfortunately, that evening, his indulgence resulted in him having diarrhoea and there were many army blankets to be washed the next morning from the tent where he had slept with the soldiers that night.

When the convoy of trucks was on the move, the bear occupied the passenger's seat at the front and loved to ride along looking out at his surroundings and alarming passers by. As the army travelled to hotter regions, which were frequented by sand storms, Wojtek felt the heat with his thick fur and would often take a shower with the soldiers to cool down. However, he managed to work out the mechanisms of the communal showers in the bath hut and eventually, this had to be locked to prevent him from using up all the army water supplies.

However, one morning when he found the bath house open, he sneaked in coming face to face with a terrified intruder, who later was discovered to be a scout for an Arab raiding party. The Arab had entered into the army camp by cutting through the perimeter wire in an attempt to find guns in the weapons store for a planned raid. During his interrogation, he was threatened with being given as fodder to the bear, which promptly made him confess and produce the names of other conspirators in the plot. As a result, Wojtek was acclaimed a hero with rewards of beer and extra time in the cool shower that day which he enjoyed until he had used up all the available water! The bear would travel with the Polish soldiers throughout their route from Iran to Iraq, Syria, Palestine, Egypt and then into the front-line action of Italy.

In the meantime, for the sisters now in Persia, Pahlavi was only a temporary holding site for the refugees. In October 1942, thousands more people arrived, having escaped from Russia, who were also in need of rehabilitation and care. The earlier March transports of refugees, who had now made good recovery, had to be transferred on in order to make room for the new people arriving.

Arrangements were therefore made for them to be moved onto the capital city of Teheran, which was some 519 kilometres away, using lorries and army trucks. The journey took two days, travelling through beautiful lush scenery, enhanced with exotic flowers such as they had never before seen. They passed rice fields and vineyards with tree-covered slopes of the Elburs mountains on the horizon. After a few hours, the scenery would dramatically change to become mountainous and the lorries and assortment of vehicles wound up serpentines between steep mountains and plunging ravines and then through a barren uninhabited plateau via Qazvin to Teheran. The refugees stopped for an overnight rest, sleeping on floors in schools on the way before proceeding onto the capital.

On arrival in Teheran, the sisters were transferred together to Camp Number 2, being the largest of the five transit camps with accommodation in tents, under the care of the Polish army and Red Cross. Washing, bathing and toilet facilities were set up in large communal barracks to cater for so many people in transit. Meals were provided in dining halls three times a day and all these amenities were a welcome change in comparison to what they had experienced during the previous two years. Some government buildings were offered for living quarters, including a disused munitions factory. There was a Polish hospital and a big Polish orphanage which was run by the Sisters of Nazareth.

Here, the hospital was looking for help on the wards and in the kitchens so the sisters decided that they could offer their services and once again find their identity, become useful citizens and at the same time, earn some money. Jania of course applied to the kitchens, where she knew that her skills would once more prove valuable. Julia and Tonia on the other hand, worked as cleaners on the wards. In the evenings, Jania took up her old hobby of embroidery and channelled her creative talent into decorating beautiful table cloths, cushion covers and wall-hangings. She found this relaxing and groups of women would gather together in the evening to sew, knit, crochet and chat.

Whilst cleaning one of the wards one morning, Tonia heard someone excitedly calling her name and looked up. To her amazement, she saw Doctor Jadwiga Kornella, her former employer from Lwów, hurrying towards her with open arms. They cried as they embraced each other, as neither knew if the other had survived the labour camp where they had last met. Jadwiga had also recently been transferred to Teheran to work in the hospital. They had not seen each other since the desperate days in the labour camp of the frozen depths of Siberia and saw how much better each of them looked in comparison to the starved remnants of women that they had been.

They had much to talk about of their terrible Gulag days and their subsequent survival and escape from Russia. Jadwiga confided in Tonia that she was now bringing up her four year old niece, Halina, whose parents had both recently died of typhus in Teheran. Jadwiga was the only relative whom the orphaned child now had, but in order to resume her work as a medic in the hospital, she needed someone reliable to help with the childcare.

Tonia would therefore once again work for Jadwiga, but instead of looking after her elderly mother and household, as she had done in Lwów years ago, she would be looking after little the little girl. Halina was a delightful child with fair hair and deep blue eyes which were sometimes very sorrowful at the recollection of her beloved parents, whom she had lost. She had been deported with her family to Siberia as a baby and had somehow managed to survive, thanks to the dedicated care and efforts of her parents. She often expressed a desire to one day become a doctor just like her aunty Jadwiga, so that she could make people well again.

Cultural and spiritual enrichment in their new country of refuge was soon established and developed. Schools were set up for children in buildings which were provided for the purpose and everything was more organised allowing life to return to some normality. There were evening prayer meetings and masses conducted by the Polish priests, who had been transferred to serve in the deportee camps. Within a few months, the exiles set up their own theatres, art galleries, study groups, Polish newspapers and radio stations. Life, as far as was possible under the circumstances, was safe in comparison to the cities of war-torn Europe, which were being bombed and destroyed.

The majority of refugees were women and children, as husbands and fathers were now in the armed forces. The men who were not in the forces were either too old or had some disability which prevented them from being accepted into the army. There were many children who had become war orphans and these were looked after by the orphanages run by Polish officials with the help of the Red Cross. The war had also turned orphaned teenagers into young carers, sometimes responsible for several siblings whilst trying to resume and complete their education, which for the large part had been disrupted since the evacuation to Russia.

In the height of the summer months, the heat of Teheran was intense (43°C, 109°F) and the nights were particularly hot to endure in the tents, whilst sleeping in hammocks covered by thick mosquito nets. Shoes also had to be put up the hammocks to avoid any vermin such as scorpions climbing into them. There were also problems with termites which were a nuisance and would destroy everything that was in their path. Vultures were plentiful in these parts and were so bold that they would swoop and steal food from people's hands, particularly from children who they knew would be too naïve to be on guard. Many times this would provide an amusing sight, particularly on one occasion when an elderly man was strolling along, carelessly carrying a paper bag of fresh doughnuts in his hands crossed behind his back. Although Tonia and Jania shouted a warning to him to look out for the vultures, he took no notice and before long, a sharp eyed bird made a dive for the bag, ripped it out of his hands and carried it off, much to the amusement of onlookers.

In the spring, Jania saw a pair of small birds looking for nesting material near their tent and she had an idea. She and Tonia found a spare tropical helmet and partly filled it with straw and grasses. They then hung it upside down in the highest point of their tent and having thrown some crumbs for the birds, waited to see if they would choose this for a home. It did not take long for the birds to decide that the helmet would make a good nest and they did not seem to mind the occupants in the tent who fed them regularly. The sisters took great delight over the next few months in watching their new lodgers putting their finishing touches to the nest, sitting on eggs and then raising their tiny chicks. Finally, after the first awkward flying lessons, the chicks and parents departed. The sisters felt a great satisfaction having provided these small creatures with a temporary house, as they knew themselves how important it was to have a place to call home, even if it was in unfamiliar surroundings.

In the mornings, Jania started work very early at the hospital and on arrival, she would squeeze oranges, lemons and grapefruits, which were now plentiful, into a huge bucket to provide drink throughout the day. By the end of the day, she would have drunk all the juice as the temperature rose into the hundreds outside and even higher in the hot kitchens where she worked.

Whilst she was working at the hospital, there was a visit to the camp from the Polish Bishop Gawlina, who travelled to these parts to visit the refugees in order to support their spiritual wellbeing. One of the scheduled places for his stop was the hospital where he visited the sick, the medical staff and he also asked to see the staff in the kitchens. As he entered the area where Jania worked, he remarked about the tremendous heat in which the cooks had to work in. Dressed in her white chef's uniform, Jania was introduced to the bishop, who shook her hand heartedly and jovially announced,

"My dear woman, be assured that any sins you commit in your lifetime will automatically be forgiven, as you have already paid your penance whilst here on earth by working in this heat of hell!"

Apart from the intense heat, occasionally, there were sand storms, which again presented a completely new experience to the refugees, and one had to find shelter and cover the head, eyes, nose and mouth to avoid choking. There was however no escape from the hot sand which blew everywhere and obliterated the daylight until the storm finally passed over and then left the task of clearing up the mess.

In the months following their arrival, many people became ill with malaria and other tropical diseases, and soon Dulab, the large cemetery in Teheran, began to fill up with thousands of Polish gravestones of men, women and children all standing in rows with identical inscriptions depicting the year as 1942. As there was such a huge volume of people dying on a daily basis, medical help was stretched beyond human capacity. Under the circumstances, there was the possibility for errors being made in the hasty diagnoses which were carried out to process those who could be saved and those who had passed away. In addition, taking into account of the blistering heat of the summer, bodies had to be buried as quickly as possible to prevent further spread of diseases.

Julia's friend Felicia Misiąg, who in Poland had been her long-standing next door neighbour in the village of Waniów, became seriously ill with typhus and was taken to hospital leaving behind her four-year old son Stan. At the hospital, having been misdiagnosed as dead, she was taken to the hospital mortuary to await burial. That night, whilst lying in the morgue, the cold atmosphere inside revived her and she awoke. She found movement restricted by a body bag which they had placed her into and she tore this open to free herself. When she managed to sit up, she realised to her horror that she was surrounded by rows of dead corpses awaiting burial. On her toe, tied on with some string, was a label with her name and date of death. She proceeded to make her way slowly out of the mortuary. The sight of her emerging out in her white nightgown and looking dazed, terrified those who witnessed the scene as they thought that they had literally seen a ghost. A soldier nearby, who was guarding the camp, put his coat around her to keep her warm, as the nights in Persia were very cold. She was then taken back to the hospital to recover from her illness, and whilst there, she met a Ukrainian man who worked there, by the name of Dymitr Hryciuk, who showed her great kindness and the two became good friends.

Unfortunately, when Felicia was returned from hospital back to her accommodation quarters, she could not find little Stan anywhere, despite frantically searching the area and camp for a whole week. She was beside herself, as having protected her son through the all the ordeals of Russia, where she had already lost her husband, the child was all she had left and now he had disappeared from her care. Finally, someone told her that they had seen a couple taking Stan away. After much searching, Felicia was able to trace them and eventually found her son safe and retrieved him.

Meanwhile, all three sisters suffered with malaria at some point, but not simultaneously which enabled them to look after each other. Jania had malaria particularly severely, but received excellent medical care at the hospital, being a member of staff. The doctors had built up a great respect for her, as she worked so hard applying her gastronomy skills into the kitchens. Whilst she lay in delirious fevers, they looked after her until she fully recovered. At the time, doctors recommended fresh pomegranate juice for reducing her temperature, which seemed to reduce the fever very quickly.

During their free time, there was the opportunity to do some sightseeing and the sisters visited the huge and impressive underground market in Teheran which sold beautiful Persian rugs, carpets and handcrafted gold jewellery. Using the money which they were now earning, they bought fine materials to have some new dresses made by the local Polish dressmakers who had quickly set up businesses. They had their hair styled, now that it had grown back after being shorn off. Tonia invested some of her money in gold which was cheap and purchased two gold wedding rings, with the intention that these could be used for her and Jędrzek's marriage, when the war was eventually over. Julia bought a wedding ring for herself to replace her own original ring which she had exchanged for food in Siberia.

On 4th July 1943, they heard the disastrous news which shocked all Polish people wherever in the world they found themselves at that time. General Sikorski, the Prime Minister of the London-based Polish Government in Exile and Commander in Chief of the Polish armed forces was killed in a mysterious plane crash along with his daughter who had flown with him. He had been on a trip to inspect his Polish troops in the Middle East and on its return flight from Gibraltar to

England, his plane crashed into the sea, leaving the pilot as the sole survivor.

Earlier that year, the Polish people had been incensed when the Katyn murders had been uncovered and General Sikorski insisted that an investigation by the International Red Cross be made into these terrible war crimes. The Polish troops who were now based in the Middle East, as part of the allied forces, were furious at the Russians for having carried out these killings and Churchill advised General Sikorski to visit the soldiers in the Middle East to offer them support and calm them down in order to get their minds focused on their engagements in battles of the allied forces. It was on the return journey from visiting the Polish troops, that Sikorski's plane was involved in the fatal crash.

Churchill opposed calling an enquiry into the crimes of Katyn, which the Russians had carried out but denied, fearing it would be detrimental to Allied unity at this point in time during the war. He calculated that without the Soviet Union as an ally, there would be no possibility of defeating Hitler and Germany. Hence, the Polish press, which during the war years was based in London, was vigorously censored to ensure that it did not print anything revealing Russia's guilt which might offend Josef Stalin and rock the boat sufficiently to jeopardise the valuable alliance with Russia.

However, the Polish press did manage to divulge the crimes of Katyn, as well as Polish feelings towards the Soviets regarding their part in these killings. Following this, Russia severed their relations with Poland's exiled government in London and shut down the escape routes to Persia. This unfortunately resulted in thousands of Polish citizens, who were waiting for transport to make their escape from Russia to Persia, finding themselves stranded on Soviet soil. Subsequently, they were forced to take on Russian citizenship, thus preventing them from ever leaving.

Julia, Jania and Tonia considered themselves very fortunate to have been in the right place at the right time, making their escape possible, as the escape route provided by the Russians had lasted for only a very limited period of time.

Special Annotation:

(Ironically and tragically, as I am writing this very part of my story on 10th April 2010, a related disaster has repeated itself with a fatal accident of the current Polish President, Lech Kaczynski and his wife, along with their entourage, who were travelling to Russia to commemorate the 70th anniversary of the Katyn massacre of 1940. Their plane suddenly crashed outside Smolensk, killing not only the President and his wife, but also ninety seven prominent members of the Polish government, politicians, high ranking representatives of the armed forces and clergy who were travelling with them to take part in the planned commemoration ceremony. Following this, President Kaczynski and his wife were buried at Wawel Castle in Kraków, the burial place of Polish kings, nobility and noteworthy citizens, where General Sikorski had also been interred in 1943).

In August 1943, there was another mass refugee transfer planned and the sisters had to once again pack their belongings and now transfer to Ahwaz on the Persian Gulf, this time travelling by train. The journey between Teheran and Ahwaz was approximately 547 kilometres, taking them through mountainous regions and through 130 tunnels to reach their destination. They travelled during a heat wave as the temperatures in Ahwaz were higher than they had previously experienced in Persia, reaching up to a scorching 54°C, 130° F.

During this time, Persia was occupied by the Russians and British who were hostile in their manner to the natives and with whom the Persians therefore did not share very good relations. However, the Polish immigrants had a genuine affinity with the Persians, as they had not arrived as invaders and were grateful for the hospitality which they received in time of crisis. Polish soldiers, for example, automatically saluted Persian officers in the street as a sign of respect for their host country and members of its armed forces, which the Persians soon noted and appreciated.

In Ahwaz, the area where the Polish refugees were based was named Camp Polonia and after the camp was closed and the Polish had moved on, it became known as Campulu even until the present day. Those who went through Persia (Iran) always recalled with gratitude, the warmth and hospitality which they had received whilst in exile there.

In November 1943, Churchill, Stalin and Eisenhower had their first face to face meeting at the Teheran Conference held in the Soviet Embassy, where part of the discussions concerned Stalin's desire to have the Eastern borders of Poland moved to incorporate them into Soviet territory and the Western allies agreed for the future of post-war Poland to fall under Soviet influence.

Their period of stay in Persia was coming to an end and a new order of departure was published at the start of December 1943 when Julia, Tonia and Jania were assigned to travel to India. The countries which were setting up Displaced Persons camps were Tanganyika, Mexico, India and New Zealand. Once more they packed their belongings and were taken along with many other refugees to port Khorramshahr, approximately 10 kilometres north of Abadan, for another sea voyage, this time east along the Persian Gulf to Karachi in India (now Pakistan)*** which lasted six days. Julia recalled the gypsy fortune teller in Waniów, at whose predictions she had laughed when told that she would be travelling to many far away countries.

In the meantime, in December 1943 Antek had travelled with the Polish army to Qassassin in Egypt and from there the Polish and British troops would be transported to the ports of Alexandria and Port Said for embarkation to sail across the Mediterranean to Southern Italy, where they would be engaging in action.

However, their problem now was Wojtek, as it was against army regulations to take animals on board ship across to Italy. The men of the Second Corps knew that the bear considered himself part of the Company and they saw him as a fellow soldier because he was so human in his behaviour. They were heartbroken at the thought of being asked to leave him behind. There was a long and anxious wait to obtain permission from the authorities of the Embarkation Office and at the very last moment, after much deliberation and bypassing of red tape, a special permit was granted for the bear to travel with his men. Finally, on 13th February, 1944 when the Polish Liner M.S. Batory was being loaded with soldiers on their way to Italy, Wojtek the large brown bear triumphantly led the Company up the ship's gangway, boarding the ship to the cheers of his fellow troops.

The evacuation of Polish exiles from Russia, organised by General Anders, took place in two phases, the first on 24th March 1942, and the second on 5th August, 1942. In total, 115,000 people escaped, which represented only 7% survival of the number of Polish citizens originally deported to the Soviet Union. Whilst in Persia, during 1942 and 1943, the Polish army in the East underwent health checks, treatment and rehabilitation, following their ordeal in the Soviet camps. They were also given intense training and preparation for battle to enable them to join the Allied Forces.
Persia came to be known to the Western world as Iran in 1935.
**The port which was called Pahlavi is now Bandar-e Anzali.*
*** In 1943, the Port of Karachi was in India and in 1947 it became part of the new country of Pakistan.*

Julia, Tonia and Jania on release from the Gulags 1942
(After disinfectant and de-lousing, with their hair cut off)

CHAPTER NINE

Next Stop India (Pakistan)

After a six day crossing of the Persian Gulf, the three sisters arrived, along with many thousands of other refugees, in Karachi on 14th December 1943 and were transferred to a huge barbed wire fenced transit tent camp near Karachi. This was run under British authority as India was under British colonial rule at that time, and had agreed to host a quota of 30,000 refugees. The camp had been temporarily set up to house the Polish exiles awaiting onward resettlement and there were many such camps scattered around India to accommodate the large numbers of displaced Polish people who were homeless. In their new setting, Christmas 1943 approached and was celebrated as best they could in the settling-in period.

In the daytime it was very hot and in the cool of the night, the hyenas howled menacingly outside the camp perimeter fencing. The surrounding countryside was quite barren in this area with vast expanses of sand and constant danger from a variety of nasty insects, scorpions and poisonous snakes. However, although conditions were basic, schools were set up to promote the education of the children and an orphanage was established to care for hundreds of children who were travelling with the Polish civilians, having lost their parents either through starvation or hard work in the Soviet gulags or more recently in Teheran and Ahwaz through starvation, exhaustion, malaria, typhoid, and other diseases.

In September 1944, after their initial stay in Karachi, their next transfer took them on a further sea voyage south, along the coast of India to Bombay during which, a tragedy almost occurred. The ship in which they were sailing had over one thousand passengers on board, mainly women and children. On this occasion, it was escorted by a convoy of military ships to provide safety against enemy submarines. In the night, the passengers noticed an atmosphere of unease amongst the ship's crew but were not given any information about what had occurred. However, next morning, the captain announced that during the night, a Japanese submarine had broken through the convoy and had come within threatening distance of their ship. On realising that it was surrounded by several armed military ships, it had thankfully retreated without any incident.

On arriving safely in Bombay, the deportees were taken by passenger trains to one of the largest of the Polish settlement camps in India, situated south of Kolhapur called Valivade. This very large temporary camp mainly consisted of single mothers whose husbands had either died or were serving with the Polish Army in Italy. There were elderly men who, having fought in the First World War and several other wars in their younger years, were now not eligible to be serving in the forces due to their age or some disability.

Accommodation in Valivade was in barracks, made of metre-high stone walls topped by matting and tiled roofs with an open veranda. This temporary accommodation was gradually transformed into colourful little homes with flowers and banana plants growing all around them. The women made great efforts to create a home in yet another strange country and furnished their barracks with rugs and pretty curtains to make them individual. Each barrack had two rooms and a kitchenette where families could prepare their own meals from produce which they could buy in the many shops of the settlement or at vegetable markets just outside the camp.

Tonia, Julia and Jania were housed in a large barrack which they had to share with another family by the name of Nejman, a couple in their late thirties with a five-year old son. They had never met previously, but got on very well and eventually became as close as family. Mrs Nejman was an extremely tall woman aged forty, five years older than Julia, and she often accompanied the sisters wherever they went, so people in the camp assumed she was a fourth sister!

Every person was entitled to an allowance of forty rupees per month, which was adequate for purchasing food and clothing. However, those who were additionally able to undertake some local paid work, had enough money to live on comfortably. Jania, Tonia and Julia enlisted as policewomen in the camp security service and they patrolled the area in smart military uniforms, dealing with emergencies, making sure that everyone in the camp wore their tropical helmets to avoid sun stroke, directing traffic and delivery vans around the camp, reuniting lost children with their mothers and calming any men who were disrupting peace and order in the camp as a result of consuming too much alcohol! They loved the work, as it enabled them to meet so many people on a daily basis and they became well known for their service and help to the community. Their police work was reasonably paid and their three combined wages allowed them to establish as comfortable a life as was possible at the time. Above all, they were grateful to have regained their health and be living in peaceful surroundings far from the war-torn cities of Europe, where at that time, civilians were enduring heavy fighting and bombing.

Everyone was issued with cooking pots and utensils on arrival at the camp and one of the standard items was a very large aluminium Indian cooking pot with a lid made by the local Hindus, which proved most useful for cooking soups and stews. All three sisters were issued with one each and with Jania's cooking skills, these were seldom empty. She was able to buy fresh fruit and vegetables from the markets, as well as some meat to cook nourishing meals for them once again. She continued to do embroidery in the quiet hours of the evenings after work and their barrack was furnished with beautiful wall hangings and intricately embroidered table cloths and cushion covers, which helped to create the atmosphere of regained stability and creature comfort. They planted a variety flowers in their small garden around their barrack and tended these together.

The barrack floors were bare ground and to deter termites and scorpions, it was customary for the locals to use cow dung, which they thoroughly mixed with water to a smooth spreading consistency, and regularly applied this to the floor areas. Although this produced an unpleasant odour to begin with, when dried, it formed a very solid and shiny veneer surface which was no longer smelly, but more importantly repelled creepy crawlies for quite some time. The Polish women would either apply this floor covering in their home themselves, or pay for the services of a local Hindu woman who came around calling for custom, carrying her bucket of smelly dung floor covering preparation which she would apply at a cost of a few rupees!

Within a year, the camp of Valivade gradually developed into a thriving little town with the building of St Andrzej Bobola Church, so that Sundays and all holy days could be observed once again. There was a cinema established, which screened Polish and Hindu films (with Polish sub titles) regularly for entertainment. A post office was opened and run by Polish officials to allow them to send correspondence and parcels to husbands and sons fighting on the different fronts. For the children there were three nursery schools, four primary schools and four middle schools, plus a grammar school. A guides and scouting movement was established for the young people and Polish shops, bakers, a restaurant and hairdressers were set up. Four medium hospitals were built to care for the sick and eight community centres were set up. Many Polish people learnt to speak fluent Marathi and likewise, the locals also learnt to speak Polish and so they all became a very integrated society. Here, far away from the world's war-torn

European cities, 5,000 Polish refugees made Valivade their little Poland in India, which was a safe and comfortable sanctuary and where they were hosted with warmth and affection by the locals.

The communication of news of developments of the war was very efficient with a regular Valivade Settlement Chronicle produced and distributed. The BBC broadcasted the war news in Polish, which was transmitted through wirelesses in the community centres, so that wives and children of the soldiers fighting on the frontlines could regularly hear of the progress and whereabouts of their men. However, this also meant that notification of casualties and deaths from the front were transmitted quickly and women feared receiving such telegrams informing them that their husbands had been killed in action. They offered immense support to their neighbours and friends who found themselves on the receiving end of such bad tidings. Julia prayed fervently that Antek would not be among the fallen or wounded.

Felicia, who had survived her ordeal in the Teheran morgue where she had met Dymitr Hryciuk, married him in Karachi where their daughter Danuta was later born and so she now had two children. As Hryciuk was a very skilled shoe maker from Poland, he soon set up a business in Valivade, repairing and making shoes. Women wanted their existing shoes repaired and new shoes made and as leathers and various skins such as lizard and snake were plentiful in supply, it became a lucrative business. The three sisters had several pairs of new shoes made by him to order, using skins from lizards, which were beautifully finished and very durable.

The business was so successful, that he employed two locals to assist him in order to meet the demand for orders. The small shop where he worked from had to be divided in half by a screen, as the two men whom he employed would not sit to work together because they belonged to different castes.

In May, the rainy season began, which was long awaited by the Indian farmers. When the downpour burst from the sky, it continued for three months. Mosquitoes bred in these periods of humid conditions which once again gave rise to outbreaks of malaria.

Valivade was set high above maize and sugar cane plantations which were plentiful that those parts. The harvest of this was in April, when the canes were cut down with sharp knives and the remaining dry leaves would be set on fire to destroy pests such as snakes and scorpions. The harvested canes would be transported by carts pulled by bullocks to mills in Kolhapur. Bullocks and cows were a vital part of rural economy and were used to paddle the rice fields, ploughing, irrigating and pushing mill stones to grind corn. However, the white cows were sacred animals of Hinduism and were never deterred from eating produce as they wandered freely through the streets markets or past peoples gardens.

The sisters acquired a very large stray black and white cat, who befriended them and whom they named Maciek. Having a pet added a homely feel to their barrack accommodation and the cat proved useful in keeping down mice in the neighbourhood and became a faithful and loved companion.

They invested some of their money in purchasing items of the local handicraft, such as carved wooden boxes made of a variety of woods including sandalwood and ebony. The Hindus also made beautiful delicately and intricately engraved containers, candlesticks and trays made of brass and silver. The jewellers were high class craftsmen and could make pieces of jewellery to order from gold coins or damaged jewellery which they were given to work with. They sat cross legged in the streets on rugs outside their shops, surrounded by piles of gold as they worked to complete orders. There seemed to be no worry about thefts and likewise the Polish people felt safe to leave doors open in their houses knowing that the locals were honest and trustworthy even though they were extremely poor.

When Jania, Tonia and Julia had made their escape from Russia, everyone was ordered to hand over any cash which they had on their person at Krasnovodsk port, to avoid taking

Russian currency out of the country. The sisters did not intend to give away their hard earned money, as the poverty they had endured had taught them a lesson for life and so they hid the money in their underwear thus managing to smuggle their gold roubles out with them. However, they now feared that at some stage in their journey, there might again be a question of having to declare these. However, if the coins were converted into jewellery, there would not be a problem. In Kolhapur, they found a reputable jeweller and ordered three beautiful long chains with crucifixes to be made out of the roubles, one for each of them. Tonia also ordered a man's ring in heavy twenty-two carat gold, with a large single ruby stone which was held in place by gold claws. She intended to present this as an engagement ring to Jędrzek Dolecki when they met after the war. He regularly wrote letters to her, enclosing photographs of himself in his army uniform from wherever he happened to be stationed and she prayed that he would return safe so when peace finally came, they could start a life together for which they had waited for so long.

The sisters sometimes travelled to Kolhapur for shopping. This was a busy and noisy place with loud local music played everywhere through loudspeakers. The busy traffic and speeding motor scooters sounded their horns constantly to clear the road ahead and the buses and trains were overcrowded to the brim with their passengers hanging on from all sides as they travelled along in the intensive shimmering heat.

In February 1945, terrible news was received of the Yalta Conference which caused great despair to all Polish people everywhere. An agreement which was ratified between Stalin, Churchill and Roosevelt, in essence meant that, because the land on Poland's Eastern borders had been offered to Stalin, its pre-war inhabitants, who had managed to survive deportation to Siberia, would not able to return home and were now homeless and stateless.

Tonia and Jania were beside themselves with grief, as their beloved city of Lwów had been given as a pawn to appease

Stalin by Churchill and Roosevelt, who were both either too blind or conveniently chose to deny seeing evil when it stared them in the face. The three sisters knew that as a result they would never be able to return to their homeland which they loved and that when the war came to an end, they would remain refugees somewhere in unknown parts of the world for the rest of their lives.

When the camp was originally set up, it was intended to provide young people with education and many practical vocational skills with the intention that they would return to rebuild Poland after the war. The teaching in all the settlement schools was delivered in Polish, following Polish curriculum and teaching styles. However, when after 1945, it became apparent that return home to Poland was not going to be a likely option, English language was introduced into the school curriculum which would give the children a vital additional skill for eventual settlement in other parts of the world.

The grief and heartache was not over yet, as towards the end of April, Tonia received a letter from Jędrzek Dolecki's brother Jozef who, along with his brother and two sons, and also Antek, were fighting in the Italian campaign with the Anders Army. As a close friend and her neighbour from Waniów in pre-war Poland, Jozef had written to Julia several times during the war with news of their whereabouts and photos in their military uniform. This time unusually, the letter was addressed to Tonia and so she opened and began to read its contents. She did not manage to finish, for the information it contained was too much for her to bear and hit her like a bolt of lightening. Before she could let out a cry of despair, she had fainted.

Jozef's letter conveyed the most terrible news that his brother Jędrzek, Tonia's intended future husband, had been killed in Italy. He had been driving at night in a jeep from the area of Monte Cassino to Bari, which because of the mountainous terrain, could only be accessed by narrow winding serpentines. Lights of vehicles had to be dimmed so as not to be easily detected by the enemy. Parts of the road on which he was driving, had sustained serious damage by previous bombardments which was difficult to detect in the dark, resulting in his jeep accidently passing over a loose cliff, the edge of which gave way, causing the vehicle to plunge down the edge of a sheer precipice, taking Jędrzek instantly to his death.

Tonia was inconsolable at hearing this tragic news. He was the only man she had ever really wanted. She and Jędrzek had loved each other since they were young and at last it had seemed to them that, when the war ended, they would find the long-awaited happiness which they had always dreamed of, but now that the war was coming to an end, their dream would not be fulfilled. In her grief, she questioned why God had saved her from death in the gulags and she wished at times that she had simply perished in the frozen forests of Siberia. She felt there was nothing to live for with Jędrzek gone, as he had been the goal which had kept her going through times of starvation, exhaustion and terror. She had focussed on him in the days when she had become detached and lost from her transport and sisters on her way to Krasnovodsk and her determination to survive for him had saved her from giving up. Her sisters supported her throughout this grieving period and they prayed in the Polish Valivade church, arranging for masses to be said for the repose of Jędrzek's soul.

In time, Tonia realised that she was not alone and looking around could see that there were others far less fortunate than herself. There were women on their own with three or four children to care for who had received similar telegrams informing them that their husbands had been killed or seriously wounded in action. She realised that she had the staunch support of two loving sisters, many close friends and her firm faith in God to see her through this tragedy and she gradually made a recovery but she never had Jędrzek far from her mind throughout the rest of her life.

Kolhapur railway station, 1944

The three sisters as camp police in Valivade, India, 1944

Three sisters with their cat Maciek in India, 1945

Tonia, Jania and Julia (India), Antek (Italy)
(Julia sent this photograph from India to Antek in Italy,
where a skilful Italian photographer attached Antek's
picture. Julia later received this in India from her husband,
depicting them all together in their respective uniforms.)

CHAPTER TEN

The Italian Campaign

Under the command of General Sir Harold Alexander, Commander-in-Chief of Allied Armies in Italy, two allied armies landed in Italy in September 1943, and advanced north on two fronts on either side of the mountain range which forms Italy's spine. On the western front, the American 5th Army proceeded from the base of Naples, making their way up the Italian boot and in the east, moving along the Adriatic coast was Montgomery's British 8th Army. The Second Polish Corps, in which Antek was serving, had sailed to Italy, landing at Taranto. They were to engage in the task of the repossession of Rome from German occupation and thus securing freedom for Italy. The terrain was difficult and weather conditions were wet followed by winter blizzards in December, which hampered speed of progress. The road to Rome from the east had been destroyed by the Germans and was impassable and therefore the only alternative route to reach Rome was from Naples.

The first Allied attack on Nazi-controlled German positions in the Italian mountain ranges south of Rome, where the Germans had a strong foothold, started on 17th January 1944. The Second Polish Corps, in which Antek held the rank of Lance Corporal in the 3rd Carpathian Infantry Division, (under the command of Major General Duch), was under the control of the British Eighth Army.

They took a major part in the fifth largest battle of World War II, at Monte Cassino, to which their contributions provided the key to its overall success. It was the biggest land battle in Europe, as Cassino proved the most bitter and bloody of the Western Allies' struggles with the German Wehrmacht on any front of the Second World War. The ultimate target was to reach and regain the freedom of Rome.

The Germans were positioned in the high mountain range south of Rome and the allies had found it very hard to break through. There was only one pass through the German held Gustav Line, which consisted of the Rapido, Liri and Garigliano valleys and their surrounding peaks and ridges. The key hill blocking the valley was Monte Cassino on top of which stood the medieval Benedictine monastery dating back to AD 524 and at the foot of this hill, lay the town of Cassino. The Germans had secured a prime advantage on the top of the hill, which gave them excellent observation points of the surrounding hills, valleys roads and below. They had fortified this with barbed wire, mines, concrete bunkers and machine guns, making it virtually impregnable. Additionally, they had destroyed bridges over the rivers and flooded the Rapido Valley north of Cassino. In order for the allied forces to move forward along the terrain, sappers needed to be sent ahead to build temporary bridges to facilitate crossing of the fast flowing rivers.

The mountains were occupied by selected German artillery marksmen and therefore the majority of those soldiers who died attempting to ascend the hill to attack the enemy, were killed outright by a single shot in the forehead. There was no cover to hide or protect the soldiers below, as bushes and vegetation had been razed to the ground by the constant artillery shelling and bombing. The Germans had the advantage of clear vision of movement of the troops below.

Although the Germans had initially refrained from damaging or occupying the abbey itself, the allies mistakenly assumed that German troops had taken over the buildings of the monastery and on 15th February 1944, American bombers dropped 1,400 tons of bombs on the monastery reducing it to ruins and rubble. However, this unfortunately encouraged the

German paratroopers to take up positions in the abbey ruins, which provided them with improved cover. Following which, between 17th January and 18th of May, the Gustav defences were assaulted four times by the Allied forces.

Fortunately, in November 1943, prior to the outbreak of fighting at Cassino, all the abbey's priceless treasures and its irreplaceable archives and paintings by Italian masters, had been transported in one hundred trucks by the Germans to Rome for safe keeping at the Vatican and thus were saved from destruction. This was organised by two German officers, Captain Maximilian Becker and Lieutenant Colonel Julius Schlegel, who completed the task under the supervision of the monks and Vatican officials.

There were four major and bloody battles at Monte Cassino before the Germans were defeated and Cassino was taken. These were fought between the German Tenth Army which consisted of the XIV Panzer Corps and the I Parachute Corps, and the allied forces under the US Fifth Army.

The first battle which lasted from 17th January 1944 to 11th February 1944, was fought between the Germans and the combined US II Corps, British X Corps and French Expeditionary Corps.

In the second battle from 15th to 18th February which started with the US bombing of the abbey, New Zealand Corps and the British 78th Infantry Division fought the Germans.

The third battle from 15th to 30th March involved the New Zealand Corps and the British 78th Infantry Division.

The fourth and final battle from 11th to 18th May 1944 involved the U.S. II Corps, French Expeditionary Corps, British XIII Corps, 2nd Polish Corps (who with great tenacity and bravery, finally managed to capture the monastery). General Anders' plan was to capture a number of key hills simultaneously to prevent Germans from co-ordinating their fire. This resulted in both sides fighting to exhaustion. Anders' men, managed to take the monastery in seven days, finding strength from their hard experience of Siberia and determined on seeking revenge for the brutal war perpetrated on Poland by the Germans. During the battles, there was no time to bury the dead and the stench of decaying bodies of soldiers, lying under the hot sun of Italy, was overwhelming for those who were still engaged in fighting.

On the morning of 18th May, Polish troops made a successful ascent to the top and raised their white and red flag over the abbey ruins. Most of the Germans had fled and those who remained were taken as prisoners of war.

The capture of Monte Casino, thus opening the road to Rome, was hugely significant to enable the allied advance to continue through Italy. For the Polish, it also had a political meaning. It proved that the Soviet propaganda which suggested that the Second Corps were reluctant to fight was a lie. It was also a big moral boost for those fighting in Poland, and in the streets of Warsaw, signs of 'V-Cassino' appeared to show their delight at the Polish victory over the Germans.

Overall, this had cost the allied forces a high price of 45,000 casualties. Additionally, following on from this, with the fighting in the Anzio bridgehead and during the advance and capture of Rome this figure increased to 105,000. During the Monte Cassino battle alone, 900 Polish soldiers were killed and 3,000 were wounded. Antek's hearing was permanently affected by the tremendous noise of the constant bombardment and artillery fire, which irreparably damaged both his ear drums, causing severe deafness which he had to endure for the rest of his life.

There was a short period of celebration following the victory of Monte Cassino during which war medals were awarded and General Sir Harold Alexander, Commander-in-Chief of the Allied Armies, decorated General Anders with the Order of the Bath in the name of His Majesty King George VI.

Addressing the Second Polish Corps as follows:

"By conferring on General Anders the Order of the Bath, my Sovereign has decorated the Commander of the Second Army

Corps for his excellent leadership and also by it expressed his appreciation for the extreme gallantry and great spirit of self-sacrifice shown by the Polish soldiers during the battle of Monte Cassino.

It was a day of great glory for Poland, when you took this stronghold the Germans themselves considered to be impregnable. It was the first stage of a major battle that you went through for the European fortress. It is not merely a brilliant beginning: it is a signpost showing the way to the future.

Today I can sincerely and frankly tell you that, soldiers of the Second Polish Corps, if it had been given to me to choose the soldiers I would like to command, I would have chosen the Poles. I pay tribute to you."

King George VI himself paid a visit to congratulate the troops in Italy on 30th July 1944.

Following the battles of Monte Cassino, the units moved up through the broken Gustav Line and into the Liri valley and up the coast to the Hitler defensive line. In the next assault which began on 23rd May, the Polish troops attacked Piedimonte, taking it on 25th May causing the line to collapse and finally clearing the way north to Rome.

In July 1944, the Second Polish Corps, under the orders of General Alexander, was moved to the Adriatic Coast. The Allies were too far north to make use of the harbours in the south for reinforcements and supply. Whilst there, the soldiers were permitted a short period of rest to enjoy the warm sea and fresh air and reorganise after the battle of Cassino. General Anders wanted to capture Ancona for its harbour as a key port on Italy's east coast. This took two days of very fierce fighting resulting in very heavy casualties on the German side and the capture of 3,000 German prisoners of war. Prior to this, Loreto was taken as a vantage point.

During action in this battle, Antek's Company had come under very heavy artillery fire during an assault in which they had been engaged, resulting in the majority of the men fighting alongside him being killed. Seeing that they were now in a very disadvantaged situation, the remaining men scattered and took shelter in some undergrowth waiting for a suitable break in which to re-join their battalion. At this point Antek, having jumped into a ditch to shelter, became detached from his remaining comrades and later, whilst returning to his battalion under cover of darkness, came across a senior officer who was lying badly injured with his arm blown off. The officer had been lying in the heat of the day for some hours and had lost a great deal of blood. Antek could see that without help that the man was undoubtedly going to die, so he hastily performed basic first aid with the basic equipment he had available and then proceeded to support and carry the wounded man back to base, thus saving his life.

Antek was later decorated with the Bronze Cross of Merit with Swords (*usually awarded for deeds of bravery and valour, not connected with direct combat and for merit demonstrated in perilous circumstances*) for saving the life of an officer in a dangerous situation. He was also awarded the Polish Cross of Valour for his contribution to the fight in the ascent to the monastery (*usually awarded for specified separate act of bravery and courage shown in battle*). Finally, he also received the special Monte Cassino Cross, awarded to those who took part in the Cassino battle.

Amongst the troops of the Polish Second Corps serving at Monte Cassino was Wojtek the brown bear, who now being two years old and fully grown, found himself in front line action with the men. In order to make his membership of the Corps legal, as pets were not permitted, he was officially enlisted and given the rank of Private with a serial number enabling him to be included in all unit rosters. During the battles, he observed what the soldiers were doing and he started to help by carrying boxes of ammunition, weighing over 100 pounds each, from supply trucks to artillery points on the front lines. He worked as hard as the soldiers and showed no fear as long as he was with his friends, even though he was in the middle of the heaviest bombardments and noise of artillery fire. One of the soldiers sketched him whilst he worked, and this drawing was later was adopted as the 22nd Company's official emblem, depicting the bear carrying a shell. This logo appeared on their trucks, caps, lapels of uniforms and equipment. When Cassino was captured, Wojtek went on with the soldiers across the Italian peninsula. He enjoyed play fighting on the beach and swimming in the warm Adriatic sea with the men, where they had been permitted a rest period between battles.

The Polish troops were given warm hospitality by the Italians as they proceeded through the towns, driving the Germans out. The soldiers found great rapport with the Italian people, whom they found welcoming and generous and many of them soon learned to speak the language and enjoyed offers of good Italian cooking and home made wines brought for them from the cellars in the villages. Some went on to marry Italian girls at the end of the war and their wives learnt to speak Polish.

In August 1944, the Second Polish Corps were involved with British and Canadian troops, in breaking the Gothic line in the battle of Metauro, the heaviest on the Adriatic side. The task of the Second Polish Corps was to drive the Germans over the Metauro River and make way for the British and Canadian troops. This started on 19th August with heavy artillery and tank combat resulting in Metauro being taken on 21st August. Subsequently, in September, Rimini was captured.

Prior to the spring offensive, the Yalta Conference had taken place in February 1945 between the Super Powers, after which the Polish troops had learned of Churchill's post-war plans for Poland which would result in their country falling under the influence of Russia. Many of the Polish armed forces taking part in the spring offensive in Italy were formed from the survivors of the Siberian deportations. They were fighting in one of the heaviest and bloodiest battles of the war and were devastated at this news and could not face the implications of this betrayal. Some wanted to lay down their weapons, as after all, although they had joined the allied forces to help free Europe, their own ultimate goal was to eventually defend and free Poland from German and Soviet rule. However, each one of them knew that their honour and duty as a soldier would not permit them to lay down their arms at such a crucial moment in the war effort to crush the Germans in Italy and they continued to fight. For the majority, it meant that they would not be able to return home, as Poland had been given over by the allies to communist rule under Russia. After the war, Harold Macmillan rightly stated that the Second Polish Corps "had lost their country, but kept their honour."

As the Polish Carpathian Division crossed the Senio River on 9th April, 1945, a tragic accident occurred, whereby American bombers, engaged in bombarding German defence points, accidently dropped bombs prematurely which fell on the Carpathian Division resulting in a number of soldiers and officers being killed and injured. However, the Division continued on with its mission fighting between the Senio and Santerno rivers. When the Polish troops broke through the Santerno River, they came into combat once again with the former German division who had previously held and fled from the site of Monte Cassino and once again fierce fighting took place. Anders' troops went on to take Bologna on 21st April, 1945. This would be the Second Polish Corps' final assignment as the war ended in May 1945. There were celebrations throughout Europe to mark this long awaited victory day

In praise of General Anders, Franklin D. Roosevelt said the following:

"As Commanding General of the Second Polish Corps, General Anders brilliantly led his men in the final overwhelming drive that resulted in the retreat of the German Army from the strongly defended Cassino. This point of stubborn resistance was captured when General Anders guided his troops in a co-ordinated and inspired Allied drive into the bitterly contested vantage point of the enemy.

Later, continuing in the eastern sector of Italy, on the Adriatic coast, General Anders again led his men in the capture of the important port of Ancona.

The outstanding leadership and tactical ability displayed by General Anders were primary contributions to the success of Allied Forces in the Italian campaign."

At the end of this campaign, the Polish troops travelled to Naples where they were occupied with clearing up operations and burying the dead of all nations. As professional soldiers, even the Germans, who had been their enemy, were given burials with respect and dignity. The Polish troops remained in Italy until decisions were taken regarding their future. For them, the end of the war could not be marked by simply packing up and going home to their families, as was the case for the troops of most other nations because they were now facing a different problem.

Post war plans for Poland had delegated for her to be assigned under the protection and influence of Russia, with a Communist puppet Government set up in Warsaw. However, the Polish army, navy and pilots, who were still in uniform and part of the armed forces, aspired to complete their professional duty of allegiance to the freedom of Poland and thought they would be able to return as a military force, with the support of their allies, to also secure freedom of their own nation. However, there were no plans for this to happen on the agenda of the British or Americans. On the contrary, Churchill labelled them as "warmongers" who were not simply satisfied with establishing peace in Europe and seeing the war at last come to an end.

At this stage, the British government tried to persuade the Polish soldiers to return to their homeland as civilians to rebuild Poland. However, the Polish troops were sure that if they did return, it was likely that under the Communist regime, they would face arrest, interrogation and quite likely would have ended up back in Siberia and so understandably, there were very few who chose this option. The small number of soldiers who did return, faced reprisals and lived in great post-war hardships for decades, as in the Communist states there was great oppression, terror, starvation and shortages of even basic necessities with ration coupons for food until as late as the 1970's.

For the Second Polish Corps, who numbered 110,000 soldiers, there was an even bigger problem, as the majority of these soldiers came from the Eastern borders which had been given away to Stalin at Yalta and as their cities were no longer part of Poland, they had become homeless. In effect, their towns, villages, homes and properties had been taken over by Ukrainians. In Antek's case, in the village of Waniów, his house and neighbourhoods in the residential area called Kolonia, were burned and razed to the ground to cover up any traces of Polish people having ever inhabited that area and this also destroyed the evidence of evacuations from those parts to Siberia. Those soldiers had no homes to return to, but it took months of stubborn refusal on their part to convince British authorities that they were not in a position to go back and the troops had a long and anxious wait while their fate was decided. At that time, many countries of the world such as America, Canada, Australia and Argentina offered to take an agreed number of soldiers and their dependents as post-war settlers.

Churchill realised that there was no option but persuade the British Government to offer these soldiers, who had after all faithfully served in action with the British and Allied Forces, special permission to travel to Great Britain for resettlement. Finally, with great reluctance, the British government allowed them to enter Great Britain to reside as civilians. Most of these soldiers had wives and children, whom they had not seen for six years, scattered in exile as displaced persons in many parts of the world, as was Julia, living as a refugee with her sisters in Valivade in India. Antek, with the Second Polish Corps left

Italy for England, sailing from Naples in January, 1946. However, he would not be reunited with Julia until November 1947.

In November 1947 Wojtek, the brown soldier bear, had been granted permission to travel with the men of 22nd Company Polish Army Service Corps (Artillery) to England. He was subsequently housed in Edinburgh Zoo, where the soldiers and veterans were able to visit him. Wojtek lived until 1963, when he died at the age of twenty-two.

At the site of Monte Cassino, a huge and beautiful Polish cemetery, for those killed in action, was established and stands separately in its own lush green valley directly at the foot of the re-built monastery. Over one thousand brilliant white gravestones of fallen Polish soldiers stand in the shape of a huge cross. A long curved monumental wall in white stone around this area reads as follows:

"Those passing, tell Poland that we died faithful in her service. For your freedom and ours, we Polish soldiers gave our soul to God, our bodies to the soil of Italy and our hearts to Poland."

A Polish military song, entitled "Red Poppies on Monte Cassino", which was written by a soldier in the battlefield, became a national song depicting the Polish losses of life in this monumental battle:

> *Do you see those ruins on the summit?*
> *There your enemy hides like a rat.*
> *You have to, you have to, you have to,*
> *Hurl him down from its clouds by the neck.*
> *They went on with rage and fury,*
> *They went on to kill and avenge,*
> *They went on as always determined,*
> *As always, their honour to defend.*

The red poppies of Monte Cassino,
Instead of dew they drank Polish blood,
On these poppies the soldier trod and perished
But his grievance was stronger than death.
The years and the ages will pass
Leaving traces of bygone days,
But the poppies of Monte Cassino
Will redden, having grown on Polish blood.

They rushed to their doom through the gunfire,
Many were hit and they fell,
Like those horsemen of Samosierra *
Like those from Rokitno ** *in bygone years.*
They rushed with impetuous madness,
They reached and completed assault
Then up went their flag white and red
Erected on the ruins in the clouds.

Do you see that row of white crosses?
Where the Pole for his honour pledged all.
Go forth, onward further and higher,
You will find more of these as you go.
The soil here belongs to Poland,
Although, Poland is so far from here.
But freedom is measured in crosses,
History's lesson costs dear.

* * * * * *

* Battle of Samosierra where the Polish charge helped Napoleon to defeat the Spanish.
** Polish charge during Battle of Rokitno in 1915 during World War I.

Jędrzek Dolecki during the Italian campaign
(Tonia's fiancée who was killed)

22nd Company band pennant
Designed from a sketch of the bear
at work made by a soldier

Wojtek playing with the Polish soldiers

Antek (far right) after the battle of Monte Cassino

The Monastery at Monte Cassino 2011

CHAPTER ELEVEN

End of the War and Independence of India

In India, the news reported from Europe's battle fronts was now looking positive and finally at the beginning of May 1945, Germany surrendered unconditionally to the allies and peace would return in Europe at last, after the long years of the world in turmoil. As all nations, the Polish refugees were relieved that the war had finally ended, nevertheless they were anxious about where they would now have to travel in order to find a country to settle down and make a permanent home, given that their home in Poland was no longer accessible. They had by now all lived in temporary accommodation of gulag cabins, mud huts, tents and barracks in a variety of host countries, and endured an uncertain nomadic existence, for over five years.

India acquired her independence on 15th August 1947 and hundreds of thousands of people gathered at India Gate by the statue of Queen Victoria in a boulevard known then as Kingsway. They all wanted a glimpse of Jawaharlal Nehru and Lord Mountbatten as they rode along in an open horse drawn carriage on the road lined with cheering spectators. As the Union Jack was lowered the Indian tricolour went up, it seemed that the whole of India erupted with joy and celebrations.

However, this happiness did not last long as the British division of India was not made with due consideration of the consequences which followed. Muslims were given the new East Pakistan in Bengal (which became Bangladesh in 1971) and the new West Pakistan in the Indus Valley. The two Muslim areas were separated by 1,600 kilometres of Indian territory, and tension between Hindus and Muslims erupted into massacre.

In what was now the new West Pakistan, Muslim extremists began killing Hindus and Sikhs and taking their properties, the Hindus blamed Muslims for the division of India and retaliated. In the unrest and rioting that followed, the natives began migrating to save their lives with Hindus escaping to India in overcrowded trains and Muslims seeking refuge in East and West Pakistan. Mobs rushed through cities and towns killing people of a different faith to their own and men who were selected as victims were often ordered to drop their pants to prove whether they were circumcised Muslins or uncircumcised Hindus. Trains were often ambushed and their passengers massacred with the result that over a million people lost their lives and several million became homeless in the conflicts which followed the gain of independence.

Jania, Tonia and Julia had to take their policing role very seriously to help keep the safety of the Valivade camp and its inhabitants during this turbulent time. There was an increase in military personnel to safeguard the citizens of Valivade and the many other settlements in existence in India at this time. Europeans did not feel safe in the unsettled and turbulent atmosphere which prevailed in India during this period.

The British rule was coming to an end in India and gradually all the refugee camps, which had been under the authority of the British government and army, were closing with the British withdrawal. Women and children, who were dependants of men serving as soldiers in the Polish Army, allied to British forces, were permitted to travel to the United Kingdom to join their spouses. Julia made arrangements to complete her documentation to enable her to join Antek who had now been in England for some while.

Although Julia was relieved that the war was finally over and her husband was safe, it was at the same time a moment of great sadness and anxiety for her, as she would be leaving her beloved sisters behind and there was no indication of how long it might be before they could see each other again. She was also anxious as she was going to have to make this journey alone for the first time in their war travels. However, she would be accompanied on the long sea voyage by hundreds of other wives and children of the armed forces, who were travelling to join their husbands and fathers in England. During that period, a total of 3,500 women and children left for England, departing from Bombay in several stages between 30th July, 1947 and 9th March, 1948 as dependents of the Polish allied forces, whose soldiers were already living in Great Britain.

The day of Julia's departure for England arrived on 1st November 1947 when the sisters had to say their tearful and emotional goodbyes. A convoy of army trucks arrived in Valivade camp to collect those travelling to England and take them with their luggage to the port in Bombay. Whilst Julia departed on her journey to join her husband, whom she had last seen in Russia five years ago, her sisters had to remain in Valivade and await their fate and onward transportation arrangements.

Tonia and Jania had to stay behind in India, as Britain was initially only accepting soldiers' wives and children at that time. Their situation was very uncertain, as they found themselves threatened with being in a position of not only stateless but also homeless, listed under the category of Displaced Persons along with approximately 19,000 unmarried or widowed women, children and elderly men, who remained in India whilst authorities decided what to do with them.

At the start of the war in 1939, when the Polish Government in Exile had escaped to Great Britain, it had smuggled gold from Poland and this had been used as part funding to provide welfare assistance for the refugees, particularly the children and orphans, with the help of the International Red Cross, and British authorities. However, because these funds were now drying up and the London-based Polish Government in Exile was no longer recognised by Britain or America after the war, this particular group of refugees became stranded and it fell to the United Nations Relief and Rehabilitation Administration to find them an alternative hosting country. There were opportunities for people to sign up to go to Mexico, USA, New Zealand or Africa and the two sisters were assigned to travel to Africa.

It was during this time that, Mahatma Gandhi was assassinated on 30th January 1948 whilst on his way to a prayer meeting. The assassin was an ultra-orthodox Hindu, whose party demanded a Hindu India not the tolerant country which Gandhi had professed. Gandhi's death left the country in deep mourning while angry riots and protests erupted, making it a very dangerous time for Europeans to be living in India. The Polish camp was guarded very heavily and its inhabitants advised against going out of its perimeters.

* * * * * *

On 4th February 1945, Churchill, Stalin and Roosevelt met in Yalta in Crimea to ratify plans for post-war Europe. At this secret meeting, in which Poland was not represented, Stalin cunningly persuaded them to assign Poland and its independence to Russian authority and protection after the war. In order to bring an end to the war in Europe, which had gone on for so long, and to avoid starting a conflict with Russia, they agreed to Stalin's demand. This resulted in the eastern side of Poland, including the cultural centre of Lwów, from which the exiles had originally been deported to Siberia, becoming incorporated into Ukraine under the Soviet Union, and Poland being occupied at the end of the war exclusively by Russian troops.

Following this, it transpired that 48,000 Polish soldiers fought and died, not for the defence of their own nation, but for the freedom of the very countries who betrayed them and they saw it as 'For Your Freedom, Not Ours'. As a result, when the war had ended and Victory in free Europe was being celebrated, Poland's victory bells were silent as she lay in ruins, abandoned by her allies and in the same position after the war as at the start of it, but this time with a different and 'approved' invader. Additionally, the soldiers who fought with the allies were unable to return home to Poland, as doing so, would put them in danger of being imprisoned or returned to Siberia by the Communist government in power. Although they fought for Europe's freedom, after the war, they were treated as an enemy by the Allies, who had betrayed them at Teheran and Yalta. As a result of the treacherous pawn moves at Yalta, the war did not end in 1945 for the Polish citizens and they had to wait another forty-five years for Poland to finally regain its independence from communist rule in 1990.

Poland paid a huge price as over half a million of her fighting men and women and six million civilians died, which represented 22% of the country's total population. Approximately 5,384,000 (89.9%) of Polish war losses were victims of Soviet and German death camps, ghettos, epidemics, starvation and excessive slave labour. Almost every family had someone close who had been directly affected. This in turn left one million war orphans and half a million invalids. Poland lost 38% of its national assets as compared to Britain which lost 0.8% and France which lost 1.5%.

CHAPTER TWELVE

Post War Resettlement in Britain

Antek arrived in England from Naples with the Second Polish Corps of the Ander's Army on 21st January, 1946 sailing into Liverpool. The soldiers were then distributed around Great Britain into resettlement camps and Antek was transferred to Witley Camp, in Godalming, Surrey. There were 265 ex-military camps all over Great Britain and Scotland, which were used to house approximately 120,000 Polish troops who had arrived in Great Britain during this period. These camps consisted of rows upon rows of black corrugated Nissan huts which had previously housed either American troops or RAF personnel and these were now needed for housing many thousands of Polish 'Displaced People' which these Polish armed forces had now in effect become. The soldiers arriving from Italy had evolved into the Polish Resettlement Corps.

In the meantime, British post-war celebrations were planned and on 8th June, 1946 a huge victory parade passed through London to which allied forces of all nations, who had taken part in the fight for peace in Europe, had been invited. However, the only nation who was strangely not present at these celebrations was Poland. The British had shamefully bowed to Stalin's specific request not to allow Polish armed forces to take part in this Victory in Europe celebrations in London. Therefore, when all countries, who had contributed to the defeat of Germany paraded with honour and jubilation through England's capital, Poland was the only country not represented, even though its army and navy had played a significant role as an ally in the defence of Europe and its air force provided a key strength in the Battle of Britain. Polish soldiers, who had come to watch, stood as bystanders on the pavements in total disbelief and humiliation. Once again, it seems that Britain feared upsetting the manipulative Russian dictator.

Additionally and unbelievably, in an attempt to hide the criminal acts of Russia from the British public, who had been made to believe that the Russians were trustworthy allies, the Polish soldiers were clearly instructed not to divulge their wartime encounters and oppressions suffered at the hands of Stalin. Such a revelation would have put Russia into a negative light, which many politicians, of the far left British government at that time, were reluctant to make public knowledge.

It took some while for the British authorities to decide what to do with these soldiers, as in effect they were still part of the Polish forces. As they were under alien status, they were issued with a registration certificate booklet which stated that any employment undertaken had to be with the permission of the Home Office and Ministry of Labour and National Service. They would not be allowed to engage in any business or profession other than the employer with whom they would eventually be matched according to their skills and pre-war trade. Until such time as they would be officially discharged from military duties, they received army pay and were accommodated and fed in the camps to which they had been allocated.

It took almost two years for the many formalities and procedures to be completed and approved before wives of the soldiers could finally travel to England to join their husbands. Having left India, Julia sailed on 1st November 1947 from Bombay on TSS Empire Brent, along with 971 army wives and children, arriving in England at the port of Liverpool on 29th November, 1947. During the period, between 30th July, 1947 and 11th March, 1948, a total of seven ships had sailed from

Bombay alone, docking in either Liverpool or Southampton, bringing the wives and children of Polish soldiers to Great Britain, thus reuniting the families.

Julia, along with a large group of women, was initially temporarily transferred to Daglingworth Camp, Cirencester in Gloucestershire to await immigration office formalities to be completed and await reunion with her husband. Those arriving in England from India, came from the tropical climates with no suitable clothing for what proved to be a very severe winter. However, at that time, clothing was only available in post-war Britain for purchase with ration coupons and the refugees were all therefore given a £40 allowance per person of coupons to enable them to buy basic winter garments such as coats, woollens and winter footwear to replace their tropical outfits. These would have been the first new garments they purchased since their evacuation to Russia in 1941, as during their refugee existence in different parts of the world, charities had donated clothes and they had been grateful to wear handed down essential outfits for seven years.

Antek made arrangements to collect Julia from Daglingworth Camp and bring her to Whitley Camp, where he was now based, in time for Christmas. The last Christmas which they had spent together had been in 1939 in their home in Waniów and they reminisced about those times. There were many gatherings and parties in the camp to make the festive season happy. All such camps had one of the barracks serving as a church and so attending the Polish masses, carol singing and dances renewed the social life and community spirit.

This was a very emotional reunion as they had lost almost six years whilst apart in exile during which time, each of them had faced very harsh experiences and fought for survival in their own way; Antek as a soldier and Julia as a civilian. There was also much readjustment to be made in order to try and piece back their lives and adapt to a new way of life together in a strange country where they did not speak or understand the language. There were many things which Antek had witnessed as a soldier in the battle fields which he did not discuss and preferred to forget and move on with his life as a civilian. Organisations of post-war combatants were set up to which some of the men were signing up to, but Antek preferred to leave the past behind. He had never planned to leave his home in Poland and certainly had not aspired to rise high in army ranks and make a career out of the tragedy of war. He had originally been a successful and contented farmer, living in a close community and having lost all this, his ambition now was to try and rebuilt his identity and economic status in order to secure a comfortable existence for himself and his wife.

Although they had been married almost ten years, Julia and Antek had only lived together for two years because of the war. They had lost their son in Russia and now decided that they should start a family before it was too late, as they were both now thirty eight years old. To their delight, early in the New Year, Julia discovered that she was going to have a baby which gave them joy and hope at the prospect of raising a family after the turbulent years they had been through. There was a further surprise, when they discovered that they were to have twins and truly felt that God was blessing them to compensate for all they had been through.

However it was not to be, as in almost her sixth month of pregnancy, Julia slipped and fell whilst hurrying for a bus, resulting in a very sad and traumatic premature birth of twin boys. Unfortunately, medical intervention was not sufficiently advanced in those days for the babies to survive at such an early stage. This left Antek and Julia devastated, as they felt that their age was against them and they could not imagine living without a family around them, Antek having come from a very large family and Julia had been brought up with two sisters and a brother.

As Antek already had farming skills, he was offered employment through the Ministry of Labour with a Mr Robinson at The Grange, Lolworth in Cambridgeshire, where there was a vacancy for a farm hand and a housekeeper. He and

Julia decided to take the positions so that they could be together and have the benefit of pleasant accommodation and so they left Whitley Camp and both were assigned to work in Lolworth on 18th August, 1948.

The Robinson's estate lay in the Lolworth countryside just off Robin's Lane and was entered by tall prestigious gates which opened onto a long private driveway at the end of which stood The Grange Manor House. In its grounds were numerous outhouses, farm buildings and beautiful extensive gardens full of mature ornamental shrubs and trees, along with a tennis court and swimming pool. The jobs were reasonably paid and included both lodgings and food and although they spoke no English, Antek was familiar with maintenance of land and animals and he loved outdoor work. Julia was a skilful and organised housekeeper, so they soon settled in with the very welcoming English Mr and Mrs Robinson, who were running this family estate with their parents.

Julia and Antek found this a very new experience, being immersed into part of an English household, where everything was run precisely to time and drinking tea was an important part of the British culture. They soon found that living away from their Polish neighbours in the resettlement camps, helped them learn some English which they could use to communicate in their place of work and they both became useful and valued employees within the Robinson estate.

Antek was officially discharged from military service on 3rd November 1948, which allowed him to settle into a civilian life although it was still a requirement for the Polish soldiers to register with the local police in their status as alliens. He and Julia were making enquiries about her sisters and decided that if Jania and Tonia were eventually come to England, they would need a place to live. It would therefore be necessary to acquire more spacious lodgings, even if it was an army barrack, in order to accommodate them. They would also regain their independence as a family to establish a life in Britain, rather than living as lodgers in an English household. They needed to find alternative employment through the Ministry of Labour and Antek found a job with a building company in Littleport in Cambridgeshire, and later with Biggs Wall Limited who were based in Huntingdon. Julia found employment at Chivers factory in Histon, where jams, marmalades and jellies were produced. They left The Grange in April 1949 with a heavy heart and the Robinsons were sad to see them go, but assured them that they would be welcome to come back and visit The Grange whenever they liked.

They were given accommodation in a disused RAF camp in Mepal, which was adjacent to the village of Witcham near Ely. Mepal camp had been built to Class A specification as one of two satellite stations for the Waterbeach cluster from which Lancaster bombers had taken off during the war. Some runways had been built and a road from Sutton to Mepal had been closed off to serve as a runway during the years of conflict. Mepal had officially been opened as an RAF camp in 1943 until the end of the war, originally housing about 30 Short Stirling aircraft of No 75 Squadron, named New Zealand Squadron. The camp sites housed approximately 2,230 personnel during the war years. The Squadron lost 104 Short Stirling and Avro Lancaster bombers in operations from Mepal.

After the war, the camp offered housing to accommodate the Polish immigrants in the area, as did all such disused RAF camps throughout the British Isles. These comprised a mixture of half-barrel shaped structures made of corrugated metal (laughing barrels) or black wooden barracks with corrugated metal roofs, known as Nissen huts. Inside they were partitioned into several bedrooms and one living room, intended as a sitting and dining room, a corner of which served as a kitchen area. This comprised of a coal-fired range for cooking, which also heated the living room, and a large stone sink in the corner with only cold running water. There were no bathing or toilet provision inside these living quarters.

Clothes-washing facilities for the whole camp were provided in a single purpose-built brick building, along the length of which ran several long trough-like white stone sinks with rows of high brass taps. In this laundry building, plenty of hot water was available and women stood with their scrubbing boards at the huge sinks, rubbing the clothes vigorously and wringing them by hand, whilst their chatter and singing, together with the steam and coloured soap bubbles, rose and filled the washroom. The vapour of bleach, mingled with the smell of washing powders, was so overpowering that it hit your nostrils long before entering the building. Boxes of Robin's starch to stiffen cotton tablecloths and sheets and little Blue bags, (a blue dye contained in a small blue and white striped muslin bag which was added to the last rinse of a 'whites' wash to enhance the whiteness) were the housewife's essential items to cope with laundry days.

As there were no bathrooms in the accommodation huts, communal toilets were provided in purpose built brick outhouses dotted around the camp site. Small children were bathed in tin baths filled with kettles of hot water in the middle of the kitchen area. A public bathhouse was open on certain days of the week, when people trooped off on a ten minute walk with towels and toiletries under their arms in search of hot running water for the treat of the week – a nice hot bath. The bathhouse had a number of cubicles with half door partitions, having gaps at the top and at the bottom. There was no possibility of lingering in the long awaited bath tub, as queues of anxious people were all waiting outside the cubicles, grumbling if you were taking too long. Indeed, on one occasion, Antek was waiting ages outside an occupied cubicle for a bath, when he heard its occupant snoring. He decided to wake the slumbering man by using a spare towel tied into a good thick knot which he threw over the top, like a grenade into a trench, onto the chap having an inconsiderate snooze in the public bath tub, which promptly produced awakened and surprised spluttering cries from the slow bather!

The camp had a large barrack which had been converted into a very attractive church and masses were conducted there on Sundays and holy days by a Polish priest, who resided in the camp. Medical facilities were housed in another barrack which had been converted into a doctor's surgery and run by a Polish doctor and his wife, who was a nurse. There was also a nursery school run by Polish teachers for children between three and five years old, which operated from half past eight in the morning until four o'clock in the afternoon. This enabled mothers to take up employment in the knowledge that their children were well looked after. All lessons and activities for the children were conducted in Polish and to support this, there was an abundance of children's Polish books available in all such camp education establishments. Lunches for the children and staff were cooked on the premises and there was a supply of old metal army beds available in a quiet room, to enable the very young children to take an afternoon nap. Adjacent to the school, was the camp Warden's office, where the camp residents went to pay for housing and sort out accommodation administration.

In the early days, the camp had a communal mess for dining, left over from the days of the RAF, which Julia and Antek found very convenient and cheap. This saved time in the evening when they returned home at the end of a long day at work. Once a week, the camp was visited by a mobile Polish delicatessen grocer who came in his van from Cambridge, which provided the opportunity for residents to purchase all their favourite Polish foods and ingredients to cook their traditional dishes. A local baker delivered fresh bread to the camp several times a week. Apart from this, there was only a small shop in the nearby village of Witcham so all major shopping had to be done in either Cambridge or Ely, both of which were accessible from the camp by public transport in the form of blue or red double-decker buses.

As the camp was situated in remote countryside, the builders collected Antek in a lorry every day to take him to work and dropped him back in the evening. Julia had a courtesy bus which was provided for workers by Chivers

Factory based in Histon, collecting her and fifty other employees from the camp early in the morning to travel the fourteen miles to the factory. In the evening, they would all be brought back to the camp.

Chivers factory at that time, employed many hundreds of people in a variety of roles. There were outdoor workers picking and sorting fruit, such as strawberries in their fields and orchards, and others employed in the preparation, cooking process and then jarring, labelling and packing. Although the Chivers brothers initially started the business with production of jam, which was seasonal work, they gradually expanded to make a variety of products such as jellies, marmalades, lemon curd, tinned fruit, custard powder, mincemeat, plum puddings and lemonade which provided work all year round. The business eventually grew into a world leading manufacturer of preserves. The factory looked after its workers' wellbeing and employed qualified medical personnel, who were on hand to look after them. They also provided free buses to collect employees who lived in remote parts where public transport was difficult to find. This was the post-war era of encouraging productivity by offering wellbeing incentives. One of the psychological tactics at that time in most factories was to play music to the workers and it was discovered that if the music was of a fast tempo, it motivated the workers to speed up and increase output on the conveyor belts. It was broadcasted by the BBC as 'Music While You Work'.

Julia loved the cheerful atmosphere of the factory where everything was run to precision time with sterile modern conditions for the processing of the food products and amazing new technological state of the art machinery which Chivers had invested in. The employees all wore crisp white overalls and hats and were rotated throughout the different stages of production. Julia would be working on the fruit quality sorting for a week and then on jarring, labelling or boxing for another. Sometimes she would be working on packing jams on the conveyor belts and sometimes boxes of jellies. At first, it was difficult to work to the speed at which the products travelled on the conveyor belts and new employees were bewildered at having to keep up. However, they all adjusted gradually and became fast and productive workers.

Julia found the English managers and working colleagues very courteous, polite and patient with those who had difficulty with English like herself. She also had the companionship of many Polish people from the camp to work with and she was very happy there. During her working day, Julia often recalled the days when she had hungrily searched for food in rubbish bins to stay alive, and here she had food of all sorts travelling before her eyes, smelling it all day whilst she packed it.

At Christmas time, all employees received a large hamper with a sample of Chivers' own products such as jams, marmalade, Christmas pudding, mincemeat and jelly. The hamper also contained a glossy book outlining Chivers' achievements and awards during that year, along with numerous photographs of employees working within the different departments. Some senior managers were depicted in comical sketches using photographs of their heads attached to amusing cartoon bodies.

The wages, which were handed out in cash on Fridays, were contained in small rectangular brass tins with the employee's name handwritten on a label on the lid. On Monday, the workers had to bring their empty tins back and leave them in a basket in the office for the finance department to refill at the end of the week.

Julia missed her sisters terribly and they wrote to each other regularly and exchanged photos. She told them about Mepal camp, her job at the cheerful English Chivers factory and life and experiences in England and they wrote to her about their very different lives far away in remote Africa where they were very happy.

CHAPTER THIRTEEN

Two Sisters in Africa

In March 1948, having been assigned to travel for resettlement in Uganda, East Africa, Tonia and Jania handed in their policewomen's uniforms and again had to pack their belongings and leave India. They had loved its fascinating culture and beautiful historical buildings, along with its gentle welcoming people, who amusingly rocked their heads from side to side when engaged in conversation. India had provided a comfortable refuge for them for almost four years and they had felt safe there, until the recent political disruptions had unfolded. They would take away fond memories of beautiful India, which they would recall and treasure for many years to come.

Now they headed for a new life in a completely different continent, this time in Africa. Many of the Polish women, especially those with small children in their care, who had been assigned to Africa as their destination, were terrified of this option. Most of them had only vaguely read about the country and what they had heard was alarming – wild animals such as lions and crocodiles, vast expanses of jungles, scorpions and numerous life threatening diseases. The majority of these people had never travelled before the war or even seen a black person in their lives and this ignorance itself gave rise to much anxiety. Their fear grew into terror at the prospect of being transported to such dangerous and remote territories. Eventually however, they were given guidance from army personnel, who had visited those areas and experienced life in Africa and this information instilled a more positive outlook for those with concerns to help them to face the prospect of this new destination.

On 2nd March, those heading for Africa were transported from Valivade camp in India by trucks to Kolhapur railway station to catch connecting trains to Bombay (now Mumbai). There, they boarded the ship U.S.A.T. General M. B. Stewart (United States Army Transport), which had been assigned to sail across the Indian Ocean to take the evacuees to Mombasa in Kenya, from where they were to travel onward to their various assigned resettlement camps which were scattered across Africa.

Whilst they sailed, they saw for the first time in their lives, flying fish which swam in small shoals, gliding near the water surface and rising above the water level, catching the lift of the wind to propel their flight. This thrilled the hundreds of Polish evacuee children who were on board, and the teachers sailing with them turned the journey into interesting geography and nature lessons when they explained to the children about the route of their crossing and the mysteries of the varied marine life which existed in the depths of the ocean over which they were sailing.

A few days after sailing from Bombay, on 5th March, the sailors and officers on board announced that the ship was about to cross the equator. At this point, to mark the occasion, the sailors organised a surprise for the passengers which depicted the ancient tradition of their marriage to the sea. Old Neptune, the Emperor of the Seas, appeared on deck accompanied by sea-nymphs. He was dressed in a fishing net and held a trident, the prongs of which represented thunder. Neptune was sturdily built, as was befitting a sea-king, with a beard down to the waist and therefore sailors of the appropriate stature were always selected for this role. Neptune's lieutenants grabbed those nearby for the ceremony of the "sea baptism". This involved placing the person on a table, pouring salty water in their mouth, sprinkling them with powder, checking their heartbeat and then throwing them into the ship's swimming pool whilst onlookers cheered. Laughing sailors watched the fun from overhead ropes, masts and ladders. When the ceremony was finished, Neptune presented all passengers with certificates to commemorate their survival of crossing of the equator.

On arrival and disembarkation in Kilindini harbour in Mombasa, the ship's crew all came out to say farewell to their passengers whom they had looked after and entertained during the voyage and they displayed the Polish red and white flag on the ship's mast to mark the occasion. The first intriguing sight for those arriving, were the native black people, from the Swahili tribe, who went jovially about their business, singing and laughing. Some carried huge heavy loads on their heads and all were dressed in bright coloured clothing with interesting patterns of African designs. The Polish children were very curious to see black people as this was quite a new experience for them and indeed as it was for most of the adults arriving.

The next part of the journey was by train to Kampala in Uganda, which was a breathtaking sight as the lush green scenery consisting of coconut palms, beautiful plants and exotic colourful flowers rushed past the windows. They saw Mount Kilimanjaro standing magnificently in the distance with its snow capped top. As the journey progressed, the scenery changed completely and they passed through golden grassland with settlements of houses made of grasses. Here, black herdsmen with spears tended their long-horned cattle in pastures. Black children ran in the fields alongside the thundering steam train to get a glimpse of the novelty of carriages filled with white children and, mutually intrigued, they all waved to each other. Then to the delight of the passengers, they passed by the Kenya National Park, where various gazelles, antelope and giraffes grazed and roamed in grace and freedom. The final journey to the destination of the Polish refugee camp in Koja, to which Tonia and Jania had been assigned, had to be completed in a fleet of lorries.

Many remote areas of Africa, which were under British colonial rule at that time, had given refuge to some 19,000 Polish exiles scattered in twenty two camps throughout south and east Africa, some of which were situated in the depths of jungles. Just to name a few, Tangeru had 4,000 Polish deportees, Lusaka 1,400, Kidugala 1,000, Ifunda 800, Rusape 600, Abercorn 600 (Southern bank of lake Tanganyika), Masindi 5,000 and Koja had 3,000. Koja lay in the Mukono region, not far from Entebbe and the capital of Uganda, Kampala. Koja was one of the most attractive sites, positioned on a picturesque hill covered with green vegetation and row upon row of neatly built huts, overlooking and sloping down to the beautiful Lake Victoria. Some huts stretched almost to the very shores of the lake.

Jania and Tonia were fortunate that their transport had arrived in Koja as late as 1948, as by that time there were houses, a church, hospital, a theatre where films were screened, schools, shops and many other amenities ready for them. However, the earlier transports of Polish people, who had been taken to those remote areas, when hardly anything existed, had to start building all these facilities from scratch in order to survive. In fact, for those arriving in Masindi, a five kilometre area of virgin jungle had been cleared between Lake Albert and Lake Kyoga, on which stone cottages were gradually built with clay flooring and thatched roofs made of woven elephant grasses, to accommodate the settlers.

The cottages had three rooms consisting of two bedrooms and a lounge/dining room. Most had a veranda attached to the front to allow the occupants to sit under cover in the fresh air. As it was not safe to have stoves in the houses because of their straw covered roofs, cooking facilities were provided nearby with a wood burning oven and baking ovens. The furnishing inside was very basic, with each hut supplied with wooden framed beds with straw filled mattresses covered with mosquito nets, a table and chairs made by the men in the camp from whatever wood was available and an oil lamp for which kerosene was provided. Camp communal bathhouses provided washing facilities as the cottages did not have running water. The toilet at the back of every cottage was a five metre deep pit in the ground covered over with wooden slats to stand on. This was not under cover so in the rainy season one got rather wet and when the wooden slats weathered and decayed they became unsafe. On one occasion, whilst using the toilet, a woman fell into the deep cess pit below because the slats simply split and gave way. Her cries for help were heard by some neighbours who quickly pulled her out.

Jania and Tonia were allocated to a cottage in camp Koja and they were to share this with an elderly widow, Mrs Aniolkowska and her grown up daughter Alicia. The four of them soon became very firm friends as they had come along the same route following their escape from Siberia, so had many common experiences to discuss and share. Both Mrs Aniolkowska and Jania loved needlework and they would sit during the evenings on the veranda, admiring the beautiful African sunsets and embroidering tablecloths, curtains, cushion covers and wall hangings to enhance the interior of their new home which they gradually and painstakingly made exquisitely ornate. Several times during the week, the four of them would walk down to attend a mass in the Koja church which was serviced by a Polish priest. Training classes were set up in various crafts and some of the women who were professional dressmakers, offered sewing classes in the evenings. Jania attended these and gained valuable knowledge to enhance her already good needlecraft skills. She borrowed a sewing machine and set about making tropical linen dresses, cotton nightgowns and bedding for herself, Tonia and the Aniolkowskas, which she could produce cheaply with materials she bought from local traders

As the sisters had neither family to be responsible for nor anyone to rely on for help in time of crisis, they extended invitations to people from the neighbouring cottages to come and have lemon tea with them, accompanied by samples Jania's delicious variety of pastries. They would all sit and talk over and share problems and concerns, celebrate occasions and commiserate losses. Eventually, all the neighbours thus evolved into a good network of close friends, who were dependable and supporting colleagues with whom they kept in touch for the rest of their lives.

They purchased some chickens from the locals and with the help of some Polish men, built a hen house and enclosure to allow the hens to roam freely and so they had supplies of meat and also eggs for baking. One of these chickens grew to enormous proportions, about the size of a turkey, and they decided to keep her aside and named her Stroosh (meaning 'ostrich' in Polish). She was very intelligent and responded to her name and commands and they loved the chicken as a pet. She had a very large red comb which, because of its height and thickness, sat tilted on her enormous head. Stroosh was given the freedom to roam around their garden and into the hut, as she proved a very useful pest controller. She killed and ate scorpions, small lizards, beetles, termites which were plentiful and anything that came into the house which might otherwise be harmful. The unsavoury items on her menu which she selected to eat, undoubtedly saved her from being eaten by her owners, as on a number of occasions, they thought that the chicken would surely die of poisoning, having eaten some venomous insect.

One day, Tonia noticed that a cobra had come into their yard and was heading for the door of their cottage. Then she saw, as if in a slow motion, the next scenario unfolding itself before her eyes. The arrival of the cobra had not gone unnoticed by the keen eyes of greedy Stroosh who, having spotted it, immediately ran after it and cornered it by a fence. The cobra fanned out its warning hood and hissed at the chicken to back down, but Stroosh was not going to be put off by this display, and struck the cobra on the head with her large beak. In reply, the cobra retracted her head and lunged forward to give the hen a lethal bite, but Stroosh flew up into the air and landed with her sharp claws on the back of the cobra's neck pinning it firmly to the ground. From this vantage point, she was able to strike the reptile's head repeatedly with her huge beak. Tonia watched helplessly as the chicken's head bobbed up and down furiously in her efforts to kill the cobra.

In the meantime, Tonia shouted for Jania and together they had grabbed a garden fork and spade in order help their poor Stroosh and save her from meeting certain doom. As they rushed to assist with weapons in hand, they saw that Stroosh had not only managed to kill the cobra by herself, but was now eating it. She was swallowing it with loud gulps and the small portion of cobra now dangled out of her beak, quickly disappeared. Jania and Tonia were sure that their pet would die, having eaten such a venomous meal and they anxiously observed her in the days that followed but their worries were proved unfounded. Stroosh continued to strut around happily, always on the lookout for any other tasty morsels which might come her way.

The pretty garden which surrounded their hut already had some established trees, papayas, pineapple plants and many exotic flowers. There were also several mango trees and having never eaten mangos before, they discovered this soft and delicately aromatic fruit was unbelievably delicious. Jania soon set about her culinary skills to use these to make compote, cakes and tarts. There were many types of bananas, including a small pink variety, which although very delicious, they proved intoxicating when consumed in large quantities. The four women began to cultivate vegetables, as the soil in that region was very rich and dark and produced magnificent crops. The cabbages which they planted grew huge and this enabled them to make their traditional Polish dish of gołąbki (cabbage leaves stuffed with boiled rice, onions and minced meat and cooked in a pot in the oven. The word gołąbki translated literally means pigeons).

As a centrepiece of the front garden, grew a magnificent plant which bore huge cream and pink lilies in abundance.

Although this in itself was something to be admired, it also attracted tiny gold frogs, who having made their way up from Lake Victoria, jumped into the lily cups and sat inside them for comfort and shade, swaying gently in the breeze whilst holding onto the cup sides with their tiny gold claws. Jania was fascinated to observe the beauty of these tiny creatures, which did not run away when approached but sat and blinked their gold rimmed eyes at their visitor. There were many fascinating new animals to discover in this new African environment, but some of course were dangerous and needed to be avoided and respected such as venomous snakes, pythons, crocodiles, scorpions and dangerous spiders.

Near their hut stood a tall tree all of whose branches were completely covered with hundreds of nests made by weaver birds. These tiny yellow and black birds made the most elaborately constructed nests which they suspended on fine threads hanging from the very ends of the branches to deter predators, of which there were many in those regions. For extra security, they made 'tunnelled' entrances to these nests from underneath. From their African garden, Jania and Tonia would observe the nest building work and listen to the delicate chatter of this avian colony in the evenings. They truly believed that they had been placed in a lush and exotic Ugandan 'Garden of Eden' along with all its amenities to compensate for their recent years of suffering.

Some of the new experiences of Africa, took a little time getting used to. At first, they found the nights, which descended very quickly in these equatorial regions, were filled with strange noises, as the nocturnal animals woke and roamed the deep jungles, which surrounded the camp, for their prey. Roaring of lions, howling hyenas, along with calls of numerous nocturnal creatures, made the camp residents realise that they were vulnerable intruders in the kingdom of wild animals. Additionally, after a day's work, when night fell, the local tribesmen, who were partially paid in rum for their employment, could be heard dancing and singing wildly around their fires to the beat of their drums, having consumed quantities of rum to lighten their spirits.

The rainy season, which arrived between March and May, was preceded by swarms of tiny flies which were about the size of mosquitoes and came in such dense clouds, that during a conversation, you could not avoid having a mouth full of them. They smothered everything and were particularly attracted to electric light. When the rain came, it was torrential and both humans and animals quickly sought shelter, for if you were caught out for a few moments in the force of this downpour, your shoulders would be bruised and painful. As the torrents of rain came down, thick mists rose from the ground making the world disappear as if in a cauldron. The artilleries of thunder crashed continuously, making the earth tremble with the force of its power. The lightening forks struck the trees and ground around the perimeter of the camp and travelled around the edge of the lake; the force of their impact completely illuminated the darkness. Storms were particularly severe around Koja, as being sited on a hill on the shores of the vast Lake Victoria, the water seemed to amplify the noise of the thunder and magnify the reflections of the lightening. Ever since she was a child, Jania had been very frightened of thunder, but after experiencing such tropical storms, she accepted them as the wonders of Africa's nature and felt no fear of storms at any future point in her life.

The Polish children, surrounded by this vast expanse of jungle, were vulnerable to many dangers. The young boys were particularly fascinated by the interesting things which could be found in the jungle and their natural curiosity for seeking some new adventures, far outweighed any warnings which their mothers gave them. The Lake Victoria itself was magnificent, surrounded by exotic vegetation and parts of it were covered in beautiful water lilies. It was very tempting to bathers and boaters, however bathing in its waters was forbidden because it was contaminated with bilharzia parasites and inhabited by crocodiles.

A terrible tragedy occurred when three teenage boys decided they would swim across the bay, despite warnings from camp residents nearby. When they had swum out a good distance, people on the shore spotted that a crocodile was pursuing the swimmers. Two of the boys somehow managed to escape with their lives very traumatised. However, the crocodile grabbed the third boy, who was not a strong swimmer, and tossing him into the air, pulled him down into the depths of the lake before the eyes of the onlookers. Although a boat was launched, nothing was ever found of the victim. The irony in this event was that the young boy who lost his life was an orphan, as his parents had died in Siberia and he was cared for by his grown up sister. The night before this tragedy, his sister had a dream in which she saw her dead mother warning her to take care of and look out for her brother. The girl was devastated by her brother's death and blamed herself for not taking more heed of the premonition and warning which she had experienced.

Termites built their mounds sometimes over a meter high and could be troublesome if they decided to enter a house as they would destroy everything in their path. However, those residents who reared chickens discovered that hens had a particular taste for termites, eating them in quantities and so lessening the problem. Army ants were quite common, and these would choose a path and follow the leader wherever he took them, sometimes through the middle of a cottage if the front and back door happened to be open. Such a determined battalion of army ants might take a whole day to march straight through a property but would not stop to damage anything, unless they were disturbed, as their leader quite clearly had a set destination in mind.

Among Tonia's and Jania's neighbours, living in one of the huts almost on the banks of the lake, was Hryciuk the shoe maker with his wife Felicia and her son Stan, who was now almost ten years old, and their daughter Dana, who had been born in India and was almost three. Hryciuk and his family had been assigned to Uganda, as he had been too old to serve with the allied forces, and therefore not eligible to travel for settlement in Great Britain with the Polish army. However, in Africa, he once again found custom for his shoe making trade and fortunately there was an abundance of material to work with, including crocodile and lizard skins from which he crafted comfortable and classy shoes. He started a lucrative business in Koja to successfully maintain his new young family. He was also a keen and skilled card player, and would join the elderly men of the camp after a day's work for games of cards which were played late into the night over much conversation and sometimes arguments.

One night, Hryciuk was returning from a card game to his hut very late by the light of his torch to help him find his way home. Nights in these remote camp areas were extremely dark with no outside lights whatsoever installed. Suddenly, he heard heavy pounding of the ground behind him and only had a split second to glance over his shoulder to realise that he was being chased by a hippopotamus, which had come out of the nearby Lake Victoria, having been attracted to the light of the torch. Terrified for his life, Hryciuk ran as fast as he could, thinking that when he got to the hut, the hippo would stop. He ran inside and slammed the door, but a kerosene lamp was lit in the hut and the determined hippo charged the door. It broke down the door, but by sheer good fortune did not manage to rush through the house and trample the occupants, as his large torso was stuck in the strong door frame. The lamp was quickly extinguished and the animal gave up and left. The huts which were sited close to the lake, although having a marvellous view and good soil, were not able to grow certain produce in their garden such as cabbages, as hippos were very partial to these. It would not be advisable to argue with an animal of that size if you found one on your allotment, munching your tasty luscious greens.

One day, Felicia's son Stan, nearly became a victim to a nest of monitor lizards, when playing with some children near the jungle. Whilst running, he tripped and fell into a deep pit which he discovered was inhabited by a group of huge lizards. Having been surprised by a free meal landing in their house, they lunged angrily towards him and would have mauled him. Luckily, some men working nearby in the camp heard his terrified shrieks and ran to pull him out of the pit, finding him unharmed but somewhat shaken. Stan had another unfortunate experience when his pet rabbit fell into the deep cess pit of their cottage toilet. In order to rescue his pet, who had dropped down a five meter hole, Stan figured out that if he placed some lettuce into a box and lowered this on a rope down to the rabbit, the bunny would be tempted to scramble into the box after the lettuce and thus it would be possible to pull him up to safety; Stan's plan worked and the rabbit survived.

The kitchens of Koja camp hospital soon beckoned to Jania's heart and she started working once again in her beloved trade. The hospital had two Polish doctors and a team of nurses to care for the sick. There were several women employed as cleaners and Tonia joined these to work in the hospital with her sister. The kitchen had a team of cooks, including Jania, and three black natives to help them in the day to day running of the kitchens and supply of provisions. All three boys had worked with the Polish settlers since the origins of the camp and therefore spoke reasonably good Polish. One of these young men was called Masunda, who was a very keen worker and always tried his best to please. Jania befriended Masunda and some evenings, at the end of a hot working day, they would sit together on the hospital veranda and Masunda would ask Jania endless questions about her journey which she had made during the war, and in particular about her city of Lwów. Jania related all she could recall and those memories now seemed so very distant and she recalled them here in Africa.

One day, Masunda had received a chastising for making some very minor error and Jania found him sitting on the steps of the hospital's kitchen crying.

"Masunda, what has happened to you?" she asked concerned.

"Oh, Miss Jania, that Mrs Lubelska was shouting at me and then she called me a **stupid blackie.**" He replied, sobbing and wiping his eyes with one hand.

Mrs Lubelska was a camp official, whose husband was some high ranking officer in the army. She was one of those women from privileged backgrounds, who used their husbands' status to puff up their own ego and armed with this superior mentality, they would try and dominate those around them.

"She had no right to call you that." Jania reassured him. "You know what, I would not swop one Masunda for ten **nasty whities** such as Mrs Lubelska." She added with a smile, patting his back.

Masunda raised his large eyes in astonishment. His sad face turned into a smile and then he grinned amusingly, showing his strong white teeth. He threw back his head and started laughing and clapping his hands like a child as Jania's reply cheered him up immensely. They stood hugging each other and laughing together. Jania always respected and treated her native work colleagues as her equals whichever country she had worked in, but unfortunately it was not the way of some white settlers at that time.

Tonia had had been delighted to hear from the medical staff at the Koja hospital, that her friend Doctor Jadwiga Kornella had also been transferred to one of the settlement camps in another part of Africa working with a medical team in a hospital. She was able to trace her and they exchanged news through correspondence.

Jania never ceased to be intrigued at the variety of nature's wondrous creatures which presented themselves on a daily basis here in Uganda. She had a surprise one day when she heard something running into their hut and when she was faced with the visitor, was unable to name what she saw and indeed the animal was looking at her with curious eyes as if to get acquainted. It was larger than a cat, with course brown fur, small ears and a long tapered tail. It moved quickly on short legs, which had sharp non retractile claws, and its face had the appearance of a weasel. She later learnt that it was a mongoose; its Marathi name was mangus. In the next few days, the mongoose returned to the hut several times and when they had established their friendship, by Jania offering him some fruit, he became a regular visitor. He proved to be a useful addition to the hut, as he would eat any insects and beetles which he found inside. However as time went on, and he became quite tame, Jania discovered that he had a mischievous character.

Jania loved flowers and there was an abundance of them in the surrounding gardens. Every few days, she would select a bunch to put in a vase on their dining table so that these blooms could be admired and provide the hut with a pleasant aroma. The mongoose carefully observed her flower arranging and decided to turn this into a game. No sooner had she carefully positioned the vase into place, he would jump onto the table knocking over the vase with his nose, together with the flowers and water, then run away with Jania in hot pursuit. He took great pleasure in repeating this several times and then would sneak around the door and peep to see if she was watching him. Jania would severely wag her finger at him with stern words as if dealing with a naughty child and thus the playful African mongoose learnt some Polish vocabulary.

Every month, the two sisters read with interest the letters which Julia sent to let them know about the life that she and Antek were leading in England. Julia had found the pace of life in England very calm and the English people very courteous and formal. She was particularly impressed by the way everyone formed such orderly queues to wait their turn to be served in shops, cafés or buses. In the evenings, one felt safe and privacy was respected by English neighbours. She had not experienced this anywhere else in the world where she had lived. She had written after the loss of their twin boys which Tonia and Jania were very sad to hear. She had told them about the work at Robinson's Grange and her new job at Chivers factory which she was enjoying. Julia and Antek now both had reasonably paid jobs and were slowly becoming more secure financially, describing their new lives as comfortable and full of opportunities for the future. Julia assured her sisters, that as their resettlement period in Uganda would shortly expire, Antek was seeking permission from the Home Office through military routes which would allow the two sisters, as dependent relatives, to come and live with them in England. Julia had made enquiries at Chivers to see if her sisters could be employed there and there were many vacancies to be filled at their Huntingdon site.

Finally, in 1950, the refugee resettlement camps in Uganda were gradually closing and on 11th July, both Jania and Tonia visited the East African Refugee Administration Offices to have their photographs taken for their identity documents to be issued, which would allow them to travel out of Uganda to England. They had to specify the names and addresses of relatives to whom they would be travelling and living with in Great Britain. Once again, there was much packing to be done and now that they had accumulated a quantity of possessions, they ordered two sandalwood trunks to be made by some of the carpenters in the camp in order to have their belongings shipped safely, to what they hoped would be a more permanent home.

They were very sad to say farewell to Africa and to the beautiful camp Koja, where they had been so happy and had made so many friends. The natives who worked with them were sorry to see them go, as this had become a small corner of Poland in the black man's land, where they had all worked together and the natives spoke Polish. Jania asked Masunda to take a few photos of them outside their Koja cottage and in their gardens, so that they could capture this period of their life and recall it with great affection. They thanked God for allowing them to survive to see the end of the war with all its ordeals which they had endured.

On 26th July, 1950 Tonia and Jania finally left Koja with very mixed feelings. Out of all the countries which they had found refuge in, they had loved Africa the most. They found it hard to leave their beautiful surroundings, but at the same time very happy to be going to join their sister in England, where they could once again restore their family unit. Those travelling were collected from Koja camp in lorries and transported to Mukono railway station from where they travelled for several days by train to reach the port of Mombasa. In Mombasa, they were temporarily accommodated in barracks to await the arrival of their ship. Finally, on 12th August, along with 1,014 other displaced persons travelling to England, they boarded the SS Dundalk Bay to sail over the Indian Ocean, Red Sea, Mediterranean Sea and Atlantic Sea, heading for the port of Hull in England.

Unfortunately, the SS Dundalk Bay was a very narrow and long ship which made the twenty-one day sea voyage extremely difficult due to the buoyancy of the vessel and the very rough seas. The first part of the journey over the Indian Ocean was very stormy from the onset with enormous waves causing the majority of passengers to suffer terrible sickness to the point that many became unconscious and dangerously dehydrated. Part of this turbulent voyage was during the night and next morning, the decks of the ship were covered with dying flying fish which had been hurled out of the ocean by the huge waves. One man died of a heart attack on board and his body was later taken off at Port Said for burial.

Crossing the Red Sea was smooth and calm with glorious weather and passengers recovered from their sickness to view the pyramids of Egypt in the distance as the ship very slowly made its way along the Suez Canal. Here, Arabs traded from boats with passengers on the ship, selling rugs, carpets and wall hangings. Passengers could purchase these by having the goods winched up to the ship in a basket and sending the money down in exchange. The Mediterranean crossing was good and when the ship reached Gibraltar, it made a stop there for three days. Three passengers were taken off at Gibraltar and left in medical care there due to severe sickness, one of whom later died of heart failure. The Bay of Biscay, notorious for its strong currents, was very stormy and therefore the final part of the journey over the Atlantic Ocean became very turbulent once more and a great proportion of those sailing suffered acute sickness.

Finally, the ship docked in Hull on Friday, 1st September at 10.14 a.m. with so many people to process and immigration formalities to complete, the disembarkation did not start until

8.00 a.m. on Saturday, 2nd September. This however was completed by 10.15 a.m. with the help of the Hull Red Cross and the W.V.S. Most of those arriving were transported to various hostels and post-war army holding camps. However, Tonia and Jania had their final destination pre-arranged, as they were going to live with their sister and so were directed to Naseby in Northamptonshire, where they had to report with their documents to the Northamptonshire Constabulary under the Aliens Order Act to register their whereabouts in the United Kingdom.

It was from here that Antek had made arrangements to fetch them and bring them to the camp at Mepal, where he and Julia had now been living almost for two years. He had asked an English work colleague, who owned a car, to take him to Northampton and transport his sisters-in-law to Mepal camp. Their trunks with belongings would follow them to the camp at a later date. Julia was waiting with great excitement for them all to arrive in the camp barrack and what an unbelievable welcome it was. There was crying and laughing with ten lost years for them all to catch up on. The journey from Uganda had been extremely long, dangerous and arduous which left Tonia and Jania totally exhausted.

When they sat down to their meal that evening, they all cried and prayed as they recalled that the last time the four of them had sat down to supper around a table was in their village of Waniów in 1940 and the events which had happened in their lives since were unbelievable and impossible to convey to someone who had not been through similar experiences. It was nothing short of a miracle that all four of them had survived against all the odds and they knew that God had been looking after them, which made possible this reunion supper. Tragically, baby Ireniusz had not been able to survive the hardships which the war had imposed on them and now, all Julia had to remember her son by, was the few pebbles which she had taken off his grave when they all left Siberia and which she still kept.

Jania and Tonia standing in Lake Victoria

Jania and Tonia outside their African cottage

Medical and kitchen staff in Koja hospital
(Jania top row, far right. Massunda
bottom row, 2nd from right)

Jania and Tonia with exotic lilies in their Koja garden

CHAPTER FOURTEEN

An Addition to the Family

The army barrack in Mepal camp was spacious with three bedrooms and a sitting/dining room and all four soon settled into a happy routine of family life. On Monday 4th September 1950, three days after arriving in England, both Tonia and Jania boarded the Chivers factory bus and were immediately offered jobs at the Huntingdon based factory. Tonia was allocated to the packing department and Jania in the jam and marmalade preparation and cooking section. For the next two Christmases, all three sisters, who were now employed by Chivers, received a Christmas hamper.

Now that there were four adults working full time and four good wages coming in, their lives became comfortable. The lodgings in the army camp, although very basic, were extremely cheap and so they managed to save their money as well as buy clothes, food and items of comfort for their barrack home in the camp. They purchased a Singer sewing machine which Jania used with her sewing skills to make curtains, bedcovers and alterations to clothes, thus saving money. They cultivated a vegetable plot around the back of their barrack with the help of their farming skills and reared some chickens which provided meat and fresh eggs to supplement their diet. Although food was still rationed well after the end of the war into the early 1950's, with the help of Jania's excellent cooking skills and their own home grown produce, they all ate healthy fresh food economically. They realised that with hard work and living frugally, it would at last be possible to regain some economic wellbeing and the possibility of purchasing their own property as post-war settlers in Great Britain.

In the spring of 1952, Julia, who was now forty-three years old, discovered she was expecting a baby in December and this welcome news provided them all with great joy and a new purpose in life. Jania and Tonia were particularly delighted at the prospect of again becoming aunts and went about purchasing baby clothes, a large coach pram and cot ready for the baby's arrival. Julia worked at Chivers until she went on maternity leave, however she was rather sad to leave behind all her work colleagues and the friendly, cheerful atmosphere of the factory.

Tonia and Jania also decided at that point to leave Chivers and found work at Pye Limited, Radio Works, based in Cambridge. Pye also supplied a bus to transport their workforce from Mepal camp and remote surrounding areas to the Cambridge factory. Before World War II, Pye had been a national leader in electronics in the United Kingdom and during the war, manufactured radar receivers and military radio communication equipment. Following this, they produced domestic wireless radios and were pioneers in the production of the first televisions and then went on to develop the first British transistor in 1956. Tonia and Jania worked on the production lines of both radios and televisions. This was skilled work which demanded great accuracy and was therefore very well paid. They were trained to do the wiring, fitting of valves into radio and television sets and Jania particularly specialised and enjoyed the delicate and intricate soldering. In the late 1960s, Pye was bought out by Philips Telecom and later by Simoco.

Although they marvelled at the variety of finished products which they were involved in manufacturing, televisions were in fact, as is usually the case with new technology, not affordable to the majority of people in the 1950's and not many households had one to enjoy. However, with the help of a generous staff discount, Jania and Tonia bought a large radio with a beautiful wooden veneer casing from Pye. The whole family could listen to programmes in Polish transmitted from Luxembourg and Lille in France. The station was called Wolna Europa (Free Europe) and it broadcasted news, music, religious services and entertainment for children to Polish immigrants throughout the world. Apart from the London printed Polish newspaper, named Dziennik Polski i Dziennik Żołnierza (Polish Daily and Soldier's Daily), the radio was their main contact with the world in their own language, as at that time, it was not possible to receive transmissions direct from Poland, because it was behind the Iron Curtain. The evening programmes broadcasted from Lille in France were the highlight of the day, when Polish families would gather around their wireless sets after a hard working day, to listen and find out what was going on in their native land.

On 30th December 1952, Julia gave birth to a daughter at Mill Road Maternity Hospital in Cambridge. She and Antek were delighted, as having waited for so many years they now had the family they wanted. Tonia and Jania were very excited at the new arrival. They collectively discussed a suitable name and, as Great Britain was about to have a new queen, with the Coronation of Queen Elizabeth II being planned for June 1953, they decided to name the baby Elizabeth (Elżbieta Zatorska) and that was me, the author of this book.

I was very fortunate to have been brought up within an unusual extended family with two doting maiden aunts, who loved fine things and regularly took me to either Cambridge or Ely on the double-decker bus to buy me beautiful outfits and toys. I had the equivalent of three mothers to love and care for me and instil in me my national identity through books, music and stories in Polish. My favourite books were by the famous Polish children's author, Maria Konopnicka. She wrote poems about the Polish countryside with its forests, mountains, vegetation and seasons of the year. There were also poems about frogs, beetles and storks, which incidentally are a cherished national bird of Poland by whose annual migration, the seasons are measured. Konopnicka was Tonia's favourite writer, as these books brought to mind her own country life, left behind long ago in the village of Waniów, where she grew up. Tonia read these poems to me regularly and the author became a very special element of my childhood quality time spent with my aunt.

Within this environment, and indeed within the camp community, it was like living in a mini Poland and my skill in the language developed to an excellent level. There was an all day Polish nursery school which I attended until I was four, where we sang Polish songs and nursery rhymes and Polish teachers taught us the letters of the alphabet. Even at three years old, I knew most of the hymns which were sung in the Polish camp church and, encouraged by my father, I sang them as loud as I could. My parents and aunts often told me about Poland, where they had originated from and their various travels and experiences during the war years, but to me as a child, it all seemed just a distant part of their lives whereas historically, it was in fact a series of recent events.

One day, whilst looking through a tin of buttons and trinkets, I came across a few ordinary looking pebbles and asked my mother why she kept them. She explained that she had taken them as a keepsake off the grave of her baby son, who had died in Siberia during the war. It was then that I learnt that I once had a baby brother.

In May every year, the Polish post-war immigrants throughout Great Britain, made a coach trip to an event hosted by a Polish independent girls' boarding school which was run by Polish nuns of the Order of the Holy Family of Nazareth, based in Pitsford, Northamptonshire. This was a prestigious school set in magnificent gardens and countryside. The event enabled them to meet people with whom they had experienced their exile years around the world and catch up on news. Ex-soldiers could also have a reunion with army colleagues with whom they had served during the war. There were open air masses with the Polish bishop in attendance, national dance displays as well as craft stalls, Polish food and book sellers, from whom my aunts purchased many different Polish books for me every year throughout my childhood.

It was during a visit to Pitsford with my aunts, when I was only three years old, that I had an experience which influenced my life. Whilst writing this book, I can step back and see how wonderful that event actually was, as I was introduced by Tonia to Doctor Jadwiga Kornella. She too, had come to the annual event, as her orphaned niece Halina, whom she had brought up during the war, was a border at the school and was studying to go into medicine. Doctor Kornella had not seen Tonia since they were in Teheran. Since arriving in England, she lived and worked in a medical practice in Birmingham. They had arranged to meet and she intrigued me greatly, even though at the time I did not know exactly who she was and how Tonia knew her. I recall her explaining to me how important it was to learn to read and write Polish, so that I would not lose my family identity and although I was very young, she made a great impression on me.

Thereafter, Doctor Kornella sent me a Polish book every year for Christmas and I recall waiting at the beginning of December for a parcel wrapped in brown paper to arrive from Birmingham, inside which would be a book signed by her in her exquisite copper plate writing. When I was young, these were story picture books which were read to me by Tonia and when I was older, Jadwiga chose books about Poland, Polish costumes, culture and classic novels which I could read myself and I persevered to do so. In exchange, every Christmas, Jania and Tonia baked a delicious Polish walnut and chocolate tort, which was carefully put in a tight fitting tin, wrapped and posted to Birmingham for Doctor Kornella to enjoy.

In 1966, at the age of fourteen, I decided to sit my O'Level in Polish and, despite having had no formal lessons, I passed this with a good grade. Although I had never attended Polish Saturday school, as most of my peers did, I read widely over the years and my oral skills were strong enough to carry me through. Every year, the names of students passing exams in Polish were printed in the Polish newspaper, following the summer results, and Doctor Kornella was delighted to see my name appear and immediately responded by sending me an additional book that year. This further encouraged me to sit and pass Polish at A'Level in only one year, again doing all the work on my own, which involved studying and analysing several classic novels, poetry and a play.

Even though Jadwiga Kornella and I had only met once on that trip to Pitsford when I was three, I wrote to her for many years and she sent me a lovely table cloth as a wedding present when I got married in 1975. In 1980, when my first son born around Easter time, he needed surgery at only one month old and in my Easter card to Jadwiga, I confided in her as a doctor. She wrote back saying;

"You need not worry. Babies and children always recover surprisingly quickly, trust me."

I took comfort in that reply and she was right. Now I always repeat this to young mothers who are anxious about their sick babies. Jadwiga sent Tonia a birthday card in June every year and when these cards finally stopped in the mid 1980's, we guessed that she must have sadly passed away as she was in her eighties. She would have been very pleased, as thanks to her encouragement for me to learn Polish, in the 1990's I became a professional freelance interpreter working for the police, law courts and the health service, eventually sitting the Diploma in Public Services Interpreting examinations.

Elizabeth Zatorska - aged 3

Pye Radio and Television factory, Cambridge, 1952
(Tonia and Jania working far left)

CHAPTER FIFTEEN

Our Own House at Last

It was predicted that the temporary army camps would eventually have to close and with that in mind, my parents and aunts worked hard towards the target of a deposit representing half the asking price of the purchase of their own house. Moving into the Cambridge property market would have been too expensive, however quite a number of their friends and camp neighbours had already purchased houses and moved to Hitchin in Hertfordshire, where there were many varieties of local industries and good prospects of employment. Hitchin was situated near several larger towns such as Luton and Bedford which offered a good selection of shops. Antek found that Biggs Wall, which was a highway and motorway construction and maintenance company, had its offices in Arlesey near Hitchin and it would be possible to transfer his job to that area. Taking all this into account, they decided to search for a suitable property in Hitchin.

I recall vividly my excitement in 1956, when I made my first steam train trips from Cambridge to Hitchin with my parents and aunts at weekends. We stayed over with my godmother in Kings Road, while we were house hunting and viewing numerous properties. She and her husband, along with her elderly mother, had moved from Mepal camp to Hitchin the year before and were happy with their choice of location. Tragically however, her husband died of cancer within a year of their move, so he had little time to enjoy the achievement of purchasing their first own house in Britain.

Although most people these days might not regard Kings Road in Hitchin as a particularly sought after area to live, to me as a child it was a most magical place on earth. Having lived in a primitive wooden army barrack all my life, the first thing that intrigued me was the carpeted staircase leading to the upstairs rooms and I specifically decreed that our new house would simply have to have stairs. The Kings Road property itself was very large and built with a narrow layout, so you went on through from room to room, lounge to dining room, through to kitchen and scullery and finally to an extension which housed an extra cooker and cloakroom.

The large garden at the back was where the magic really began, as the little gate at the end of it opened onto huge communal allotments beyond which, lay the most beautiful park (Ransoms Park) with tall humming poplar trees, lime trees, and enormous swaying weeping willows on whose branches children swung themselves across the river that ran through the park. There were vast open green spaces with swings, a very tall slide and a high suspended carrousel type roundabout. Around the perimeter and overlooking the park, stood a row of very unusually designed and quaint looking Victorian cottages which had been built many years before for the railway workers. Above the rooftops of these, one could see the steam trains travelling to Cambridge, London and Scotland with their rhythmic clutter and shrill whistles echoing around the park below.

There was however one thing which greatly disturbed me as a child at Kings Road on Friday nights, and I shall never forget the unpleasantness of the experience. The park which appeared to me so beautiful in the daytime, was unfortunately adjacent to a large brick building which was an abattoir. On Friday nights, the pigs were delivered from local farms for slaughter and throughout the night, as we tried to sleep, the distressed animals shrieked their last cries in the process of being stunned and killed and to me they sounded like terrified screaming people. The bedroom windows had to be closed, as the smell of gutted pigs filtering from the slaughter house was quite pungent and nauseating.

After much careful property searching, we found a semi-detached house which we all liked in Bearton Road, and to my great delight, it had the stairs I so desired. It was a very large property with three reception rooms and three double bedrooms. At the back was a two hundred foot orchard with twelve mature fruit trees, various coloured lilac trees and garden mainly laid to lawns. I recall visiting this in late September and Mr Williams the owner, who was a local architect, was about to move to a new house which he had designed, took us around the orchard to explain the different types of apple and pear trees which grew therein. All around me on the grass lay ripe gold and red apples which gave out a delicious aroma. There were several varieties of Cox's apples, Bramley cooking apples, plums and three varieties of pear trees including William's, Conference and Comice pears. Alongside the length of the garden ran a public footpath which linked Bearton Road to Lancaster Road and Lancaster Avenue and provided a short-cut for children walking to Wilshere Dacre School and the Hitchin swimming pool, for shoppers to the town centre, and from it was the access to our back garden via a very wide wooden gate.

On 22nd September, 1957 an enormous green Deamer's removals lorry arrived at Mepal camp to collect and transport our family to our own home at last. Having packed our shabby wartime army surplus cooking pots, mosquito nets and wooden trunks brought from the tropics, army furniture which had been provided at the barracks, including metal army beds, khaki army blankets and quilts and horsehair filled mattresses, we said goodbye to the camp and our friends and neighbours and made our way to our new life in Hitchin.

What a joy it must have been for my parents and aunts to at last arrive in their own hard-earned home, complete with the luxury of a bath and toilet, after being in exile and homeless for over seventeen years. As for me, I ran up and down that long awaited staircase all day long. The architect, who had moved out of the house, had left behind a collection of small replica houses in the shed made to scale that must have been models which he had created in the design stage of his work and the detail of these fascinated me greatly.

On 23rd September, I accompanied my father to Hitchin town centre to visit the police station in Bancroft, where various documents were stamped and exchanged. I was four years old and did not understand why we were at the constabulary, but I do vividly remember feeling extremely hot and having an unbearable headache whilst there. After walking back home, I was put to bed ill with a very serious bout of flu which lasted over a week. Later that week, the whole family was struck down one by one with the vicious flu epidemics which was going around at that time and we were all in bed for a week, luckily each person at different times.

Then came our first Christmas at the new home and for my parents and aunts this must have been very special having spent the last seventeen Christmases in a variety of temporary accommodation including mud huts, tents, jungle huts and army barracks. The Polish Christmas Eve tradition with breaking and sharing of the white bread was celebrated with exchange of wishes under their own roof. There was a feeling of great achievement and pride at having come this far from the ashes of 1940 and all miraculously surviving as a family to see this moment.

In December of that year I had my fifth birthday and immediately in the new year of 1958, I started at Our Lady's Catholic School in Nightingale Road. This placed me into a situation out of my comfort zone and was a complete cultural shock which I shall never forget, as I started primary school without the knowledge of one word of the English language. Fortunately, my first teacher in that class, Miss Hazelwood, was extremely patient and kind and by the time I progressed to the next year, I was speaking quite well and completely fluently by the end of the second year. I received no help with school work at home, as nobody could speak English and there was no-one who could even hear me read when reading or spelling homework was set, but I persevered. Extra English support for ethnic minority children in schools was unheard of in those days.

Later, when I was eight years old and spoke good English, I became the family interpreter and accompanied my parents everywhere, even to school on parent's evenings to interpret what my teachers had to say about my progress. This led to me becoming a local community interpreter, as I was asked by my parents' friends and Polish neighbours to interpret at doctor's surgeries, dentists, vets and even funeral parlours. This always resulted in being given rewards of chocolate or even a half-a-crown and certainly lovely Christmas presents every year from those whom I helped. Juggling the two languages became second nature and it developed my maturity by giving me insight into many situations which an eight year old child simply would not normally experience – how to arrange a burial, what styles of coffins and linings were available and their prices, how dentures were fitted, how pensions were arranged and even how to complete my dad's income tax form.

When I was nine years old, my most amusing interpreting incident took place when my dad asked me to write a note in English for him to take to the local farmer in Ickleford village near Hitchin in order that he could order a lorry of pig's manure to be delivered for spreading onto our garden. My parents and aunts had turned half of their enormous garden into a vegetable patch and grew most of their own vegetables, but in order for this to produce crops, it needed fertilising every few years. My dad gave me precise instructions of how he wanted the note written.

"Write it bold and clear, not your usual tiny print." he specified.

Having sat down and given this matter some careful thought, I realised that although I knew the correct Polish terminology for 'manure' or 'fertiliser', having learnt these words from adults at home, I would not have come across this in my English school vocabulary. I therefore decided to improvise the best I could and in big, bold print, according to my dad's instructions, I wrote "ONE LORRY OF PIG'S SHIT!" Having decided that this should do the trick, I folded the note neatly and sent my dad off with it on his bicycle to the farmer. Later that day, a large lorry did indeed arrive and delivered the very smelly order – my parents were pleased that they could enrich their vegetable garden, I was proud that my choice of wording had successfully produced the correct goods and everyone was happy. However, many years later, when I was a teenager, I realised my selection of vocabulary should have been a little more subtle and with amusement I visualised the farmer's face unfolding my carefully written note. However, we were regular customers for many years at the Ickleford Farm shop which sold beautiful free range eggs and we purchased sacks of potatoes in bulk every year to last all the winter months which the farmer delivered.

When they purchased the house in 1957 for £3,000, my parents, helped by my aunts, had managed to save half the asking price, which was some achievement, bearing in mind that my dad's salary would have been approximately twenty pounds per week and my aunts earned ten pounds per week. Building Societies were few and far between and in any case, they would not have been eligible for a conventional mortgage, as they had banked only with the Post Office Savings Bank. In order to secure the balance therefore, they opted for one of the local authority short-term loans, which at that time were available for purchases of older properties, but were repayable over a time span of only ten years. Even with three adults working, this would be a difficult task in such a short period and they decided to take in lodgers in order to help pay off the loan in that time.

In 1956, the Hungarian revolution took place and thousands of Hungarian refugees fled to Great Britain to seek political asylum from the Communist regime which had taken over their country. This provided our family with an opportunity to increase our income by renting out the top part of our house to paying lodgers. We had many of them living with us over the next six years and sometimes as many as five people occupying the upstairs of our house. One tiny bathroom and one kitchen served ten of us at one stage, but my parents were used to living modestly and managed without complaint. They sympathised with the situation of these refugees, as they had experienced their hardships first hand and we treated them like family. Some of these were very young boys barely in their twenties, who had left their parents and families behind and escaped to safety in England. On Christmas Eve, all our lodgers were invited to take part in our Polish festive meal around our family table. They found Christmas an emotional time, thinking about the families left behind in Hungary and some would cry when they reminisced after a few festive drinks. Without exception, all these refugees managed to find jobs in the various local industries and earned good money. They all possessed big powerful motor bikes which roared through our wide gate into the back garden, where they were lined up and parked for the night. As a child I was fascinated by these awesome machines and grew to love the noise of their engines and the characteristic smell of warm motor bike oil. After living with us for a few years, many of the Hungarians learnt to cook Polish dishes and some learnt to speak Polish very well indeed. In turn, they taught me Hungarian songs which I still remember to this day.

The property in Bearton Road was situated within easy walking distance of most amenities such as the town centre, the Catholic Church, next to which stood Our Lady's Catholic Primary School, and both Lister and North Herts Hospitals. When buying the house, the distance to the church was of particular importance to my parents and aunts, as they were devout Catholics and went to church every Sunday to Polish mass. This provided them with not only spiritual support, but it also formed a large Polish community meeting place which was vital to maintaining their identity and communication links with other families.

Sundays in our home were always set aside as a day of religious observance and celebration of family unity. Tonia and Jania would together attend an early morning mass and return home to start cooking a sumptuous and delicious Sunday lunch, whilst my parents and I attended the Polish mass at one o'clock following which, we returned to an inviting smell of lunch all ready and waiting for us. Jania always made great efforts over Sunday lunches and took trouble to make deserts according to her recipes of years ago, such as she had prepared in the elite houses of Lwów before the war. Amazingly, she remembered all these and never referred to any written recipes or cookery books, nor did she use scales to weigh ingredients. She made cooking and baking look so easy and never appeared flustered for time or daunted by large numbers of people to cater for.

Our house was surrounded by several good shops, one of which was the large Co-operative store just three houses away which sold most things including fruit and vegetables and where fresh bread was delivered every day by local bakers. It had a fresh cheese and meat counter where sausages hung up in bunches and ham and bacon was freshly sliced and weighed to order. There were no self service supermarkets until the late sixties and the shop assistants took everything off shelves, weighing and wrapping them for you, taking time to exchange polite conversation. Large jars of sweets lined the shelves in rows and I would often go and make a selection for the assistant to weigh and bag for me. At the top of the footpath leading to Lancaster Road was a small grocer shop Lancaster Stores, owned by Mr Payne and down the road to that, in Bunyan Road, was Foskett, an excellent family butcher. At the other end of Bearton Road was a large Mace's grocers shop and finally, across the road to this, a newsagent and tobacconist run by Mr and Mrs Burgess, which delivered our Polish daily newspaper and where my father would take me at Easter to choose the largest Easter egg in the shop, usually one with the most colourful ribbon and bow.

When supermarkets were eventually established, Stitchers was one of the first to open in Hitchin, offering incentives of pink or green savings stamps for every pound a customer spent. They issued books into which the stamps were stuck and glossy catalogues from which to choose gifts, which indicated the number of books of stamps required when ordering the items.

In addition to these local stores, there were several mobile shops such as the delicatessen lorry, which years ago visited the Mepal camp, came from Cambridge every Thursday to supply the Polish community with their traditional breads, smoked meats and sausages, cheeses, pastries and cakes. The doughnuts from that van were legendary, well cooked, completely filled with jam and not at all the doughy undercooked variety which are found in bakeries today. There was also a horse and cart which came around regularly selling fresh fruit and vegetables. Harrison the bakers sold bread out of a dark green van, and once a week a delightful cream coloured mobile Notts Bakers van hooted his arrival and pulled down steps at the back of the vehicle to enable customers to go up into the van and select their purchases. When one entered the van, the aroma of fresh breads, iced buns and assortment of cakes, all displayed in large sliding wooden drawers, was unforgettably delicious. Occasionally a lorry with household and cleaning items came, which also sold blue and pink paraffin and people would go out with canisters to fill up and purchase paraffin from taps at the back of the lorry to use as fuel in their heaters. As the houses all had open fires, the coal lorries were regularly seen stacked high with their huge black sacks which were carried through the back gates to the houses by strong, very sooty coalmen all dressed in black boiler suits.

In 1963, we paid off our loan well before the time allocated and I remember my parent's delight when they were handed the deeds of the house, displayed in a folder tied with pink ribbon and sealed with red wax, which indicated that they were now its true owners. After translating these deeds, I helped them to arrange for the safe keeping of these documents with a local solicitor. By this time, the lodgers had all moved on with their jobs and some had bought their own homes which left us with the freedom of our house to ourselves at last and it was only then, at the age of eleven, that I was able to have my own bedroom.

My dad worked with Biggs Wall for the next twenty years until his retirement in 1974. Although this was very hard work, he enjoyed being outdoors in all weathers, both the scorching heat of summers and bitter cold winters, which in the fifties and sixties were extremely severe. He would never have changed for a job inside a factory, despite my mother's encouragement to do so for his own comfort. His job took him all over the country according to where roads were being altered or repaired, underground pipes were being laid or new motorways were being built. The lorry from Biggs Wall would collect him at six o'clock in the morning and return him at six in the evening, Saturdays he worked until midday. Sometimes the work would be somewhere far in London and other times more local in Luton. He worked with the teams involved in the huge project of building of the new dual carriageway which formed part of the A505 from Hitchin to Luton. This improved the route for traffic, particularly buses, which no longer had to make the arduous painfully slow climb on a single road up the steep Offley Hill.

Both my aunts Jania and Tonia, found jobs at Lister Hospital in Hitchin, situated off the Bedford Road at the top of Maxwell Path which conveniently, was only a ten minute walk from our house. Jania once again found herself looking after one of the hospital kitchens, preparing snacks and refreshments for the surgeons and consultants. She enjoyed working with leading surgeons Doctor Talbot and Doctor Young and every Christmas, received lovely gifts from the medical staff for looking after them with such dedication. When she herself had to undergo major emergency surgery in 1963 to remove a life threatening blood clot on the brain, the medical staff with whom she worked, performed the operation and saved her life. I remember going to visit her whilst she was recovering in the hospital and you would think the patient in her bed was a film star, as she was surrounded by the most beautiful flowers sent by the doctors and nurses. Jania worked at Lister well over her retirement age, when she left at sixty-five in 1963 and then turned her skills to sewing, cooking and making jams and preserves from fruit grown in our garden.

Tonia on the other hand, worked on Ward 8, which was the gynaecological women's ward. She was part of a team in the ward's kitchen and as a cleaner on the ward itself. She was also very much appreciated by the medical staff whom she worked with. In 1960, when she also had to undergo surgery for gall stones, which in those days was a major operation, she was cared for by her familiar medical team which made the whole experience much less traumatic.

As a child during school holidays, I often went to meet Tonia at the hospital and walk home with her. She had introduced me to Sister Grant, the Sister on Ward 8, who got to know me well. Tonia always volunteered to work on Christmas Day and I was sometimes invited to come to the hospital on Christmas morning to see all the unbelievable fun that went on. The wards were beautifully decorated and the doctors and nurses would be dressed up as fairies, pixies and colourful pantomime characters. I remember seeing the chief surgeon dressed as a baby, complete with nappy, bonnet and dummy, being wheeled by the nurses in a large coach pram around the wards and corridors. Another surgeon was dressed as Father Christmas visiting all the wards and handing out gifts to the patients. One year, I was surprised to hear my named being called out by him and went to collect a present, which I later discovered was from the Sister Grant, who had given me a beautiful gold plated charm bracelet with ballerinas hanging all around.

Although the hospital buildings were mostly made up of rows of army style wooden barracks coming off very long corridors, it was a close community where everyone knew each other and there was a homely atmosphere and team spirit. Tonia worked there until 1968 when she retired at the age of sixty-three and she and Jania were then always busy in the kitchen or the vegetable garden enjoying their retirement together. The large administration and geriatric blocks were the only brick built buildings, which were later used specifically to house elderly patients in care after the closure of the main hospital. Lister Hospital moved to its newly built site in Stevenage in 1972.

Whilst I was at primary school, my mother did not go out to work as the big house and enormous garden took a lot of time to keep maintained. She did the washing all by hand using the traditional metal washtub and washboard with the exception of the bed linen. Once we had the lodgers, there were sometimes seven beds to change so we resorted to taking the bed linen in bulk to Innisfail Laundry in Queens Street Hitchin, where it was professionally washed, starched, ironed and ready for us to collect in special transportation boxes.

In 1963 when I started secondary school at the Sacred Heart Convent, which was situated in Verulam Road, my mother started a job at my school along with a Polish friend Maria, whom she had known for years back in her village in Waniów. They served out the school lunches, did the washing up and cleaned the school premises. The school housed boarders as well as day students and the dormitories had to be cleaned in the afternoon while the students were in lessons and then the classrooms were cleaned after three-thirty when the day students had gone home. After school, I would stay behind and do my homework or paint in the art room and then walk home with my mum at five o'clock when she had finished her work. She enjoyed the atmosphere of the school and after eleven long years at home as a housewife, she regained her confidence out in the world of work. The nuns were always very appreciative of her help and meticulous attention to detail. She worked there until 1976 and retired at the age of sixty-seven when the

Convent was sadly sold to property developers who demolished the building and its beautiful grounds and in its place built a housing estate, naming it Convent Close.

In June 1967, when I was fifteen years old, I accompanied my parents on an annual visit to Fawley Court, which was an independent Polish school for boys run by Marian Fathers in Henley-on-Thames, where Polish post war veterans from around Great Britain gathered once a year. There in the crowds, I found my father speaking to a distinguished looking man to whom he introduced me. The man put out his left hand to greet me and I realised that his right arm was missing. Later that day, my mother told me that the man to whom I had spoken was the high ranking officer whose life my father had saved during the battle at Ancona, when he had found him with his arm blown off and helped him to safety, and for which he had been decorated with a high military award.

My parents and aunts decided to sell the property at Bearton Road in 1972, before its huge garden became too much to manage and they purchased a new and attractive house nearby in Bowyers Close just before their retirement. Although the house itself was spacious, the gardens were smaller and more manageable and this was a very admirable achievement, looking back at their humble beginnings when arriving as refugees in Britain.

In 1973, when I was twenty-one and about to become engaged to my future English husband Graham, Tonia searched through her wooden trunk, which she and Jania had brought from Africa, and inside she found a small red box lined with purple velvet which she gave to me. The box was marked with the name of an Indian jeweller in Kolhapur and inside was the gold ring with the ruby stone which she had ordered in 1944 in India for Jędrzek Dolecki, her intended husband, who tragically lost his life in Italy. She suggested that the ring had waited twenty-nine years for an owner and she now wanted me to give it as an engagement ring to my future husband, whom it actually fitted perfectly. Our wedding followed in 1975,

when Graham and I bought our first house in Hitchin and my
parents and aunts were delighted to see our first son Stephen
born in 1980. I inherited the aluminium cooking pots which
had been issued to my mother and aunts in India and I use these
to this day for cooking gołąbki (stuffed cabbage leaves). Even
though they have been regularly used for almost seventy years,
they have never lost their shine.

The war, along with its terrible years of hardships, followed
by twenty of heavy labouring work in the building trade had
eventually taken a heavy toll on my dad's health. On 3rd
February 1983, after a very short illness with a chest infection,
Antek Zatorski passed away suddenly at the age of seventy-
four. Julia and Antek had been married for over forty-four
years. My mother was devastated, her health deteriorated and
she seemed to lose her will to live without him. Just two and a
half years later, on 1st November 1985, All Saints Day, she also
died at the age of seventy-six of a kidney failure. They were both
laid to rest in what has become the Polish section of the Hitchin
cemetery and at that point, my aunts Jania and Tonia requested
that I arrange to purchase the plot which was vacant next to
Julia's and Antek's grave, to enable them all to eventually rest
together.

Although my aunts were both considerably older than my
mother, they were much fitter and had a very positive outlook
on life. They enjoyed each other's company and shopped, went
to church and socialised together all their lives. They possessed
a frame of mind which helped them take things in their stride
and this greatly contributed to their longevity and enjoyment of
life and they lived to see my second son Andrew born in 1990.

Jania remained remarkably physically fit and had all her
own perfectly strong teeth and excellent eyesight into her
nineties, but sadly she developed Alzheimer's. Her dementia
made her incoherent and it became difficult for her to
communicate with her sister or indeed any of us. Her speech
and memory was diminishing and when she knelt down to say
her evening prayers, she cried because she realised that she

could no longer remember the words of prayers which she had recited all her life. Tonia would help her by saying the words for her to repeat. However, because she was physically fit and strong, she would wander off long distances and often got lost, which caused everyone great concern searching for her. Sadly, she died in September 1990 at the grand age of ninety-two.

Tonia, who had cared for Jania during the last few years of her life, suddenly found herself without the sister with whom she had lived, worked and survived hardships throughout her life. They had lived together longer than most married couples and had been inseparable. At that point, Tonia seemed to give up and within four months of Jania's death, she also passed away in January 1991. They were buried together in the plot which they asked me to purchase for them beside Julia and Antek. I was suddenly bereaved threefold, having been brought up within my unusual extended family which consisted of the equivalent of three mothers. The epitaph which I chose for my aunts' gravestone reads "*Together in life and in eternity*" because that is exactly as I remember them.

Looking around the Polish area of the Hitchin cemetery amongst the tall pine trees, I found it extraordinary to notice that at least six of these graves belong to neighbours of my parents from their village of Waniów. When one considers the unimaginable distances that these people had wandered during their perilous exiles around the world, amazingly they found their final resting place in such close proximity of each other. After surviving their turbulent trials and challenging experiences of life, may God have them in his keeping and grant them all eternal rest.

Antek, Elizabeth, Julia, Jania, Tonia
(At their home in Hitchin 1966)

Antek outside Bearton Road house, Hitchin

Outside the wards of Lister Hospital, Hitchin 1967
(Tonia far left, a student from France and Mrs King who
worked in the kitchen of Ward 8 with Tonia)

Foskett Family Butcher shop, Hitchin 2011

CHAPTER SIXTEEN

Return to Lwów

After my parents and aunts passed away, as the only surviving child, I was left with the task of sorting out their estate and related paperwork. Many years later, whilst going through two carved wooden boxes, which had been made for my mother and aunts in India during the war, I found documents inside which inspired me to write this book. Although I had always considered that their life stories were worth recording in some way, I could not decide from which perspective this account would best be portrayed and therefore delayed the project until well into my fifties. Additionally, I suspected that this would involve a great deal of research, which I knew might prove to be a very complicated task to undertake. In any case, having been incorporated into Ukraine after the war, Lwów and Waniów were behind the Iron Curtain, which made it completely impossible to visit the areas where my family had actually lived. However, what had I discovered in the two mysterious document boxes which would prove so useful?

In my parents' box, I found two small grey identification booklets entitled Certificate of Registration and on examining the details of these, I was completely shocked and moved to tears at the implication of the wording of their contents. These had been given to my mother and father when they had arrived in England. They had been issued as a form of identity, under the "Aliens Order", to ensure registration and tracking of anyone who was considered an alien and residing in Great

Britain after the war. There were regulations specified in this booklet to state that soldiers discharged from the Polish Resettlement Corps were not allowed to set up their own businesses or take up any employment without the consent of the Ministry of Labour and National Service. There was also a legal requirement that any change of personal circumstances such as marriage, divorce or death of husband or wife, including change of residential address within the United Kingdom, had to be reported to the nearest police constabulary within forty-eight hours of the move and failure to comply was punishable by a fine of £100 or six months' imprisonment. (The fine would have represented a fortune considering my father would have been earning approximately £10 per week).

I could not believe, that having served faithfully as part of the Allied Forces, the Polish soldiers had not only lost their country to Russia, but post-war, were given the status of aliens in Great Britain as if they represented the enemy. I suddenly realised the implication of that visit, when as a four year old child I had accompanied my father to the Hitchin police station on 23rd September, 1957, the day after we had moved house. The purpose of our visit to the constabulary had been to fulfil the legal requirement of reporting our change of address from Cambridgeshire to Hitchin, as we were regarded as aliens. Even today, I feel extremely embittered and outraged that my father should have had such a reward for his military contributions to help the allies secure victory in Europe. It was not until the Aliens Order of 1960, fifteen years after the end of the war, when the booklets were stamped "*The holder is exempt from registration with the police*," that we were no longer subjected to such tracking.

These little grey booklets however, also provided me with useful details and address of my parents' first employment in Great Britain, when they had worked together for Mr Robinson at The Grange in Lolworth in 1948. In the summer of 2010, I travelled to Lolworth to visit the property which my parents had so often fondly recalled and although the

Robinsons no longer resided there, it was a very impressive place to visit.

I also came across a small brown envelope marked "not important" in my mother's handwriting and this contained the purchase deeds signed by my grandparents in 1925 when they bought the house in Waniów in Poland, in which my mother and aunts had been brought up and where my parents had subsequently resided after they married. This included the detailed plans and measurements of the agricultural land belonging to the property which had all been abandoned when they were evacuated to Siberia by the Russians on that fateful night of 10th February 1940. Amazingly, when one considers the journey around the world and circumstances through which those deeds had travelled and survived, I realise that my mother must have kept them safe all during the most gruelling period of the war in the constant hope that she would one day return to her property. Finally, years after the war had ended, she must have realised that this was a past which they could never return to and it would be fruitless to pursue any post war reclaiming of what the Russians had stolen. Recognising this, she had simply marked the property which her parents had bought, the home where she grew up in and later rebuilt with Antek, as "not important".

Although there are organisations who specialise in securing post war compensations for properties lost in Poland as a result of the upheaval of the conflicts of World War II, my tentative enquires led me to believe that it could be a very long drawn out process lasting many years. It would also be an extremely costly business of trying to go through overseas courts for what would ultimately be very little gain and I have not pursued this idea, particularly after my visit to the village in 2009. Additionally, I somehow sensed that my parents would not wish me to take that option on their behalf.

However, this was a significant turning point which made me decide that, in their name, I needed to return to their village and accomplish what had been impossible for them in post war years. It was unfortunate that they had not lived to see Poland restored to freedom from Communist rule. Although I would be visiting their home regions of Lwów and Waniów, these were no longer even part of Poland but were now in Ukraine. I hoped that retracing my immediate family's history, which would be a considerable achievement, would also enable me to piece together my own identity by seeing for myself the part of the world where my parents came from and to which they referred as having been their home.

The second wooden box belonging to my aunts also held documents which helped me to investigate further. I found the two black identity booklets which had been issued to Jania and Tonia in 1937 in their city of Lwów. These had proved extremely valuable verification of identity throughout their years of exile around the world and had saved them many endless hours of waiting in queues when making arrangements to travel from one country to another, as was the case of refugees who had no documents to verify their identity.

The booklets contained the names, addresses and signatures of the employers at whose residences Jania and Tonia had worked in Lwów, including Professor Halban and Doctor Jadwiga Kornella. It also gave the names and addresses of the general practitioners with whom they had been registered for their medical care. On examining all these, I was determined to try and return to their beloved Lwów and in some small way take them back with me. As Lwów was now in Ukraine, I realised that all the street names would be changed completely and furthermore they would be written in Cyrillic Russian alphabet, which would add an extra challenge to my task.

At this point, I was thankful that in my school holidays in 1967, whilst a teenager, I was looking for something to occupy my time and decided to purchase a copy of Teach Yourself Russian from which I taught myself to read basic Russian. However, at that time I could never have imagined that this skill would ever prove to be useful. I managed to find a pre-war Polish street map of Lwów and a renamed Ukrainian version to work alongside, which would help me find the residences of the Halbans and Doctor Kornella, where Tonia and Jania had worked and lived. In order to undertake this expedition into my family history, I sought assistance of my English husband Graham, who fortunately not only has an interest in the history of World War II, but as an ex scout, is also an excellent map reader.

In May 2009, having only the booklets which I had found in the boxes and a satellite picture which we had printed of the village of Waniów, Graham and I decided to travel to what is now Ukraine, flying from Luton to Warsaw and then onto Lwów. We went with a completely open mind knowing that we might not find anything which we could relate to, but it was worth a try for the adventure. Coincidently, our journey happened to fall on the one hundredth anniversary year of my parents' birth.

In order to make the trip to Lwów meaningful, as far as the memory of Jania and Tonia were concerned, I had decided to take something of theirs with me which I could leave behind in their city. I found Jania's rosary beads and Tonia's prayer book and put these together with their pre war photographs, copied from their black Lwów identification books, which depicted them as young and beautiful women. I placed these carefully into a tin along with a photo of Doctor Jadwiga Kornella, as she too had been a faithful citizen of Lwów. These three remarkable women's were linked with the years during which they had lived and worked in Lwów and no doubt they all would have longed to return there. Finally, I labelled the tin "Children of the Polish Lwów" and planned to bury these items in some relevant place for which purpose I had packed a small trowel. I prayed that my cases were not examined too closely, for if detected, would have required some creative explaining on my part to Ukrainian airport military personnel.

When we landed in Lwów, we were immediately fascinated by the grandeur of its tiny airport building which from the outside looked like a theatre or opera house, made of stone with tall pillars and beautifully etched glass in all the windows and doors throughout the building. Inside, the entrance hall was circular with an extremely high ornate domed ceiling. The city reflected the atmosphere of class which had gained Lwów its pre-war fame and reputation and despite sixty years of architectural maintenance neglect under Soviet rule, this splendour was still very much evident in what had survived.

Having booked into the beautiful Grand Hotel in the heart of Lwów, which would have been a very prestigious place to stay in the days when Jania and Tonia were living in the city, we set about finding our way around using our Polish and Ukrainian maps. To our amazement, it did not take much effort to trace and find the exact residence in the city centre where the Halbans had lived and it looked prestigious, so one could only imagine how lovely it must have been in the 1930's. We also found Doctor Jadwiga Kornella's property, where Tonia had lived and worked before the war. This very grand building, which formed the corner of a main street, had now been converted into a building society and I was tempted to go inside to look around. The floor was covered in polished granite tiles and in the corner of the banking hall, there were curved roped-off steps spiralling down underneath the bank, probably for staff or housing of the vaults. I presumed that during the war, these would have been the steps which led to the cellar underneath the building where the residents, including Tonia and Jadwiga, had sheltered in 1939 during the German air raids.

As we walked outside the building, I found an open gate which I was tempted to enter in order to get a view of the gardens at the back of the property. This led me into an enclosed courtyard garden with enormous mature trees providing a lovely cool and quiet sanctuary from the busy street which the property faced. It was a strange feeling to imagine that the comforts of these residences, must have contained all my aunts' possessions which had been left behind, as they had been staying at my mother's house in Waniów the night when they had been evacuated. This must all have stood waiting, frozen in time, in the years that Tonia and Jania had been lingering and suffering in the depths of Siberia, followed by exile in Persia, India and Africa.

We then made our way to the beautiful Łyczakowski cemetery, where famous and noteworthy citizens are buried in the grandest tombs imaginable amongst tall trees full of birdsong. This is one of the oldest cemeteries in Europe and spans an area over forty hectares. Here it was relaxing and a pleasure and to wonder around the acres of parkland on the warm sunny May morning that we had chosen for our visit. It was at Łyczakowski cemetery that I decided to bury my tin with the mementoes of Jania, Tonia and Jadwiga Kornella to symbolise their return to their city which they had so loved. There could not have been a more honourable or fitting place to leave these items, as they had often mentioned walking in this parkland in days when they had been Lwówian citizens. At this point, it finally dawned on me that my book about their lives would obviously have to start from Lwów and nowhere else.

Later that morning whilst wandering through the famous writers section, to my great delight we came across the tomb of Maria Konopnicka, the children's author from whose books Tonia had read me poems all my childhood years and I found this quite an emotional discovery. Here I left a candle in honour of this writer whose books I had enjoyed as a child and which had undoubtedly inspired me to later read Polish literature.

As the cemetery was so extensively large, I decided that if we were to have any chance of finding the burial place of Professor Halban, if indeed it still existed, I needed to enquire at the archives office which was sited in the grounds. As he had died seventy-five years ago, and the war years had caused Lwów to suffer serious bombardment and destruction, I was uncertain whether anything whatsoever had survived. The officials were extremely helpful and efficient in the archives building and to my amazement within seconds found the record card giving us the directions to follow.

Graham and I walked up high near the military graves and found that this area of the cemetery was being completely renovated and the gravestones were being systematically polished to reveal their original beautiful white stone. It did not take very long before we saw a comparatively short surname in a row high up and climbing up nearer, we discovered that it was indeed the grave of Professor Halban, whom I personally had not known but heard so much about from my aunts that I was delighted to find it. Here I also left a candle to symbolise Jania and Tonia's reunion with this noteworthy man who had been their much loved employer and friend.

We spent a whole morning walking around the beautifully paved walkways among the most exquisitely designed and carefully tended monuments. The grandeur of this place was breathtaking and the atmosphere tranquil and relaxing. Walking in the cool shade of the tall trees left us refreshed and most happy that we had found some tangible evidence of the important part of my aunts' lives which had been disrupted and left behind incomplete as a result of the war.

When we returned to the city centre, we managed also to find the buildings which prior to the war had contained the doctor's surgeries where Jania and Tonia had been registered with Doctor Margol and Doctor Frisch and these were now used as office buildings.

Quite by chance, we discovered a fascinating pharmacy museum dating back to 1735 just off the Market Square at Drukarska 2. Stepping through its doorway, we felt that we had entered a beautifully furnished pre-war chemist which had been locked in a time capsule. Although this was still functioning as a retail pharmacy, it was possible to go behind the scenes and see the rooms where old pill boxes, bottles of medicines, potions and doctor's prescriptions of bygone days were displayed. There were also old photos of the city's pharmacists mounted on the walls. Below the chemist, we visited its cellars, where the temperature was quite cold, which would have been an ideal storage for chemicals used in the production of medicinal products. We wondered whether Doctor Kornella might have used this pharmacy to purchase medical supplies relating to her work.

In the city centre, we visited the only Catholic Cathedral which now remained in Lwów dating back to 1360. We attended a mass here, which I requested be dedicated for the repose of the souls of Jania and Tonia, and I found it an emotional experience to be in the church where they would have worshipped almost seventy years ago. It was in this cathedral that King Jan Kazimierz nominated the Virgin Mary as Queen of Poland in 1656 during a war and she has been regarded as Poland's queen ever since.

We made several stops in the various cafés to try the coffees and fantastic assortments of cakes and pastries, including Café Veronika, which turned out to be a cake lover's paradise. Their cakes were not only delicious, but also intricate works of art. However, photographing the specimens was not permitted, as we found out from an annoyed waitress. We also sampled the Viennese Café which dated back to 1829 when Lwów (Lemberg) had been a key city in the Habsburg Empire and Viennese confectionary was world renowned.

Before the war, Lwów had always been famous for its production of superb liqueurs and chocolate and we discovered that these were still being produced and we were able to purchase both in the local retail stores to bring home.

Linked with the discovery Halban's grave, we visited the lovely and extensive buildings of the University of Lwów where the professor had taught. The place was very busy that day with hundreds of excited students collecting their exam results. We spent some time in the grounds and building itself recollecting that at the onset of the Second World War, many professors from Lwów University and Polytechnic along with doctors and surgeons had been systematically and brutally murdered by the Germans, with the help of Ukrainians, to deplete Poland of its most highly educated citizens as they feared that their knowledge represented power.

During my research, I had learnt that prior to her deportation to Siberia, Jania's last residence of employment in Lwów had been with Professor Stefanowicz in Nabielaka Street near the Abrahamowicz Institution of Education, opposite Wulecki Heights. Before the war, this residential area of Lwów had housed many of its professors, who later fell victim to the Nazi extermination programme. Commencing on the night of 3rd July, 1941, neighbours living in Nabielaka Street had witnessed from their windows, with the help of field glasses, a pit being dug by the Germans on the slope of Wulecki Heights. Having rounded up many of the professors from their houses in Nabielaka Street, along with their wives, children and domestic staff, the Nazis led them in batches before a firing squad and shot them so that they fell directly into the freshly dug mass grave which was covered quickly to eliminate any traces of their crimes. These systematic executions went on for several nights during which, many talented and educated Polish citizens lost their lives solely to destroy the knowledge which they possessed.

From this account, I realised that had Jania remained in the service of Professor Stefanowicz and not been deported by the Russians to Siberia in 1940, she would undoubtedly have met her death in front of that firing squad as part of her employer's household. Instead, although she almost died of starvation and disease in the Soviet gulags, she did at least have some small chance of survival and had fortunately gone on to live to a very old age and tell her story.

The next task which we had set ourselves was to find my parents' village of Waniów and also its adjacent town of Bełz. I also planned to visit the railway station of Ostrów from which their village had been deported to Russia in February 1940. We decided to hire a vehicle from a car rental in Lwów to make this trip and with Graham driving and me reading the Ukrainian road signs in Cyrillic script and recollecting names of towns and villages which my parents had mentioned years ago, we came off the main city roads into the country roads.

Here the driving was extremely challenging because of the atrocious road surfaces and we could easily imagine that we had gone backwards in time about one hundred years. As there had been heavy rainfall overnight, we had to continually steer the car around huge pits filled with water to avoid getting our wheels trapped in these remote places, where we would not have felt safe to ask for help. At one point, we noticed that the bus which was travelling in front of our car was having difficulties steering straight and assumed that the driver was drunk. However, it transpired that the suspension was broken and the body of the bus was moving sideways over the rear axle. As a result, the driver was unable to keep the vehicle straight and we realised that the pot holes which the bus had driven through must have caused the damage.

Finally, we arrived in Bełz, which before the war had been a thriving town with many shops, banks and businesses, which had been owned by the 3,600 Polish Jews who lived there. However, during the war, the Jews would all have been deported by the Germans and met their doom in the Nazi extermination camps and this in turn depleted Bełz of its wealth and as a result, there was now hardly anything to see. The Catholic church where my parents would have worshiped was now sadly a derelict and decaying ruin, probably destroyed during the war and there would have been no incentive for post-war Ukrainian residents to restore it. One small pretty church called the Church on the Castle (*Kościół na Zameczku*) was still well maintained but was now an orthodox church where Ukrainian residents worshiped. It was from here at Bełz that the famous miraculous painting of Poland's Black Madonna resided until 1382 and was later transferred to Częstochowa, where it is currently housed and displayed for pilgrims to visit.

Our next task was to find my parents' land and ascertain where their property had been located. We did find a muddy track that led to the edge of where their road called Kolonia had existed. However, in 1940, immediately after the people in my parents' village had been taken by cattle trucks to Russia, all their properties had been systematically destroyed and burned down to erase any trace of their existence and thus the evidence of Stalin's crime lay undetected.

This was the closest that I managed to trace my parent's house and land and so it was here by the roadside in a field, to symbolically bring them home, that I buried a Golden Virginia tobacco tin belonging to my father containing a photo of him in his soldier's uniform in Italy and a photo of my mother in her police uniform during her service in India. This was both an emotional and disappointing moment because I had not succeeded in finding as meaningful a resting place for this tin as I had done in Lwów with my aunts' box.

Finally, we drove to Ostrów railway station and imagined what this journey from Waniów must have been like for my family during that winter night with temperatures -30°C, when they had been taken in sledges and were herded onto the cattle trucks. We found the station, which consisted only of a tiny raised bank and white line as its platform. As I stood by the rails which stretched out into the distance as far as the eye could see, my emotions hit rock bottom and I cried bitterly for all the evil which had begun here and which had devastated so many years of my parents' and aunts lives, not to mention the elimination of my grandparents, baby brother and dozens of my relatives. They could not have known the distances that they would travel around the world when they left Ostrów station that night and certainly never would have imagined that their exile would last the rest of their lives.

At that point, I gained an insight of the magnitude of what had happened to them, which even now is not common knowledge to people of other nations who had not been affected. I realised that this had to be recorded, given that the perpetrators had never been held to account for their calculated and systematic ethnic cleansing of Eastern Poland. Numerous films have been made over the years to portray the crimes committed by the Germans and commemorative events are held regularly for the victims of the Nazi holocaust. However, the Soviet extermination gulag camps, which claimed so many millions of lives, have never been acknowledged or publicised to any degree. Even today, when I mention my family's deportation and incredible survival in Siberia to people who are knowledgeable in history, they reply that they had no idea that this took place during World War II, which shows to what extent the superpowers suppressed details of these crimes for fear of upsetting Stalin. Indeed, the post war government in Great Britain was very left wing and pro-Russian which provided plenty of opportunity for the cover up of Soviet war crimes.

I recalled the words of the camp Commandant in Siberia who addressed the prisoners and told them that hair would grow on the palm of his hand before Poland regained its independence. Unfortunately hundreds of those who listened to his speech that day, did not live to see that he was grossly mistaken; sometimes it takes many patient years before evil is finally conquered.

When I returned to England after this incredible journey, I was amazed how many members of the local Polish community expressed interest and amazement when I mentioned that I had travelled to Ukraine and visited the Eastern borders which were formerly part of Poland. The people I spoke to were either quite elderly and would have lived in those towns before being evacuated, so remembered those areas well. Others had been taken to Siberia as small children and could recall the gulags and further travels during their exile years in Persia, India and Africa. One lady, to whom I was speaking in a supermarket about my trip, actually hugged me and said, "Thank you for going back to my hometown. It was something I have never been able to do and I am so pleased that you have done it on my behalf."

This led to further interesting developments when I shared this information with Stan Misiąg, who had survived Siberia as a small child and also his fall into the monitor lizards' nest in

Africa. Now in his seventies and the grandfather of five, he came to visit us and was able to contribute many details of his life in the Koja camp in Africa and the incident of his mother's misdiagnosed death in Teheran, when he had been taken away, assumed to be an orphan. His visit included a most unexpected surprise for me as he had brought with him an old pre-war photograph of a wedding to see if I could identify anyone on it. To my astonishment, I immediately recognised my own mother and realised that this was a picture of a wedding in the village of Waniów, which had taken place in the early 1920's. This is the only photograph I have ever seen of my mother as a young girl in Poland, as all family photographs and belongings were left behind in the confusion and panic on the night of the evacuation by the Soviets.

The photograph generated further interest and brought valuable information, as I emailed it to my father's relative, Father Władysław Gurgul, a Marian priest who lives and works in America. He too was deported to Siberia at the age of nine, so remembered many details of his Waniów village. Although he thought that he knew nobody in the photograph, he sent it to his elderly aunt in Australia. She was able to name all those present at the wedding including, to his great surprise, his own grandmother. His aunt also sketched out a map showing most of the properties and names of the families who resided in Waniów before their evacuation. This map, along with the photo, suddenly brought the residents of Waniów back into life, as I had heard their names many times when my parents talked about their life before the war. This information provided many important links which helped me with certain aspects of writing this book.

Father Gurgul also gave me the name of a lady living in Leeds, Janka Winnik, who had also been evacuated from Waniów with her family to Russia as a young girl. Although she was in her eighties, her memory was remarkable and she could recall the finest details. Immediately on my return from Ukraine, I went to visit Janka in Leeds to show her my photographs of the trip and she was very pleased to share information, providing me with details to complete gaps for my story. As a child, she had known my father and his family when they were neighbours in Waniów. Her very elderly husband, who originated from Lwów, had served in the army in Poland before the war. When he heard that I had just returned from a visit to that region, he expressed great joy that I had gone to see the city.

"If you ever go back again," he said, "please give Lwów my love."

Sadly, shortly after my visit to meet Janka and her family in Leeds, she suffered a stroke and subsequently passed away. I was so very glad that I had taken the opportunity to visit and acquaint myself with her in time to share my findings.

I was very surprised by the reaction of people whom I spoke to about the trip and it confirmed in my mind that I had indeed accomplished a big milestone in the name of many Polish immigrants. I am certain that my mother Julia, my father Antek and aunts Jania and Tonia would have said exactly the same, as I had specifically made the trip in their name.

One year before my visit to Lwów, I flew on holiday to China with my husband and two sons. Whilst flying over Siberia, I looked down upon miles of desolate snow covered wasteland and tried to imagine what it must have been like for my parents and aunts during their barbaric imprisonment there all those years ago. At that time, they could not have imagined that they would ever survive those hardships and that one day their daughter and grandchildren would be flying in an aircraft over those territories.

Writing this book has enabled me to produce a witness account of what was an unpublicised and skilfully covered up Russian holocaust. My research provided me with an insight into what my immediate family had endured during the turbulent years of the war and how they adapted, strived and made the best of the terrible situations in which they found themselves on numerous occasions. This was certainly an example of their strong faith in God which kept them from losing hope, even when there was not an immediate light visible at the end of the tunnel. Subsequently, they spent the rest of their lives thanking God for sparing them and allowing them to live a long and meaningful life which had somehow been enriched and strengthened by their experiences. It gave me a sense of discovery of my own identity in being able to return to my parents' village, which I had heard about for so many years but had never been able to see for myself. It also provided me with an opportunity to turn their long-held dream into realisation.

The following photos were all taken during our visit 2009

University of Lwów

Latin Cathedral of Lwów (2009)

257

Łyczakowski Cemetery Lwów (2009)

Lwów Railway Station

Lwów Airport, airside entrance

Church on the Castle (*Kosciół Na Zameczku*) in Bełz

Lwów Pharmacy Museum in Market Square

Lightning Source UK Ltd.
Milton Keynes UK
UKOW050210170712

196082UK00001B/9/P